80/20 DAILY

Selected Books also by Richard Koch

The 80/20 Principle
Unreasonable Success and How to Achieve It
The Star Principle
The 80/20 Manager
The 80/20 Individual
80/20 Your Life
Beyond the 80/20 Principle
Superconnect°
Simplify°
The Financial Times Guide to Strategy (5th edition)
Suicide of the West*

°Richard Koch and Greg Lockwood
*Richard Koch and Chris Smith

80/20 DAILY

Your Day-by-Day Guide to Happier, Healthier,
Wealthier, and More Successful Living

RICHARD KOCH

Author of *The 80/20 Principle*

First published in Great Britain by Nicholas Brealey Publishing in 2024
An imprint of John Murray Press

1

A CIP catalogue record for this title is available from the British Library

Trade Paperback ISBN 978 1 399 81456 0
ebook ISBN 978 1 399 81457 7

Typeset by KnowledgeWorks Global Ltd

Printed and bound in Great Britain by Clays Ltd, Elcograf S.p.A.

John Murray Press policy is to use papers that are natural, renewable and
recyclable products and made from wood grown in sustainable forests.
The logging and manufacturing processes are expected to conform to the
environmental regulations of the country of origin.

John Murray Press
Carmelite House
50 Victoria Embankment
London EC4Y 0DZ

John Murray Business
123 S. Broad St., Ste 2750
Philadelphia, PA 19109

www.nicholasbrealey.com

John Murray Press, part of Hodder & Stoughton Limited
An Hachette UK company

For the three happiest and most 80/20 families I know:

Annie and Jamie, and Grace, Sal and Tom

Marie-Louise and Jon, and Noah and Jake

Guy and Nicky, and Romilly, Ben and Otto

PREFACE AND ACKNOWLEDGEMENTS

This book would not have existed were it not for Ryan Smith, so my first tribute must be to him. He had read *The 80/20 Principle* and thought I should write a book of daily readings based on the principle. I agreed. And rather to my surprise, so too did my editor-publisher, Iain Campbell. So, I wrote it! Thanks, Ryan! Appreciation also to Iain, whose editing has been meticulous, fast, precise yet imaginative, and well beyond the course of duty. If all editors were as good as Iain, authors and their readers would be so much happier. And great credit to my marvellous agent Sally Holloway for her many talents and ability to get things sorted with the minimum of fuss – 80/20 indeed.

80/20 Daily, I confess, has taken me far longer than I imagined. I loved writing it, but as I dug into the work, it became clear to me that the range, scope and power of 80/20 goes far beyond what I had previously covered, or been aware of, and required extensive new research and thinking.

The great bulk of *80/20 Daily* is totally original; although based substantially on themes in about a dozen of my books, I was challenged to think again about most issues, and for the first time about some of them. I wrote each reading anew, only very occasionally quoting myself.

There are new subjects in the book, including 'opportunity-ism', moods, growth, the theory of personal monopoly, self-love, how to invent your own virgin territory, how to compound yourself, the right place to live, time oases, the nature of luck (what it is and is not, contrary to popular views), choosing and creating your hubs, making 80/20 decisions, hunches, Pascal's wager and asymmetric bets, and finally a chapter on the black swan and history.

My biggest debt of all, and that of 80/20 – if we imagine it as a sentient force – is of course to the imitable and seminal figure of Tim Ferriss. Over the past two decades, nobody has done so much to promote 80/20 so tirelessly and influentially. I am particularly grateful for the endorsement that Tim has given me, quite against his normal (and sensible) policy. My books and I have also benefitted enormously from my two appearances on his legendary podcast *Show*, and I recommend – perhaps rather too blatantly – that you listen to my two blogs with Tim.* In the recent one, Tim graciously came to visit me in Portugal, and we had great fun doing it across my kitchen table. Wow, Tim!

A very large debt is due of course to Perry Marshall, whose has kindly written the Foreword to this work. Perry is, of course, the author of the very successful *80/20 Sales and Marketing*, which ranges well beyond sales and marketing, and could be viewed as *The 80/20 Principle Part Two*. It's entirely complementary to my work and brilliantly does many things that I could not have attempted. If you like this book, please read his!

Equally, there is my gratitude to my friend Marx Acosta-Rubio, who has been a tireless supporter and constructive critic of my work. Marx reads extraordinarily widely and encouraged me to read several great biographies, which led me to write my most recent book before this one, *Unreasonable Success and How to Achieve It*. Marx is a wise polymath, a noted libertarian and a person of enormous goodwill. *Unreasonable Success* and all my books, especially this one, have been greatly improved by his influence.

Finally, I warmly thank all my friends who generously made the time to read drafts of this book and made valued contributions. I hesitate to name my friends, for fear of omitting someone, but really vital ideas came from Guy Bowles, Tom Butler-Bowden, Hugo Delgado, Dr Chris Eyles, Nicholas Ladd, Jamie Reeve and Jamie Stirrat.

Enough! Please get stuck into reading the book, reflecting on it and indeed the whole life process of getting happier, healthier, wealthier, more successful and more of a force for good.

Richard Koch

October 2024

---

* The links to the blogs are as follows:
https://tim.blog/2020/09/22/richard-koch/
https://tim.blog/2023/07/05/richard-koch-2/

CONTENTS

About the author xi

Foreword by Perry Marshall xiii

What is 80/20? 1
Intelligent and lazy 9
Time 23
Happiness 29
Ambition, self-belief and your career 37
Creativity 43
Optimism and opportunity 51
Difficulties, stress and moods 59
The subconscious mind 71
Growth 79
Success and 80/20 85
The theory of personal monopoly 93
80/20 and the boss 99
Fantasy mentors, failures, winners and sex 105
More on happiness … and romance 111
A short course on self-love 123
Money and happiness 127
Friends 131
More on optimism and opportunity 137
The time triad 151
More on creativity and how to invent virgin territory 159
Growth and how to compound yourself 167
How to increase your effectiveness with less effort 181
The art of 80/20 Thinking 191
Decisions 205

Networks   221

Territory, hierarchy and how to thrive in the
brave new world   235

What is the source of meaning in your life?   247

Evolution's lessons for you   259

A genetic perspective on how to make more money
and have more fun   271

Niches and breast-beating   287

Risk, possessions, experiences and relationships   295

Neuroplasticity, tit for tat and the right place to live   305

Time oases, thinking and chaos   315

Parkinson's laws   323

Fibonacci's rabbits   327

Luck and good fortune   341

Live in a small world   351

Choosing and creating your hubs   361

Hunches   367

Fortune favours the bold   377

Pascal's wager and asymmetric bets   385

The black swan and history   391

Thank you and fare well   403

Endnotes   407

ABOUT THE AUTHOR

Richard Koch is the author of *The 80/20 Principle*, which has sold more than a million copies and has been published in over 40 languages. He is one of the most successful venture capital investors of his generation. Richard was previously a partner of Bain & Company, and co-founded LEK Consulting. He has lived in seven different countries, most of them sunny, enjoys cycling, walking, tennis, swimming, reading and gambling, and his most faithful partner is Sooty the Labrador. He is a Visiting Fellow of Wadham College, Oxford University.

FOREWORD BY PERRY MARSHALL

When Richard Koch asked me to write a foreword for his new book *80/20 Daily*, I was bemused. Doesn't saying 365 things about 80/20 seem a little anti-80/20?

After all, 80/20 isn't about saying more – it's about focus. So, would it be more in line with 80/20 to boil it down to one? Or 73, which is 20 per cent of 365?

But then again, maybe there's a depth to 80/20 that begs a daily drip of wisdom to truly mine its depths.

The Principle is profound. You can explore it each day for a year and still find more to discover. Do you just want to be an 80/20 'brown belt'? Or a third-degree black belt? The depth and breadth of 80/20 suggest its complexity is worth embracing too.

I decided 80/20 is deep enough to mine daily. Each application reveals a new angle on familiar problems. A single insight can radically shift your thinking and strategy.

Now if anyone can make each of those 365 insights count, it's Richard Koch. He wrote the first book about 80/20 in 1997. It sold more than a million copies, was translated into 40 languages. He's written 25 other books, some on 80/20, most across a spectrum of other ideas: how to become happier and wealthier; how to attain zen-like elegance in your life, and more.

He started to invest his savings of around $500,000 in 1983. This little pot of wealth has now grown to around $1,600,000,000. His annual growth in assets has been around 22 per cent per year, compounded, which is slightly better than Warren Buffett (although Buffett has vastly more wealth as a result of starting earlier).

Richard does this by spending less than a day a week on his investments.

He has no office and only two employees. He never uses spreadsheets – he doesn't know how to, and thinks they are misleading. He does his sums on an ancient HP12c calculator. He gives a lot of money away (but only to friends and family) and has no idea how to spend his wealth and doesn't care. He has only one extravagant habit (a secret).

He cycles two hours a day and takes his Labrador for long walks, often by the sea. He plays tennis, gambles, shares meals with friends several times a day and reads two hours a day too. He lives in almost perpetual sunshine. A good life.

Each day's entry in *80/20 Daily* promises you payoff in terms of happiness, relaxation and absence of stress, a healthy mind; ability to help friends and family and your wider community. And yes, eventually even in wealth as a result of finding a great career.

Sometimes, even the 80 per cent that seems like excess carries value that you only recognize upon deeper examination or in hindsight. I acknowledge the irony: the deeper you reach into 80/20, the more you appreciate the full 100 per cent. Each layer of nuance builds upon the last.

Richard's *80/20 Daily* might be the routine your mind needs to stay fit. And in a world saturated with information, a principle-focused daily ritual may be precisely the discipline that cuts through the deafening noise. Richard will teach you to think simply, powerfully and happily.

Dive into it – one day, one rich 80/20 insight at a time.

Perry Marshall
author of *80/20 Sales & Marketing* and *Evolution 2.0*

www.perrymarshall.com

CHAPTER 1

WHAT IS 80/20?

What is the 80/20 Principle and why is it so wonderful in daily life? We're going to explore exactly what 80/20 is, why you should use it and how. For people who like analysis, there is 80/20 Analysis, which is extremely useful in statistics and business. 80/20 Thinking, however, is far more neglected and far more powerful. It can greatly lift our lives to new levels.

1   The universe is wonky!

What is the 80/20 Principle ('80/20' for short)?

80/20 tells us that in any population some things are likely to be *very* much more important than others. A good benchmark or hypothesis is that 80 per cent of results flow from 20 per cent of causes, and sometimes from a much smaller proportion of powerful causes.

Take everyday language. Sir Isaac Pitman invented shorthand after finding that just 700 words and their variants account for 80 per cent of common speech. The 700 words account for less than 1 per cent of all words in the dictionary. This is an example of an 80/1 relationship – 1 per cent used 80 per cent of the time.

It's a pretty safe bet that of all the clothes in your wardrobe, you wear fewer than 20 per cent of them 80 per cent of the time. Daily life is full of relationships like this. Some of them are curious but not that important; some affect your happiness and influence you greatly. It is these 80/20 events, facts and hypotheses that you are going to be learning about every day.

We tend to think that life is 50/50 rather than 80/20. It sometimes happens that 50 per cent of people have 50 per cent of a scarce resource, such as money or influence, but this is rare. Does every hour of work you do have the same value, or are there a few things that have great results while most do not?

The universe is wonky! Results and causes are skew-whiff, but predictably so, following an 80/20 pattern. When you discover asymmetries in your life, you can find ways to multiply results with much less effort, stress, time or money.

Are you familiar with 80/20? Do you get the idea? You will see a large number of ways in which to multiply what you want with little pain and – perhaps – great enjoyment.

2 Some other illustrations of 80/20

- A study of 300 movies released over 18 months found that 4 of them – 1.3 per cent of the total made – took 80 per cent of box office receipts.

- On the stock market, the top 10 stocks in the Standard & Poor's Index – 2 per cent of the total – typically account for 92 per cent of all gains.

- There are 5 per cent of US share-owning households who own 75 per cent of the total value of shares.

- If you go to a concert, be it rock, jazz or classical, a very small proportion of songs or music – the old, familiar pieces – will be played more than 80 per cent of the time.

- Of the 6,700 languages in the world, 100 (1.5 per cent) are used by 90 per cent of people.

- Americans comprise less than 5 per cent of the world's population, yet consume more than 50 per cent of its heroin, along with some other very harmful substances.

- Police spies in Europe between 1847 and 1917 listed several thousand 'professional revolutionaries'. Yet only one of them – Lenin – actually pulled off a successful revolution. History is full of events on which a handful of people have enormous impact, both for good and ill.

- Betfair, the world's largest person-to-person betting exchange, reports that 90 per cent of the money staked comes from just 10 per cent of its clients.

- There are thousands of new inventions emerging all the time, yet a tiny proportion of them have an impact on our lives that is greater than all the others put together – for example, nuclear power, the computer, the internet and now artificial intelligence.

Can you think of examples in your life where 80/20 applies?

3 Why is 80/20 so life-enhancing?

When you spot a cause that has an enormous effect, you may be able to use it to achieve extraordinary results with ordinary effort. *The essence of 80/20 is to identify activities that have a high ratio of results to effort, time, money or any other scarce resource.* 80/20 is also about doing things that make you and other people happy, and create no stress.

Life is full of 80/20 possibilities of this kind. You will see over the course of the book, for example, that:

- a small proportion of your time generates most of your valuable results;
- fewer than 10 decisions you make in life are truly important and in terms of results overwhelm all the thousands of other decisions you make;
- there are four factors which influence your happiness – or lack of it – far more than anything else;
- it is always possible to greatly improve your life by using 80/20 Thinking.

Until recently, 80/20 has been used mainly in business and economics. My mission is to get 80/20 used in all areas of your life to greatly increase your peace of mind, joy, achievements and positive impact on people you know.

Are you ready to learn how to be much happier and kinder? Do you agree that huge effort is not always necessary for great results?

4   80/20 Analysis and 80/20 Thinking

There are two different ways to use 80/20:

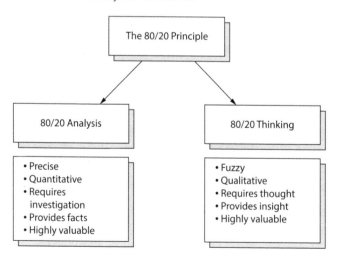

80/20 Analysis has traditionally been the main use of 80/20. Maybe I'm just not a very good analyst, but I use 80/20 Thinking more.

80/20 Thinking means embracing the basic idea behind 80/20 – that there are actually very few important inputs in life or any aspect of it. That's quite liberating when you think about it.

80/20 Analysis is primarily a business tool, but 80/20 Thinking can be used to great effect both in business and outside it.

Do you like the idea of '80/20 Thinking'? Read on and you'll soon become an 80/20 Thinker.

5   How to start your 80/20 Thinking

You need to constantly ask yourself: *What is the 20 per cent in my life that leads to 80 per cent? What works brilliantly, that I should do more of, or that I should expose myself to, placing me in the slipstream of its warm current?*

Never assume that you automatically know the answer. Take time to think creatively about it. What are the *few vital* inputs or causes, as opposed to the *trivial many*? What are the little hinges that swing big doors? Listen for the haunting melody being drowned by the background noise.

Once you have the answer, or at least a good hypothesis, try it out. Does it make a big difference? You know 80/20 Thinking is working when it multiplies effectiveness and good feeling. Action from 80/20 Thinking should lead you to getting much more from much less.

When you use 80/20 Thinking, do not *assume* that its results will be good or bad, or that the powerful forces we observe are good. Drugs are powerful, but not necessarily good. It's the same with any important change to your routine. *Decide whether the results are good for you.* What is the effect on your *inner self and your visible performance!* Then decide – do you give the minority of powerful forces a further shove in the right direction, or frustrate their operation?

We like little causes and big results. That is what you are searching for. These little causes, small changes for big gains, are all around you. External and internal opportunities surround you every day, whether you notice them or not. Notice, test the results, see if they are good and, if so, multiply them.

Keep thinking 80/20. It is the biggest and best new habit in your life.

Have you started thinking 80/20 yet?

6   80/20 turns conventional wisdom upside down

With 80/20, you:

- celebrate exceptional results, rather than raise average efforts;
- look for the quality shortcut, rather than run the full course;
- are selective, not exhaustive;
- favour brevity over verbosity;
- strive for and praise excellence in a few things, not all-round performance;
- delegate and outsource as much as possible in your daily life;
- choose your careers, employers and bosses with the utmost care;
- employ rather than are employed;
- use relaxed reciprocity, not formal contracts;
- think, in everything, where 20 per cent of effort and money leads to 80 per cent of returns;
- stay calm, target a few very valuable goals and opportunities, and work less;
- make the most of your rare lucky streaks (often more than luck) where you are at your creative peak and the stars line up to guarantee your success.

Are you unconventionally wise?

7   80/20 Thinking combines extreme ambition with a relaxed and confident manner

We have been conditioned to think that high ambition must go with thrusting hyperactivity, long hours, busy-ness, ruthlessness and the sacrifice of self and others to the cause. We pay dearly for this association of ideas. Ambition does not need to involve the rat race.

A much more attractive, and equally realistic, combination is extreme ambition + confidence + humour + calmness + a civilized manner. Most great achievements come through steady application, deep thinking and sudden insight. Think Archimedes in his bath. Or Newton escaping the plague in

London to sit under a tree in Lincolnshire and be hit by (or, more likely, to observe) a falling apple. Think Einstein daydreaming about passing trains. Darwin watching mockingbirds in the Galápagos Islands. Henri Poincaré chatting to a friend while boarding a bus. Bertrand Russell pottering around Cambridge to buy some pipe tobacco. Would science be the same if they had been chained to a desk or frenetically directing a team of scientists?

Most of the breakthroughs of high achievers come in a very small part of their working lives. 80/20 makes this clear. You have more than enough time if you have enough curiosity and ambition and you *think*, rather than rush around aimlessly. Achievement flows from sudden insight and selective action, from divergent thinking, visions of eternity and solitary pondering. Though there are some exceptions, most of the seminal books in the world took just a year or two to write, and most of the music which endures took less than a day to compose. Elton John says he wrote 'Candle in the Wind' in 20 minutes. Discoveries, inventions and mental leaps take seconds, hours, days or months, not lifetimes. They come like a hot knife through butter, not blood from a stone.

We have our best ideas when we are feeling good and relaxed. The still, small voice of calm has a bigger place in your life than you realize. Leave the rat race behind and do some solitary pondering.

Do you want to do that? Start today.

CHAPTER 2

INTELLIGENT AND LAZY

This is classic 80/20 territory: contrary to what many people believe, it's best to be intelligent and lazy. Intelligent-lazy people are selective and use 80/20 to decide what to do and – more importantly – what NOT to do. They know how to achieve superior results with less effort, leading to greater happiness, and increasing their influence and impact. The world would be so much happier and better run if we were all intelligent and lazy. You can make a start today …

8   The von Manstein matrix

	Stupid	Intelligent
Lazy	Leave alone	***Stars***
Hard working	Fire immediately	Excellent staff officers

Field Marshal Erich von Manstein was a commander in the German army during the Second World War. He despised Hitler. He said there were four types of army officer:

- First, there are the lazy, stupid ones. Leave them alone, they do no harm.
- Second, there are the hard-working intelligent ones. They make excellent staff officers, ensuring that every detail is properly considered.
- Third, there are the hard-working, stupid ones. These people are a menace and must be fired at once. They create irrelevant work for everybody.
- Finally, there are the intelligent lazy ones. They are suited to the highest office.

Where do you belong on the matrix? Are you, or can you become, intelligent and lazy?

9   Intelligent and lazy

The most effective people are intelligent and lazy.

The key to becoming highly effective – and to having a life full of enjoyment *and* achievement – is lazy intelligence.

Intelligence is a necessary condition both for doing something worthwhile, and for being able to enjoy a full life, not one based on toil.

But why is being lazy important?

The essence of 80/20 is 'more with less'. If 20 per cent of people or forces achieve 80 per cent of valued output, it follows that they are many times more effective than the other 80 per cent of people. The 20 per cent of people could therefore achieve their output, if they chose, with less time, less effort, less stress or less of some combination of all of these.

Since stress, beyond a certain point, is harmful to mental and physical health and to happiness, high achievers, if they are sensible and not addicted to work, should be lazy. Even if high achievers really do love work to the exclusion of other activities, they are likely to cause unhappiness in co-workers and in people who try to maintain close personal relationships with them. Anyone who is intelligent but not lazy may be missing out on some valuable human experiences, including love.

Lazy intelligence is a sensible personal strategy, and it benefits other people.

Are you intelligent and lazy? If not, why not?

10   The big, lazy boss who achieved the Earth

It's no accident that the two people I have seen create the highest value in business are also the idlest I've ever met.

The first was Bruce Doolin Henderson, a big man in every sense. Not fat, but tall, vast, intimidating. His thing was ideas. Ideas, he fervently believed, created wealth. He revolutionized business strategy as a set of elegantly interlocking ideas, pithily expressed. Before Bruce, there were huge unreadable tomes on corporate strategy, useful only to insomniacs. Bruce reduced it all to two one-page charts. I still use one of the charts all the time.

He created arguably the best and most influential consulting firm in the world. He created the whole freaking industry of strategy consulting, which has given more opportunity, thinking power and money, to more bright, wet-behind-the-ears young people in the world ever.

Did he work hard? Nope. Hardly at all. As soon as he set his firm up, he hired other people to do all the work. Two years into the firm he created, he stopped doing any consulting. All he did – and he had a real nose for unlikely talent – was recruit, and write those little green tracts ('Perspectives') on strategy.

Bruce stayed in his office or at home, writing those tracts. He toured all his international offices like a mafia boss. He had set the whole shooting match going, selected fantastic vice-presidents, written the industry bible, seen the visions of eternity and witnessed his disciples spread to every land around the world. Idleness had its compensations.

How much do you use ideas to create great wealth and influence?

11   The second laziest person, and the best money-maker, I have known

For better or worse, the person who had the most influence on me was Bill Bain, a genius without any qualifications apart from a history degree. Bill died in 2018, and I remember him with great affection. He was also the second laziest person I've met.

Bill was enormously creative. He was the co-inventor of the growth-share matrix with its cows, stars, question marks and dogs. His greatest insight, however, was that the best way to sell and operate strategy consulting was in a close personal partnership between the lead consultant and the client's Mr Big, the CEO of the whole shooting match. This ensured incredibly valuable information flowing to the client CEO from the work of tens or hundreds of consultants, a way for him to overcome resistance from powerful 'barons' within his organization, and therefore to multiply the value of his firm. For the consulting firm it was a recipe for endless growth in billings and profits.

The Bain formula was so powerful that Bill was able to command the loyalty and hard work of truly exceptional people such as Mitt Romney. Bain did this through the mechanism of a monthly meeting of all worldwide partners.

Save for chairing the monthly meeting and mentoring his disciples, Bill did nothing – no meetings with clients, no case-team meetings, no memos, *nada*. He led a charmed life. Everyone else in his empire would be working 60- or 70-hour weeks. Everyone else felt stressed. Bill exported stress; he did not import it. His calendar was bare or filled with meetings that never happened. One Bain partner told me, 'I can never get in to see Bill to discuss a client situation; his diary is full of artificial constraints.' That was how Bill liked it. You would see him in the elevator, immaculate in tennis regalia. He would smile or make a joke, feeling not the least embarrassment at the contrast between his life and ours. He was the cat that had cornered the cream.

Could you emulate Bill in some way?

12 David and Jacques: a tale of two bosses

The two top people in a large consulting firm, David and Jacques, hated each other. They represented different factions: David was English and supported by his countrymen and the Americans, while Jacques was backed by the European offices and the profitable and fast-growing Telecoms Division. In my hearing, David once called Jacques 'the laziest man alive'.

David was right. You see, Jacques was charming, French and indolent. He arrived in the London office between nine and ten, having walked eight minutes from his luxury apartment overlooking the park, which the firm paid for. He made a few phone calls to France, Germany and Italy, put his feet up to read the papers and chatted amiably to people in the office. He had a leisurely lunch with some old friend, also on expenses, and always with fine wine. He then left work well ahead of everyone else. Challenged once on why he left so early, he turned and smiled: 'But think how late I arrive!'

Yet under the cloak of indolence there was a first-rate mind. He knew which very small number of consultants in his company were worth their weight in gold. He selected, promoted and mentored them, making them 100 times more effective. His flashes of spontaneous insight were stunning. None of this required large tracts of time; if he had worked more with his board colleagues he would have achieved much less. And he was magic with clients too; they loved and respected him.

David worked eight to eight, and then often rushed off to a work-related dinner. He chaired the firm's many committees and supervised all the emergencies, of which there was a constant stream. No wonder he resented his French colleague, who was paid more.

A few months later, Jacques and the head of the Telecoms Division resigned to set up a new venture, which became much more successful than the original company. They lived happily ever after, while David and his colleagues were always staving off imminent collapse.[1]

How can you be more like Jacques?

13   Bing Crosby – the golfer who sang

80/20 and lazy achievement extend far beyond the domain of business. Lazy achievement is possible in any walk of life, including entertainment, media and other spheres that are viewed as immensely competitive, requiring long hours and constant toil.

Bing Crosby was one of the most popular and influential singers and actors of the twentieth century. His signature style of intimate singing was copied in various forms by greats such as Frank Sinatra and Elvis Presley. His work touring for Allied soldiers in the Second World War earned him the accolade of being voted the 'most admired man alive'.

But there was another side to Crosby. He was a fanatical golfer. He viewed his professional obligations as secondary to golf, which is why his wife called him 'the golfer who sang'.

Crosby's agent would tear his hair out trying to get Crosby to agree to recording schedules and performances. Golf came first.

So, he was unusually lazy, but was he also intelligent? Oh, yes. To be able to play more golf, he devised a way to avoid the work of planning and coordinating live radio broadcasts. Bing was the first singer to copy motion picture techniques and pre-record his broadcasts. This is an example of a 'virtuous trade-off', where a seemingly inevitable trade-off can be avoided and transcended.[2]

Crosby used innovation to remove the conflict between his work and his most pleasurable leisure pursuit. Could you do the same?

14   Intelligent laziness increases achievement

Intelligent laziness is the strategy most likely to increase your *happiness*. But there is another benefit of intelligent laziness – it is also likely to increase your *achievement*.

Most high achievers think a great deal before they act. This is incompatible with a great deal of action, which leads to hard work and long hours. Action drives out thought – so laziness is the perfect antidote.

Very few of the high achievers I know are workaholics.

The hallmark of high accomplishment is original, deep thinking – which is almost impossible if you are too busy.

Getting great results also requires *selectivity* and on *a narrow front*, which laziness also facilitates.

Of course, you could be lazy and not think much. That is not recommended!

Are you trying to become intelligent and lazy?

15   Intelligent laziness benefits society

Bertrand Russell wrote an essay called 'In Praise of Idleness'[3] in which he said, among many other thought-provoking statements, 'The road to happiness and prosperity lies in an organized diminution of work.' His argument went like this – suppose that a certain number of people work eight hours a day to produce all the pins the world needs. Now, suppose through technological innovation that it is only necessary for the workers to work four hours a day to produce the same number of pins. Why shouldn't the workers only work four hours for the same pay and spend the other four hours on leisure activities?

Russell was a socialist, so his argument ignored the way that capitalist societies operate. Perhaps he was pointing out the inequity that most of the benefits of higher productivity go to capitalists rather than workers. In any case, his point, shorn of its politics, is basically right – progress operates through finding ways to make better or cheaper goods with less work.

If you need another example to convince you of this, take the world's experience with Covid.

Most people stopped working, but somehow living standards did not collapse. This was partly because of government borrowing and payments to people who were not allowed to work, which will have to be partially recouped in the future via higher taxes, but clearly valuable output did not fall anywhere near the reduction in the level of work. The same happened in the world wars. This suggests that most work is of marginal value, and when push comes to shove, we can do without it. That is precisely what 80/20 implies.

If you work more intelligently with less effort, you deserve to take more leisure.

Why don't you?

16   How unusual is 'intelligent and lazy'?

Very.

Most intelligent people, especially those who aim at great achievements, work very hard – by which they mean working not only intensely and with full attention, but also long hours. In Silicon Valley, where the Protestant work ethic is pretty universal amongst those of all faiths (and none), the only people who don't work hard and long are playboys (and playgirls) and trust-fund beneficiaries whose ambition is to spend money rather than make it. It is assumed that anyone seriously ambitious must work hard and long, at least for a sustained period of time until they have 'made it' – and probably long after that too. As the legendary Silicon Valley entrepreneur Sam Altman says, the religion of hard work is necessary because only 'extreme people get extreme results'.

Yet there have been times in history when 'intelligent and lazy' was not unusual. Two of Britain's most successful prime ministers in the nineteenth century – Disraeli and Gladstone – enjoyed life to the full and limited their hours of work. Disraeli was a playboy, dilettante and novelist. Gladstone was always slipping away to his beloved Italy anonymously and out of touch with Downing Street even when prime minister. But as the twentieth century rolled on, such brilliant indolence became increasingly unfashionable, and even impossible for people in top jobs.

Today there is no template or respect for people who are intelligent and lazy. Even most people who practise intelligent laziness and high achievement are, so to speak, in the closet – that is, concealing the terrible sin of laziness rather than being proud of it. My mission is to change that. I personally have worked hard and long for other people, and didn't enjoy it much nor achieve great things. Since I was 33, I have worked for myself. The less I have worked, the more I have achieved, and the more I have enjoyed life.

Would you like to join me in setting a new (old) trend?

Rejoice in being different, right and happy.

17   Ruskin on happiness at work – and laziness

John Ruskin was one of the nineteenth-century's greatest polymaths – a writer, philosopher and art critic of the very highest order. If you are intelligent and lazy, use some of your spare time to sample his enormous range of works.

He wrote:

> 'In order that people may be happy in their work,
> these three things are needed:
> They must be fit for it.
> They must not do too much of it.
> And they must have a sense of success in it.'[4]

You must be fit for the work (intelligent), not do too much of it (lazy) and successful. These three things don't have to go together, but if they do, you will be happy in work. Do you know anyone who is intelligent and lazy, and not successful and happy?

Are you suited to your work? Do you not do too much of it? Are you happy in it? Practise the 'holy trinity' of work!

18   Intelligent laziness and determination

Would you expect an intelligent-lazy man or woman to also show great determination? Perhaps, paradoxically, that seems to be the case.

If you are super-intelligent and super-lazy, you also need to be super-determined and super-ambitious. Not everyone who is intelligent is ambitious or gets things done. Nor are the great majority of lazy people. But intelligent-lazy people need to have the spark of genius, and genius involves not just creativity, but also curiosity, and perhaps even insatiable greed – a desire not necessarily for money, but for reputation and achievement, and to wrest the secrets of the universe, or a tiny portion of them, from the gods jealously guarding them.

The determination to find a much better way of doing things, or finding much better things to do, is the pure gold of 80/20, the gospel of more with less, the pulsing heart of intelligent-laziness.

Have you hit the trifecta of laziness, intelligence and supreme ambition?

19   Intelligent laziness and selectivity

The heroes who are lazy and intelligent must also be *selective*.

If you are lazy (as well as intelligent) you must be selective, and you can also afford to be selective.

You cannot get more with less unless you are selective – selective in using 80/20 people, methods and insights. Therefore selectivity and success are also bedfellows. Once you know that very few people, actions and decisions will have a disproportionate, wonky and warped impact on your fortunes, your career and your happiness, then what must you do?

You must find and capture the big breaks in life. You don't flail around with indiscriminate and urgent actions because actions drive out thought. You don't sweat the small stuff because small drives out big. You don't cover the waterfront because the real action and growth is very local. You don't behave like a dilettante, or spread your chips all around the roulette table, because only one number will win, and to beat the odds you must know it.

You don't try everything because that will have average returns. You don't diversify because you understand 80/20.

For success, to stand even a chance of a jackpot in the lottery of life, you need to be selective. And unless you are selective, you are not intelligent, at least not the 80/20 way.

And because you are selective, it is possible also to be lazy.

Intelligence requires selectivity. Selectivity permits laziness.

How selective are you?

20 Intelligent laziness and creativity

Intelligent-lazy people usually have qualities such as thoughtfulness, originality, insight and vision. They may sometimes also have flaws, such as arrogance or smugness. Lazy and intelligent people may be self-possessed, jealous of their time and attention, disdainful of mundane obligations, strong-willed and even dictatorial.

But the characteristic that runs through lazy and intelligent characters, like a seaside town's name through a stick of rock, is above all *creativity*. To be lazy but super-effective requires creativity.

Creativity itself has its high mountains and lower peaks, but one thing about creativity is that it does not have to be sustained for very long, and sometimes not more than once.

Think of Bruce Henderson inventing the concepts of strategy, the experience curve or the BCG matrix. It may have been highly demanding, but it only needed doing once. The same is true of Bill Bain's idea of close partnership between a many-handed strategy ship and the chief executive of Megacorp, and the way he ran the monthly partners' meeting. Do these two things once, or once a month, then coast downhill to the tennis club whenever you want. Creativity is mandatory for the lazy-and-intelligent, yet it is ideally suited to them too.

And finally, creativity is of enormous value to human expression, to all art, all science and all humanity.

Stoke up your creativity to Olympian standards, if you want a fascinating, rewarding and important life.

21   How to acquire laziness

I assume that if you have read this far, you are intelligent.

I also assume that you buy into the virtues of intelligent laziness.

But what do you do if you are not currently lazy?

For a start, rejoice that you were not born lazy. There is no virtue in that. Virtue lies in not being lazy, and then making yourself lazy.

To make yourself lazy, there are just three steps:

- Stop working such long hours. Limit yourself initially to 40 hours a week, then reduce to 30, then 20, then 15, then 10. But what do I mean by work here? I don't mean work you would rather not do. If you don't enjoy something, stop doing it altogether, find a disciple or several, or otherwise outsource or delegate the work. If you work 10 hours on the most vital questions and opportunities, which you enjoy, you will add far more value than you do now. You will be far more selective. You will be much sharper. You will be far more creative.

- When you are down to 10 hours, it is then fine to increase the hours, but only if your degree of enjoyment of work increases, if your valuable output does not decrease, and if you enjoy the work more than anything else you could be doing.

- To keep yourself honest, go back to, or take up a hobby which you love, and which is time-consuming. Tennis, golf, cycling, rock-climbing, writing, reading, touring, speaking, helping friends and their families, collecting anything rare or beautiful, learning a new language, studying at a college or university, playing music ... anything where the hours go by happily and quickly, and where you are learning or teaching something new.

If you are serious, start the steps NOW. Today. This is the moment of truth.

CHAPTER 3

TIME

Time, especially the 'jerky' quality of time, is a fundamental 80/20 theme. Little particles of time can have an enormous impact on our lives and on history. Our experience of happiness may be greatest in relatively short periods of time. This imbalance means that the next period of our lives can be one of intense happiness, quite disproportionate to the time involved, if we structure our lives creatively. There is no shortage of time: realizing this can transform our lives.

22   Time revolution

Time revolution is the fastest way to make a giant leap forward in happiness and effectiveness, and to capture opportunities.

Consider these 80/20 hypotheses:

- Most of any individual's significant achievements – the value they add in personal, professional, intellectual, artistic or athletic terms – are achieved in a minority of their time. Crudely, 80 per cent of achievement is attained in 20 per cent of time taken; conversely 80 per cent of time only leads to 20 per cent of output value. If you double your time on your top 20 per cent of activities, and if you are in control of your time, you can work a two-day week and achieve 60 per cent more than you do now.

- Most happiness occurs during quite bounded periods of time – or happiness islands – whether the period measured is a day, a week, a month, a year or a lifetime. The idea of happiness islands both tests this hypothesis and also provides support for the hypothesis, given that anyone who takes the idea of happiness islands seriously is able to increase their happiness markedly.

What is the 20 per cent of your time that is super-productive, and the 20 per cent of your time when you are much happier than usual?

23   High versus low value output

Most of what we do is of low value relative to the rare interventions we make which are of incredibly high value.

Consider Albert Einstein. In 1905, he wrote five seminal academic papers, including one advancing for the first time the concept of relativity in physics. During the rest of his life, he remained very creative. Yet if he had died in 1906, he would still have rocked the scientific world to its foundations. A very large proportion of his lifetime achievement occurred in just one year, less than 2 per cent of his working life.

Similarly, it has been observed that the very best mathematicians complete their best work by the age of 30, and after the age of 40 they might as well just stop working for all the impact they will have.

The same is true of top sports people.

For anyone who is truly creative, who is going to change the world to any measurable degree, there are small dollops of time during which they make a breakthrough. Times when you are literally hundreds, thousands or almost infinitely more productive than other times. This may be when you are young or when you are old, but the time taken will be a small part of your working life.

Some of the work you do is only worth, say, 10 or 20 dollars an hour. But some of the work you do – or could do – may be worth hundreds or thousands of dollars an hour. Typically, this happens when you make a decision or come up with an idea that not only transforms your life, but also that of other people.

So why waste your time on the trivial things?

You can make hugely better use of your time.

Think how you might do that. Come back to this question when you have some spare time to think. That in itself could be one of the best uses of your time!

24   There is no shortage of time

The most liberating implication of time revolution is that there is plenty of time. If you only make good use of 20 per cent of your time, there is no shortage of it!

This runs counter to everyone's view of time. Yet it is totally logical. Different periods of time in our lives – whether measured in days, weeks, months or years – have wildly different results in terms of our happiness and usefulness. In this sense, time is not time. The value of certain amounts of time varies enormously. It is not time that determines how much you value life, but your attitude to time and the uses you put it to.

Time spent being happy is not time wasted. But time that neither makes you happy, nor generates good results for yourself or other people, *is* utterly wasted. And for most of us, most of the time, what we do with time is either trivial or worse.

So, take a deep breath. You may be extremely busy and harried. But if you cut out trivial activities – this does *not* include things you really enjoy – you will find that you have plenty of time.

What are the useless activities that you could cut out of your life, to give you more time to do the things you enjoy and are good at?

25   Treat time as a friend

Time gone is not time lost.

The good things you have done in life – the love you have given and received, the useful things you have done for yourself, for friends and family, and for the wider world – have not gone away. They are deeply integrated into the flow of life, they have had good results and will continue to do so now and in the future.

Time is a sustainable and renewable asset. Time will always come round again. This is why there are seven days in a week, twelve months in a year and why the seasons recur. Insight and value come from placing yourself in a comfortable, relaxed and collaborative position with time. It is your use of time, not time itself, that is the enemy.

Time is also forgiving. If you have made bad use of time, if you are still making bad use of it, you have the freedom to change your habits, your attitudes, your beliefs and your actions. Once you realize that time spent adding value to your life and the lives of people around you can have enormously and permanently beneficial effects, you will not want to squander your time. Every small particle of time you use to great effect is enormously valuable. And there are millions of these particles of time that are ahead of you. Used generously and wisely, they will make you happy.

Relax! Think what it means to treat time as a friend.

26   Act less

Action drives out thought. Thought before action is always more valuable than action without thought.

It has often been observed that the most productive time on a project is the last 20 per cent, simply because the work must be completed by a deadline. It follows that productivity on a project could be doubled or more, simply by halving the time for its completion.

When time is limited, when it really matters, we think more and are more creative. This is not evidence that time is in short supply.

Plan more. Think more. Think more intensely. Think more creatively. Think in terms of desired results. Act less, but act with greater purpose and confidence.

How are you going to act less and think more?

CHAPTER 4

HAPPINESS

Happiness is the most fundamental 80/20 theme. Across the ages, from Aristotle to the American Founding Fathers, happiness has been recognized as pivotal: nothing is more important for you and the world. And, oddly, the pursuit of happiness is infectious and altruistic.

27   Happiness in the world starts with you

Happiness has some odd characteristics.

It is not just valuable in its own right, it is also both a cause and a result of success, and even of money. Just like money, but rather less obviously, happiness compounds furiously. Happy parents are likely to generate and nurture happy children – who themselves will probably have happy children. The effect of this over generations is enormous.

The same phenomenon can be observed within companies, factories, offices, clubs, pubs, shops, social gatherings, schools, colleges, churches, orchestras and just about every group imaginable. Some are reliably happy and jolly; others are not. Happiness is not just an individual trait; it is a collective one too.

Happiness and unhappiness are infectious.

Happiness, therefore, is your most vital duty.

If you want to serve other people well, you owe it to them to be happy. (This is truer the higher your position, the greater your responsibilities.)

To benefit the people around you, and the world at large, *strive to be happy*.

Happiness in the world starts with you. Decide that you will be happy, because, apart from being good for you, it is your duty.

You are talented enough to generate a huge increase in happiness for other people and the world.

Will you choose to do so?

28   Happiness islands

Identify your happiness islands – the small amounts of time that contribute a disproportionate amount of your happiness. Find a peaceful place to think, take a clean sheet of paper, write 'Happiness Islands' at the top, and list as many of them as you can.

Deduce what is common between all or some of them.

Some of them will be the 'usual suspects' of pleasant times – holidays, travel, celebrations with friends, sporting events or something more intimate.

But often what makes people happy is deeper or more unusual. It could be exercising a skill, learning something you are really into, walking the dog somewhere beautiful, reading, writing, painting, cooking or doing a good turn for someone in need.

When you have identified your happiness islands, *double the time spent on them.*

To go beyond this, you may need to change something structural in your life – career, lifestyle or relationships, for example. Rule nothing out.

Ideally, make the islands the centre of your life. Turn the islands into the mainland.

What are your happiness islands?

29   Unhappiness islands

The best way to start being happy is to stop being unhappy.

Unhappiness islands are the small amounts of time that cause you the most grief, unhappiness, worry, stress or lack of confidence and zest for life.

Identify what they are and any common denominator between some or all of them.

Unhappiness islands are blighting your life.

Whatever it takes, remove them.

What are your unhappiness islands?

What are you going to do about them?

30　Become happier by changing your self-image

Psychologists say our happiness is related to our sense of self-worth. A positive self-image is essential for happiness.

Here are three ways to improve your self-image:

- *Do the right thing*

  Follow your conscience. When do you feel good about yourself? When you help someone else? When you do good work? When you feel proud of yourself for any reason? When you walk in the light?

- *Do maximum good with minimum effort*

  Do things that don't exhaust your goodwill.

  We have a finite amount of love, care, attention, time, money and ability. Focus love on the few people you care about most.

  For the rest, do small things with a high ratio of impact to effort. Smile! Greet strangers! Be polite and respectful! Be considerate! Arrive on time! Look for the good in other people! Look for opportunities!

- *Do what you do best*

  Some people write funny thank-you notes. Some are good with a quick phone call. Others are natural extroverts and make people feel good and valued. Then there are people who can take someone out of their funk and blues.

Whatever you do best, do more. Do less of everything else.

What will you do today, to feel good about yourself?

31　Daily happiness habits

Cultivate daily happiness habits. Happiness is profoundly existential. It exists only now. You can remember past happiness, or look forward to future plans, but the pleasure this gives can only be experienced in the 'now'.

Here are seven daily happiness habits. Cultivate them all and experience them every day.

- *Exercise.* But make it exercise you positively enjoy, such as walking or cycling.
- *Mental stimulation.* Reading, puzzles, quizzes, talking to an intelligent friend about something abstract, or writing a short journal entry or conceptual email are all examples. Watching television or a video, even a documentary, are not.
- *Spiritual or artistic stimulation.* For example, going to a concert, theatre, movie, art gallery, museum, reading a poem and any form of active art.
- *Do a good turn.*
- *Take a pleasure break with a friend.* This could be going for a cup of coffee or a drink with them, going for a walk or just having a natter.
- *Give yourself a treat.*
- *Congratulate yourself* on anything good or useful you have done today.

Try these out!

32   Structural happiness

Happiness is strongly influenced by four 'structures' that you can put in place.

Based on decades of research in the US, Charles Murray performed the great feat of showing that there are only four important 'structures' we need to put in place to make it likely that we will be very happy.[1]

The two equal greatest contributors to high happiness are:

- Having a very happy marriage (or other long-term relationship)
- Having a very satisfying job

The next most important are:

- High social trust
- Strong religion

High social trust means social activities, principally being an active member of a group or club, giving and volunteering, informal social interactions or getting involved in electoral politics.

If you have any two of the four attributes, you are more than likely to be very happy.

The top two attributes together almost guarantee high happiness.

Long-term relationships are a gamble, but the odds favour them making you very happy.

Does this help you decide how to structure your life?

33   The fortunes of flow

Flow is the concept identified by psychologist Mihaly Csikszentmihalyi. It happens when you are so absorbed in an activity that you give it your undivided attention. Time stands still – you operate outside time. Extreme effort is effortless.

Flow goes beyond enjoyment. It is the ultimate in creation. You express the core of your expertize, fusing your mental and physical limits. There is a deep sense that you are destined to express yourself. You are powerful and in command.

Pinballers ping like rattlesnakes; surgeons sew like seraphim; footballers boot beautifully; dancers dance; teachers teach; writers write; composers compose; painters paint; boffins beget breakthroughs; but the Muse on their shoulder dictates.

When you stop, you know you have been in the zone. You radiate authority and assurance. If you do nothing else today, you have done far more than enough. The 80 per cent can exit; the 20 triumphs.

Flow often happens in teams but it can also be solitary – scuba-diving, bird-watching, skating, visiting an art gallery or walking in beauty.

If you have experienced flow, you may become addicted to it. This addiction has no side-effects. Flow moves you to deep happiness. If you are ever fortunate to flow, do it more. If you can make a career out of it, even if it is dangerous, you will die happy.

How will you flow?

CHAPTER 5

AMBITION, SELF-BELIEF AND YOUR CAREER

These three are all recurrent themes in 80/20. Ambition is good, but self-belief is even better – the sky's the limit! Your career matters, but must *never* make you unhappy.

34   Think big

One of my favourite books, *The Magic of Thinking Big*, was published in 1959. Author David Schwartz said that outrageous achievements could happen if someone believed in them.

He gave two examples which then seemed improbable – that we could travel safely into space and that a tunnel could connect England with the European Continent.

If you really believe it can be done, you will defy doubts to find a way.

The difference between very successful people and less successful ones has little or nothing to do with ability. It has everything to do with the scale of ambition and self-belief.

Belief delivers power and determination. Your personal skill is irrelevant. If you believe something is possible and will it to happen, you can co-opt amazing people to work out how.

What outrageous ambition do you truly believe is possible?

35   Believe in yourself

In *Unreasonable Success and How to Achieve It*, I studied 20 people who changed the world, including Winston Churchill; Marie Curie; Walt Disney; Bob Dylan; Steve Jobs; Madonna; Nelson Mandela; J. K. Rowling; Helena Rubinstein; and Margaret Thatcher, to name a few.

They explained their mission succinctly.

Churchill's was to stop Hitler – nothing else mattered.

Thatcher aimed to avert Britain's national decline.

Disney created unforgettable characters.

Rubinstein invented cosmetics to make women beautiful – 'there are no ugly women, only lazy ones.'

By far the most important attribute they had was self-belief. Nobody ever changed the world without being totally convinced that they could, and they should.

To achieve something great, *you cannot have too much self-belief.*

How much do you have?

Multiply it.

36   Turbocharge your self-belief

Half of the twenty people I profiled in *Unreasonable Success* had terrific self-belief from the get-go. The other half acquired it during life's journey.

They had a 'transforming experience' – usually one or two incredible years of personal growth. They entered the period as one person; they emerged as someone completely different.

Some joined a small, high growth organization with a new way of doing things. Some met people with knowledge that nobody else had, and worked with them.

When the transforming experience finished, they had new vision and objectives.

They started to do unusual things that attracted attention and positive feed-back. They became accomplished at something innovative – a novel way of making music, a new art form or web technique, a proprietary means of analysis, a terrific idea for a venture, anything innovative and useful.

They ultra-specialized, and developed a recognizable and unique signature approach.

Then – their actions and success changed their self-image. Truly, utterly, they believed in themselves.

You can follow in their footsteps.

Will you?

37   Self-doubt can be good

Self-doubt and self-belief often go together. If you don't have self-doubt, that is fine, but if you do, it can be very valuable. Self-doubt raises the question, 'Am I on the right track to my destination?'

Steve Jobs was very conscious that he was adopted as a child. This made him especially ambitious. He felt abandoned, yet chosen by his non-biological parents and loved by them. This combination, Jobs felt, made him special.[1]

The sense of abandonment fed his desire for total control of the product. He needed to provide both the software and the hardware for Apple devices, which in the end became a differentiator and source of huge competitive advantage.

If you have self-doubt, do not repress it. It could prove magic.

38   Ambition is good

In his amusing and opinionated book, *A Mathematician's Apology*, G. H. Hardy argues that almost every great achievement increasing human happiness – medical discoveries relieving suffering and everything that has lowered the cost and increased the quality of what we consume – has been driven by ambition.

The desire for reputation, position or money may not be the most admirable motive, he says, but who cares? If the ambition of one person leads to the happiness of many, who can deny that ambition is good? If someone has talent, they should be ready to make any sacrifice to cultivate it fully.[2]

Ambition is good.

Are you ambitious? It is something to celebrate.

What is your life's ambition?

If you don't yet know, or are not sure, take whatever time is necessary to ponder and get to the bottom of this.

CHAPTER 6

CREATIVITY

Creativity is 80/20 because of its tremendous effects on you and the world and because creativity is the opposite of hard work. What you need to do to be creative is misunderstood: it is not a property of individuals, it is the result of deliberate strategy, conscious or unconscious.

You can be creative – if you follow the 80/20 way to become creative, then why not? It is fun and produces great results for little angst.

39 You can be creative

People do not divide into 'creative' and 'uncreative' people.

There is no such thing as a creative personality, ordained from birth. There are only people who create something new and valuable, and those who do not.

There are few of the former; many of the latter. Over time, though, many more people have created than in earlier ages, and the proportion of creative people in the population has increased. You can be one of this select group.

Do you want to create something new – for example, a novel, a useful theory or idea, a painting or sculpture, a poem or screenplay, a new social trend, a business or charity, a new territory of investigation, a way of doing anything to higher standards or with less effort, *or something never done before*?

80/20 will show you how …

40 To become creative, first define your 20 per cent spike

Your 20 per cent spike is your uniquely powerful and creative strength, the few characteristics which will become your trademark creative signature.

Everyone has a unique 20 per cent spike.

Introspection is a good start. Yet defining your spike will take trial and error, experiences and relationships, learning from brilliant people and almost certainly some sort of training or apprenticeship.

Learn everything possible. College may help. But knowledge is almost freely available from cyberspace. The greatest learning comes from experimenting and from practice. If you want to write, write. If you want to paint, paint. If you want to be a public speaker, speak. If you want to make music, play and improvise. If you want to be a philosopher, think. If you want to make money, invest. If you want to be a leader, lead.

Attach yourself to the best individual, company, network or group in your field. Keep narrowing and redefining it.

Go beyond what has been done before, thought before, imagined before.

Then, if you create something entirely new, life will move to a higher plane.

Fully defining your 20 per cent spike may take a long time.

Start today!

41   How Bjorn-Ingvar found his 20 per cent spike

Bjorn-Ingvar was a professor at Gothenburg University. He also belonged to a Lutheran mission church, which had a loss-making business publishing prayer books. The church asked him to take charge of it on an unpaid basis.

He knew prayer books were toast. He looked for wholesome secular titles to supplement them. It turned out that he had an eye for unlikely bestsellers.

He loved the work and agreed to do it full time, giving up his professor's salary for a small honorarium.

His books always sold well. The publishing house became larger than the church that had founded it. Bjorn-Ingvar's pay was miserly – linked to a church minister's pay – but he was having so much fun, he didn't care. 'I work for the cause and the church. If I have created a business worth tens of millions, is that more valuable than the work of a pastor who saves souls?'

Bjorn-Ingvar's spike was an instinct for what his specialized audience would buy in droves. He delighted in finding inspiring, spirited books that would sell surprisingly well. *His greatest reward was in making a difference.*

What difference could you make, that would also make you feel great?

42   How Rachel found her 20 per cent spike

At school, Rachel was bored. The only subject she liked was maths. She left as soon as she could.

She loved clothes. She couldn't afford to buy them, so she decided to sell them. She worked for a large department store in Miami and ended up in The Designer Room – 'Sheer heaven,' she told me. 'Selling to rich women was great fun!'

With a head for numbers, she discovered that margins on the most expensive garments were higher than on the other stuff. The most beautiful clothes took no more effort to sell, often less. She realized that they were hugely profitable.

Starting as a clerk, she talked her way into sales. She always upsold to customers and became the top salesperson.

'You might say I was daydreaming,' she said to me. 'A girl with no credentials could never become the boss. But it's funny. I knew that if by some miracle I became the managing director, I would be a great boss. I'd commission great merchandise that would sell instantly, and train everyone to focus on the most profitable lines.'

'I told myself, "Cinderella, you *will* go the ball." I was destined to head a big brand womenswear business. The hardest part was getting there. It's been smooth sailing ever since. I feel more "me" at work than I do at home.'

Where do you feel most 'you'?

43   What is your territory?

Know what you love doing.

That's your key to creativity.

Can you apply your 80/20 spike to what you love doing?

The convergence of what you are best at, and what you love doing, is *your territory.*

Your territory is your own proprietary sphere of influence. It's the battlefield where you have bled and survived, and where winning has given you authority.

What is your territory?

This may take some time pondering.

Once you have defined your territory, it's all plain sailing from there.

44   Learn everything about your territory

Have you defined your territory yet? Once you have defined it, learn everything about it. Do not reinvent the wheel.

Identify the 'greats' in your territory. Read, listen, watch everything they have already discovered.

Take your time. It may take months or even years of study and learning. It will be a labour of love.

Once you have learned everything about your territory, you are ready to create.

How will you learn everything about your territory?

45   Albert Einstein's dirty little secret

'The secret to creativity', said Einstein, 'is to conceal your sources.'

Einstein is synonymous with genius. Yet he started out as an average student. He was slow to learn to talk. He seemed backward. His grades were poor. Zurich Polytechnic was not the city's best college, but when Einstein first applied to study there he was rejected.

He made it into the Poly the next year but graduated near the bottom of his class. His mathematics were shaky and his girlfriend had to check all his calculations.

He realized, however, that the new, counterintuitive ideas of quantum mechanics demanded a total revision of physics. In 1901, he read with ecstatic delight Philipp Lenard's paper showing that the accepted theory of light was dubious. He considered Lenard's experiments alongside Max Planck's work on radiation wavelengths, coming to the startling view that light could be described not only as waves but also as 'light-quanta' particles. From there the key to relativity was within Einstein's grasp.

It was his identification of a red-hot new scientific area, his 'sources', together with his relentless curiosity, that made Einstein a genius.

If your sources are new and revolutionary, you too can make a breakthrough.

What are the most exciting things you have recently discovered, that have not yet been applied to your territory, but could be?

46   Genius made simple

Einstein's breakthrough in relativity came from applying exciting new ideas in quantum mechanics to his virgin territory, relativity.

History repeated itself when Niels Bohr and Max Planck's theories about quantum mechanics were applied by young scientists to other new territories: astrophysics, biology, chemistry and electrodynamics. As a result, John Bardeen, Subrahmanyan Chandrasekhar, Manfred Eigen and Linus Pauling all won Nobel Prizes.

Their discoveries were monumental, but the process was simple. They took a super-powerful idea and applied it to a new territory.

So, range far and wide outside your own territory. Search for powerful and innovative concepts to apply to it. *The value of this key to greatness cannot be overstated.*

Could you turn this key?

CHAPTER 7

OPTIMISM AND OPPORTUNITY

Optimism produces great results for little effort.
Optimism made humans a biological success against
all the odds. Even if you are not naturally optimistic
you can learn optimism.

Opportunity is optimism on steroids but it is different
from optimism. Opportunity exists out there in limitless
amounts – you just have to notice it and take it.

47   The benefits of optimism

First, optimism is inseparable from the view that you have free will and can make decisions about how to lead your life. If you are optimistic, life is an adventure. The future can be better than the past. The essence of adventure is optimism plus uncertainty.

If you could design your plan for life, and knew how it would pan out, it would be utterly boring. Yet equally, if you don't think you can influence how your life unfolds, life feels pointless.

Second, optimism makes better things happen. If you believe you have influence, you will work more intelligently to make good things happen. You will explore more options, be more creative, inspire more people to collaborate with you and develop the most important life skill – the instinct to calculate the odds and plump for the way with the greatest return for the least time, effort and money.

Third, optimism gives you resilience: the power to overcome setbacks. Life is not a rose-garden. Optimists expect kicks in the teeth yet take pride in surmounting them. Optimists find a better way to reach their objective, or a better objective which can succeed.

Fourth, optimism results in better health and a longer life.

Finally, optimism is fun. Optimists have a genuine smile whatever happens. Pessimists wear a long face. Optimists are more attractive, have more personal power and win more of life's games.

Optimism is more important than your background, education, intelligence, diligence, ability, money or other personal attributes. Optimism is open to all.

Are you optimistic?

48   The power of positive thinking

You probably know that this is the title of a book written by Norman Vincent Peale (in 1953). Here is my summary in modern language:

- Our thoughts are super-powerful. There are two kinds: positive and negative.
- Self-confidence generates positive thoughts.
- A positive view of your psychological assets also generates positive thoughts.
- Negative thoughts come from lack of self-esteem, imaginary obstacles, worries and fear.
- Each day there is a war within us of positive versus negative thoughts.
- If you are optimistic and think you are going to win, you probably will.
- If you think about your doubts, obstacles and fears, they will probably triumph.
- You should picture your success, desires and happiness constantly.

Summary: *trust yourself and the universe. Be relentlessly optimistic.*

Try this today and for a few days. See if it works for you.

49   The power of non-negative thinking

Professor Seligman, who has written the best book on how to become more optimistic, thinks that the key thing is not positive thinking, but rather *the power of non-negative thinking*. What really matters, he says, is what you do when things go badly. When setbacks happen, the key thing is to avoid and change the self-destructive thoughts you may have. He describes this as *the central skill of optimism.*[1]

If you find that the daily battle between positive and negative thoughts doesn't help you, try Dr Seligman's prescription. It has the great merit of being economical, stripping away trivial and unproductive thoughts.

Today and for the next few days, be on **red alert for setbacks**. Don't let them terrorize, overwhelm or depress you. Remind yourself that setbacks are usually temporary, specific to particular circumstances, and rarely your fault.

Don't be set back by setbacks!

50   Optimism and the psychology of the West

Optimism is pre-eminently Western. Psychologist Richard Nisbett says, 'To the Asian, the world is a complex place ... subject more to collective than to personal control. To the Westerner, the world is a relatively simple place ... highly subject to personal control. Very different worlds indeed.'[2]

Optimism is supremely 80/20. Most of the achievements of the world since the sixth century BC were achieved with the benefits of optimism. Progress has been greatest in optimistic times. Optimism is one of the greatest assets of any civilization or group within a civilization, and of successful individuals.

The opposite is also true. When civilizations turn pessimistic, as they did during the first half of the twentieth century, bad things happen – very bad things indeed.

Do you personally feel optimistic?

Are you optimistic in your professional life?

Are you optimistic about the future of your country and civilization?

51   Ancient Greece and optimism

Ancient Greek philosophers started the idea of *individual autonomy* – people can be self-starting and take charge of their destiny, shaping the world around them for their own benefit.[3]

Humans, they said, were the only creatures that could reason. This was immensely valuable. Individual minds could link with other human minds and with divine intelligence. The rest of nature was passive. Mankind could be active, optimistic, creative and self-advancing.

They also believed in human potential for goodness and progress – creation was good and getting better. Aristotle originated the concept of *potentiality* – the deepest reality was not in the here and now, but in what could be in the future. What matters is what the world and its people could *become* on reaching their full potential.

What you could become is greater than what you are now. This philosophy is immensely optimistic and invigorating.

What is the one most important dimension on which you could become better than you are now, the one dimension to focus on now?

How will you seize the opportunities to improve that are available to you?

52   Optimist islands

Optimism operates at three distinct levels – that of individuals, of groups of individuals and of societies.

If your society is not optimistic, that is a pity. But it still does not stop you from voting for genuinely optimistic leaders. Nor does it stop you from being optimistic as an individual, or from working in optimistic networks or organizations.

If you are optimistic, you are much more likely to be happier and more effective. If you increase the extent to which you are optimistic, you will likely become happier and more influential.

If you work with other optimistic people, life becomes even better. You can live on 'optimist islands'.

Optimists of the world, unite; you have nothing but your chains to lose; you have a wonderful world to win.

What will you do to advance optimism?

53 'Opportunity-ism'

We have seen the huge value of optimism, in helping to win the battle between positive and negative thoughts, in overcoming setbacks and, by becoming increasingly optimistic, advancing our happiness.

But there is something even better than optimism – the conviction that life is full of wonderful opportunities, the systematic search for them and, by taking them, lifting your life to ever-higher levels of existence. 'Opportunism' is a dirty word, so I call the thing that goes beyond optimism 'Opportunity-ism'.

Could you coin a better term?

The first element of opportunity-ism is being aware that beyond our existing blinkers lie fields of unimaginable and unimagined opportunities. A friend once told me that it was only by pairing up with a teammate at a college that he found a new activity he did not know existed. He now enjoys extraordinary success in this very specialized field.

The conviction that there are hidden or unexplored opportunities 'out there' enables you to see things that you would never otherwise have noticed. Look for opportunities that are at least 10 times what you would normally expect or imagine. It must be something you would enjoy doing and think you would be good at, and must also involve or benefit at least one other person whom you like.

As Jordan Peterson says *'What you aim at determines what you see.'*[4]

What unimagined mega-opportunity could you aim at?

CHAPTER 8

DIFFICULTIES, STRESS AND MOODS

Life is difficult but that is good – it is better than it being easy because challenge is good for you. However, stress is bad if it makes you unhappy and feel oppressed. You can and *should* avoid bad stress.

There are four basic moods; one is best. You can cultivate it and be happier and more influential.

54   Life is difficult

'Life is difficult' are the famous first words of M. Scott Peck's great work *The Road Less Travelled*.[1]

The idea is both simple and paradoxical. If you expect life to be easy, you will be disappointed and frustrated. But if you expect life to be difficult, you can take the difficulties in your stride and take pride in overcoming them. By expecting life to be difficult, it is no longer difficult. The difficulty is discounted. It no longer matters, except as a stepping-stone to greater self-confidence.

Thus, the attitude we adopt to difficulty itself dissipates difficulty. This is an extremely smart encapsulation of the 80/20 philosophy. Life's difficulties do not matter, because the one thing that does matter in dealing with adversity is expecting and surmounting it.

The relationship to stress is obvious. Stress, beyond a certain point, destroys happiness. Therefore, you should overcome stress. Yet stress can only be overcome by believing that you *can* overcome it. The enemy of such a belief is fear. But fear can be overcome by believing, and demonstrating, that you can overcome fear.

We go to extraordinary lengths to make our lives more comfortable and to remove life's difficulties. This is all to the good. We quell infant mortality, conquer hunger and some diseases, extend lifespans and increase enjoyment. Yet once you fall into the trap of believing that difficulties and stress can be entirely removed, for example by money or relationships, you set yourself up for Peck's dilemma. *Only by expecting difficulties and not being fazed by them can you be happy. Only by relishing life's insecurities can you become secure.*

Do you truly understand and accept that life is difficult, and that this is good?

55 Can we reconcile 'life is difficult' with optimism?

Is there a consistency problem with 80/20?

We know that 'life is difficult', that we should fully expect this and that happiness requires us to overcome difficulties by anticipating them.

But we've also seen 80/20 extolling the virtues of optimism, because only by being optimistic and sensitive to opportunities can you reach your potential and make the world a better place.

Are these two 80/20 views inconsistent?

No. The point that is common between 'life is difficult' and optimism – the essential and most fundamental 80/20 philosophy – is that it is your attitude that partly creates reality, a better reality for yourself and the universe. Reality is a slippery concept. There is reality 'out there', such as all the good and bad things about creation – sunshine, the beauties and dangers of nature, the rivers of life, the miracle of new births … and cancer, natural disasters and death. An important part of reality 'out there' is also other people. Then there is reality 'in here', the reality of your consciousness, your thoughts, your hopes, your fears, your experience of life, your actions.

To a significant extent, 'reality out there' is impervious to your 'reality in here'. But not entirely. We cannot control 'reality out there', but we can influence and change it. We can build houses, for example, to shelter us from the elements. You can also influence and change your 'reality in here' by your beliefs about yourself and the world, which in turn will have an impact on 'reality out there'.

'Life is difficult' and optimism may seem contradictory, but in a more fundamental way they are complementary. Your expectation of difficulties and your optimism both contribute to your happiness. They are twin cherries on a single stalk, the stalk of beliefs that work to make life better.

Can you combine 'life is difficult' and optimism? Do you agree that this will increase your happiness and the good you can do?

56   Challenge versus stress

Do you agree that challenge is good, but that stress is bad?

Technically, stress is neither good nor bad. Stress, pressure, whatever you call it, can be good. Children who have too little stress, because their life is too easy, with everything handed to them on a plate, may well find even trivial setbacks in later life distressing and overwhelming. Motorists on a long straight road – such as North Dakota's Highway 46, which stretches for 123 miles – may have too little stress and doze off or run off the road because of lack of attention. That is why engineers build unnecessary bends (curves) into roads. Ian Robertson, a clinical psychologist and neuroscientist, has written a splendid book which says that each of us needs the right level of stress or challenge.[2]

Nevertheless, in common usage (and in most dictionaries) 'stress' is identified as a bad thing, a 'constraining force' (*The Concise Oxford Dictionary*) or even a disease suffered by managers. Challenge, on the other hand, is something we can all welcome, at least in theory. I will use 'stress' to mean 'stress which is more than we can or should endure', and 'challenge' to mean something that makes us stronger and sharper, along the lines of the philosopher Friedrich Nietzsche's dictum 'What doesn't kill me, makes me stronger.'

And here is a simple 80/20 rule: *If stress is making you unhappy, remove the cause of the stress.* Not 'remove it if you possibly can', because for some reason we often allow stress to ruin our lives. No. Remove the cause of the stress. Period. *There is always a way to remove this kind of stress.*

Have you ever suffered from this kind of 'bad' stress? Did you remove it fast enough?

57   Avoid undue stress

Some people get stressed very easily. Others can cope with difficult challenges and thrive on them. Wherever you are on this stress continuum, it is true that certain circumstances reliably activate your feelings of stress.

I can feel stress coming on whenever I am stuck in a traffic jam or on an underground train that is not moving. I react badly to queues. Even in pleasant restaurants, I feel stressed by poor service, even a tiny thing such as waiting too long for the bill to arrive. I am stressed when talking to lawyers or pedantic, plodding people.

None of this stress is functional. It helps nobody. On the other hand, because I know what situations cause me stress, I take steps to avoid them. I avoid roads that often get jammed, and if I see a line of cars ahead, I turn off and find a longer route that is clear. I avoid restaurants with poor service. We all know what stresses us out and develop our own avoidance tactics, but sometimes we don't realize how important they are.

One secret is to take more time. 80/20 teaches us that we have oodles of time, even though our lizard brain tells us to hurry up. Feeling undue stress will chop more off our life than cultivating a relaxed attitude to time.

There are two main sources of stress – work, and other people you need to please. The two come together in 'the boss'. Find a likeable, understanding boss. If they are also very demanding, that's good too – it brings out the best in you. Perhaps true perfection lies in being in control of your time. But that too can be stressful if you have an over-developed conscience.

80/20 insists on doing the most important and valuable things. Intelligently seeking happiness is uppermost. Anticipating, avoiding and defusing stress is one of the essentials of happiness.

You know how to avoid stress. Make sure you do it.

58   Will this matter 10 days from now?

What you're going through right now may seem important, but will it matter in 10 days? Or in a year? Or 10 years? Will you even remember this moment in the future? These 'time warp' questions are imagined by Richard Carlson in his book *Don't Sweat the Small Stuff – and It's All Small Stuff*. The answer to these questions is generally 'No', which indicates that we shouldn't worry too much about current problems. Carlson is right, don't sweat the small problems. But do sweat the small opportunities. They can have big effects.

The maverick economist John Maynard Keynes said that in the long run we are all dead. Except, of course, that in a sense both Keynes and Carlson are not dead. They have followers who are alive and their legacy lives on.

Is that a contradiction? Perhaps, at least if you achieve something – and *everyone* achieves something in life, not least in their impact on other people – it is not all small stuff and when you part this mortal coil you are not simply dead. 80/20 squares the circle. You see, the trivial things in life, especially the things we fret and sweat about, don't matter, but some things, a small minority of things you do in life, really do matter. It's why you are alive, and believing that everything is small stuff seems too pessimistic and ultimately defeatist. All lives matter.

It is not just writers or artists who leave a lasting legacy. It is anyone who brings up their children badly or brilliantly. It is you and me and everyone on the planet who has daily interactions with several people. Every good and bad act has multiplicative consequences, some much more than others.

Because of their often-lifelong effects, good and bad acts to infants, children and young people have powerful repercussions. This is why nurturing and protecting them are among the most far-reaching actions you can take.

Kindness and unkindness to everyone matters. When you ask, will this matter in the future, think of yourself as someone endowed with god-like powers that can be used for good or ill. What you do every day matters; if it doesn't, you might as well be dead.

Do you think that what you did yesterday, or will do today, matters? What kind or powerful and useful action will you take today?

59   Remove a source of stress now

Someone once remarked about one of the most successful people I know, 'Bob is a genius, but he can't handle stress' – as though this was a fatal flaw. We often think the ability to take stress is a virtue. Close behind, often, is the thought that anyone who can't handle stress is a wimp.

This is stupid. Stress that makes us nervous or unhappy is not something to be endured. It is something to be eliminated. Enduring stress is the opposite of 80/20 – it requires a great deal of effort and angst for a negative return, which is the possible impairment of your health, and the certain subtraction of joy and pleasure from your life.

The intelligent person using 80/20 will make it a priority to kill this canker before it starts eating you alive. Tolerating stress is not a sign of mental health, but the reverse. More broadly, anything that detracts from your enjoyment of life also detracts from your ability to achieve more with less.

What is the number one source of stress for you in life and work?

How will you remove it?

60 Improve your mood, improve happiness and improve results

Moods matter enormously. And they can be influenced to give you much greater confidence, energy and optimism. Mood moderation is one of the great 80/20 secrets.

Psychology professor Robert E. Thayer is the world expert on moods. He says that moods are at the core of our being. He divides moods into four categories, shown in my FOUR MOODS CHART below:[3]

	Tired	Energy
Calm	Winding down	Confident, optimistic
Tense	All used up	Racing to deadline

The star box is the top right – Calm-Energy. Body and mind are welded together, so to increase Calm-Energy without side-effects every day, exercise (even a brisk 10-minute walk can raise your mood and increase energy), listen to music, have plenty of social interaction (even a phone call with a friend) and sunlight, eat healthily and sleep well and long. Avoid sugary snacks, which deplete energy and raise tension. The good news is that you can greatly raise Calm-Energy.

How will you increase your Calm-Energy?

61   80/20 moods

Everyone has moods. Good moods. Bad moods. But what are 80/20 moods?

If you could chronicle your moods in the last 100 days and rank them from the best moods (1, 2, 3 …) down to the worst (98, 99, 100), and you took the best 20 moods (1–20), versus the bottom 20 (81–100), what do you think your difference in happiness and productivity would be?

The 80/20 hypotheses are obvious. On the top 20 days it is likely that:

- you will have done your best work and been most creative;
- the result from at least one of those would have been outstanding, far above the norm;
- you will have been happiest;
- you will have made the right decision on any vital issue;
- you will have made other people happy.

And on the days when your moods were worst, the opposite.

Moods produce results. And moods pass. Therefore:

- Always strive to be in a good mood.
- If you are in a bad mood, stop. Do something to change your mood. Don't try to do any important work. Avoid significant decisions.
- If you are in a good mood, make important plans, take vital decisions and think of the best opportunities that could possibly be available to you. Magnify your impact on the world.

Recall the last time you were in a great mood. Did it have great results?

62   What causes your good moods?

It may seem that moods are beyond your control. But whether you realize it or not, your actions and the environment around you may predictably influence your moods.

Try to think whether your good moods coincide with any of the following, and whether they may in part have been *caused* by the following:

- Exercise, such as going for a walk, swim or bike ride, or playing sport
- Visiting a beautiful place or an art gallery
- Seeing friends and doing something together
- Going to a sporting event or a concert
- Reading a good book
- Meditating
- Doing something creative

What causes your good moods? What is the single most reliable and easy way to put yourself in a good mood? Do more of that!

What puts you in a bad mood? Could you do less of that?

Do you find it wonderful that moods can be changed by what you do?

63   Bad moods are selfish

A final word on moods.

Whenever you get trapped in a bad mood, remember this:

Bad moods are incredibly selfish.

If you are in a bad mood, I guarantee that *you will make other people unhappy*.

Perhaps you would have a 'right' to be in a bad mood if it only affected you. But it doesn't.

So, if you possibly can, just decide that you will not get into bad moods, as it's not what decent people should do. I'm sure you are a decent person. So, don't have bad moods.

You may retort that bad moods are beyond your control.

But that isn't entirely true. Perhaps not true at all.

For two reasons.

One is that you can study what causes your good moods and then put yourself more frequently in the path of a good mood. And, you can study what causes your bad moods and avoid those causes.

Secondly, and finally, *whenever you find yourself in a bad mood, appeal to your better nature.* Do you want to harm your friends and anyone you meet in the next few minutes or hours? If the answer is no, have a rueful smile to yourself and drop your bad mood. At the very least, it is bad manners.

Will you do that for me please, the next time you are in a bad mood?

Thank you very much!

CHAPTER 9

THE SUBCONSCIOUS MIND

The subconscious mind is so 80/20 because it does amazing things, with no effort on your part. It is the source of creativity; it exists outside time; it does not think like the conscious mind; it is emotional rather than rational. The conscious mind has to think and direct the subconscious, like a lion-tamer and a lion (I am not a lion).

Learning how to tap into the subconscious is easy and wondrous if you know how. You will see how.

64 The 80/20 asset par excellence

The greatest miracle of 80/20 is the subconscious mind (also known as the unconscious mind). The subconscious is humankind's greatest asset. Besides many other things, the subconscious is the source of your creative thoughts and intuition.

Everything that we have created – language, mathematics, cities, art, science, engineering, music, cathedrals, rules for civilization, social equality, democracy, the conquest of diseases, trade, exploration, dams, canals, pipelines, bicycles, cars, powered boats, trains, aircraft, space shuttles, artificial intelligence and cyberspace – flows from the subconscious mind.

Neuroscientists estimate that 92 per cent of our brain is subconscious, versus only 8 per cent conscious. The subconscious is by far the dominant driver of your life.[1]

What makes the subconscious so *very* 80/20 is that it operates 24/7/365 with little or no effort. Conscious thinking is hard and requires focused attention; it can only do one thing at a time. By contrast, the subconscious can perform trillions of operations simultaneously, delivering fantastic results with almost no effort.

Learning how to use your subconscious can change your life.

Do you know how to use your subconscious?

65 How scientists use the subconscious mind

Scientists and thinkers often use the subconscious to make breakthroughs, following a common pattern. They work on a problem for years. The answer won't come. They set their work aside. Then, one day, when doing something mundane, the answer suddenly pops up.

For French mathematician Henri Poincaré, the answer came to him when boarding a bus in Paris and chatting to a friend. 'I went on with the conversation,' he said, 'but felt a perfect certainty that the problem had been solved.' Philosopher and mathematician Bertrand Russell was buying a pouch of pipe tobacco when illumination struck.

August Kekulé saw dancing atoms and molecules while daydreaming on a horse-drawn omnibus in London, and thus completed his theory of chemical structures. Four years later he dreamt of snakes catching their tails, leading him to posit that carbon atoms in benzene form a ring.

The conscious mind is great at collecting and ordering data. But the final step in changing a scientific theory usually comes from intuition.

Can you remember a time when your subconscious solved a problem for you? What happened?

66 Artists, the Muse and the subconscious

Nancy C. Andreasen's fascinating book *The Creative Mind* shows how poets, playwrights and musicians are inspired by their subconscious minds.[2]

Playwright Neil Simon says he doesn't write consciously – the Muse sits on his shoulder and dictates. He simply writes it down.

Samuel Taylor Coleridge fell asleep and when he woke instantly wrote over 200 lines of his epic poem *Kubla Khan* without any conscious effort.

Mozart wrote his music, he said, in a pleasing lively dream.

New compositions came to Tchaikovsky suddenly and unexpectedly, generating a great sense of bliss without any effort on his part.

I know that this process is not confined to geniuses. When I sit down to write a book the same thing happens. I may have read and thought a great deal before I start to write, but I don't make notes. As soon as I sit down to type, the words flow effortlessly. If this doesn't happen, I give up and write a different book.

If I can do it, you can too. *Feed your mind and your works will write themselves.*

Knowing how to prime your subconscious mind is the secret to creativity.

67   The subconscious exists outside time

The subconscious is a little weird.

It exists outside time, in the eternal present. The subconscious has no sense of the past or the future. Your past, present and future are all the same to the subconscious. Let me try to explain this with an analogy.

Imagine that you are watching a movie. It has a past, present and future, but they are all compressed into 90 minutes. At any given time, you are part way through the life of people in the movie, yet it is always the present for you. Ignore the fact that the movie takes 90 minutes of your life – imagine you are viewing it all at one moment. That is how the subconscious operates. All time is flat. All time is the present.

If you want something to happen in the future, you have to present it to your subconscious, as if it has already happened. For example:

- 'I am a successful novelist/scientist/playwright/songwriter/broadcaster/ musician finalizing my work and about to write it down.'

- 'I am the leader of a wonderful new social movement/company/ political party which is changing the world for the better.'

- 'I am a rich philanthropist.'

- 'I never had any doubt that I would attain my goal, even though it looked impossible.'

- 'I feel strong, generous, joyful, happy and at one with the world.'

Can you translate your wishes into the 'triumphant present'?

Can you believe you are already what you want to be?

68   The subconscious is a weighing machine, not a thinking machine

Another peculiarity of the subconscious is that it does not apply a filter to information. It is literal-minded, taking everything that you tell it at face-value. It cannot distinguish between current reality and imagination. If you tell it strongly enough what you want, it will work to make that a reality.

The subconscious cannot tell the difference between true information and false information, or between important and unimportant information. It weighs information. It pays most attention to information which is presented with emotional force, which is frequently repeated and which is recent.

The subconscious pays most attention and works best with the following.

- You present your beliefs and wishes with great emotional force and passion.

- You have presented your beliefs and wishes recently: current views 'sit on top of' the subconscious.

- You repeat, repeat and repeat your views and wishes. This is why advertisers pay to repeat their message again and again. Your conscious mind may be bored, but your subconscious is enthralled. This is why Goebbels, the Nazi communications 'genius', said 'a lie repeated often enough becomes the truth'.

Have you translated your wishes into subconscious-friendly terms?

69 The 80/20 way to tap into the subconscious Stage 1: decide what you want the subconscious to do for you

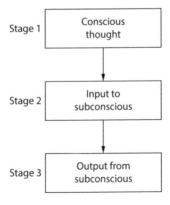

Do you want it to help you be creative, realize a personal goal or increase your serenity?

Now be more specific. Tell your unconscious mind what you want it to do for you. Write down exactly how you will be creative, what your goal is or the thought which will give you peace of mind.

See the following readings for stages 2 and 3.

70 Stage 2: input your wishes to your subconscious

- Relax and daydream
  - ☐ Sit in a comfortable chair in a quiet, private spot, preferably outdoors.
  - ☐ Put all thoughts (apart from the message you are about to transmit) out of your head.
  - ☐ Send the message to your subconscious – say it out loud if you can.
  - ☐ Daydream during 'automatic' exercise – something such as gentle walking or cycling you do often, without thinking about it, with no stress or strain.
  - ☐ Repeat the message, preferably out loud, during the exercise and immediately afterwards.
- Before sleep
  - ☐ A couple of minutes before you go to sleep, voice the message.
  - ☐ Look forward to a good sleep and sweet dreams.
  - ☐ Repeat the message as the last thing you think before sleep overtakes you.

Try this today!

71 Stage 3: receive output from your subconscious

The subconscious will try to communicate its answer to you. Unless you crowd the answer out with vigorous activity, a preoccupation with unrelated matters or a restless mind, you will get the message.

To help the subconscious get through, relax and daydream at times during the day.

The answer often comes at night, or during the morning in that time of semi-slumber during the hour before you awake. Sometimes it comes in the middle of the night and wakes you up. To capture the insight before you fall asleep again and forget it, have a notebook and pen on your bedside table.

Have you gone through all three stages yet?

Make it a habit.

Once you have learnt the power of the subconscious, help your family and friends to do the same and reap great benefits with minimal effort.

CHAPTER 10

GROWTH

To get the most out of life, you have to understand the power of growth. Growth makes life easy and fun; you need to find growth and thrive in it.

But, as 80/20 observes, growth is very much a minority sport. Growth hogs growth and makes non-growth prevalent and stultifying. Seek growth or wallow in mediocrity – not a hard choice if you understand that growth is *everything*.

72 Growth is everything

From time immemorial until a few centuries ago, there was no growth in the economy. Population and living standards were flattened by nature, above all by hunger and disease.

Then, in Western Europe, there was a slow growth in free cities, oases of commerce in a sea of feudal agriculture, followed by the colonization of the Americas, the invention of printing by movable type, then the steam engine and machines which could multiply human and animal power hundreds, thousands and eventually millions of times.

Industry and its self-perpetuating, permanent growth has transformed history, the human experience, and even the geography and population of our planet to a degree unimaginable just three centuries ago.

Every country which has industrialized has experienced growth of 2–3 per cent per annum ever since. This may not sound much, but 3 per cent growth is enough to double living standards every 23 years.

Albert Einstein was once asked, 'What's the most powerful force in the universe?' He replied at once, 'Compound interest.'

Compounding is truly miraculous. Yet there is a problem with it.

Can you guess the problem with compounding?

Clue: it is closely related to the 80/20 Principle.

73 Compounding – problem and opportunity

The problem with compounding is that it is unequally distributed. But that problem is also the opportunity.

If Henrietta the hairdresser is 18 and saves $1,600 a year and it grows at 10 per cent a year (roughly the rate that stock market values have grown over time), how much will she have at age 65? Without compounding it would be 47 years times $1,600, which is $75,200. But with compounding it comes to a whopping $1.5 million.

But what if Henrietta puts the money in the bank instead of the stock market? Bank interest rates have been all over the shop in the past. But let's take a reasonable estimate of 2 per cent a year, compounded annually. When she retires at 65 Henrietta will have $122,987 – a tidy sum, perhaps, but nowhere near $1.5 million.

Long-term savers are on the right side of compounding. The more they save and invest, and the longer they leave their savings compounding, the richer they will get.

People who save little or nothing are on the wrong side of compounding. People with credit card debts paying exorbitant interest rates are in the hell of compounding.

Are you exploiting the joy of compounding or suffering the hell of compounding?

74   Growth in companies

The economy grows because businesses – companies – grow. The economy does not grow because of the public sector (this is essentially society consuming, which is not necessarily a bad thing – but it does limit growth).

But, as in everything connected with compounding, growth is unequally distributed.

High growth companies – those increasing revenues at more than 10 per cent annually, say around 30 per cent overall (some companies are growing at 50–100 per cent and lift up the total growth sector) – probably represent no more than 5 per cent of the total economy. Yet they are a perfect illustration of 80/20 in dynamic action over time.

If the low-growth 95 per cent of the economy grows each year at 3 per cent, and the (initially) tiny high-growth sector grows at 30 per cent, what would the picture look like in 10 years?

The answer is that the 5 per cent fast-growth companies take 81 per cent of total growth over the 10 years – an 81/5 relationship!

At any one time, the overwhelming preponderance of growth belongs to a very small minority.

Compounding is the greatest ally of 80/20. The vast majority do not grow very much, but the few that grow a lot also hog the most absolute growth.

80/20 suggests that there is no point working outside the very few areas of high growth. Yet more than 9 out of 10 people are stuck where growth is limited.

Are you one of them?

75   Why work for a high-growth company?

- It will be more fun.
- You will get promoted faster.
- You will learn far more.
- You gain satisfaction from being part of a winning team.
- You may make far more money, through pay increases, bonuses and, perhaps, stock options.

Are you convinced? What are you going to do about it?

CHAPTER 11

SUCCESS AND 80/20

Authentic success doesn't accept the rules; you write your own rules and voyage into uncertainty, experimenting and job-hopping.

Your flaws are your destiny, your source of triumph: you win hugely or not at all. This may suit you better than following the rules and having modest success which is not your own doing and not gratifying.

To succeed beyond all expectations, you must limit your focus but hit the stars. 80/20 will guide you.

76   What does school success predict?

When I was 14, one of our more unconventional teachers dropped a bomb-shell on us. He asked us who in the class would be most successful when they left school. We voted for those who were at the top of the class in their exams, spoke up most in class, were captains of sport or were most popular. But Mr Hunt surprised us. 'I don't know who will be most successful in life,' he said, 'but I know who *won't*. It's none of the classmates you mentioned. The person who will achieve most is someone obscure, someone you would never suspect. *Success in school does not equal success in life.*'

Sitting squarely in the middle of my class, shy, unnoticed and unremarkable, but having a deep desire to be successful, this was music to my ears. And Mr Hunt was right. Class and school captains became lawyers and estate agents, got married and were never heard of again. They may have been deliriously happy for all I know, but they were never rich or famous.

Now US research has substantiated Mr Hunt's intuition. High school success predicts college success. A good college degree is nice: 9 out of 10 graduates go on to have professional careers, with 4 out of 10 in the highest tier jobs. The benchmark for high school success was a grade point average of 3.6 out of 4.0. By contrast, a survey of 700 US millionaires showed an average score of only 2.9.[1] The researchers concluded that good high school students are diligent and follow the rules, but people at the very top get there by breaking the rules, doing something original and different.

Don't work too hard at following the crowd and being obedient. It's not much fun and doesn't pay as much as doing your own thing. Did you care about your grades in school and college? Did they matter later on? If you have children, what do you tell them?

77   Filtered and unfiltered leaders

Harvard Business School professor Gautam Mukunda has some intriguing views about leaders. He says that great leaders do not have the same qualities as good leaders; they are not souped-up versions of the same thing. It is not a matter of 'more' – they are fundamentally different people.

Filtered leaders are people who work their way up the greasy pole, conscientiously paying their dues, respecting the conventions, reliably following the party line and never rocking the boat.

Unfiltered leaders don't work their way through the ranks; they barge in through the window. They are the people who were *not* head of their school, and they often have poor qualifications or even a track record of failure. They are entrepreneurs who do their own thing and create their own power alley. In politics, they are like Winston Churchill, who would never have become prime minister of Britain were it not for Hitler and the threat he posed. Or they may be like US vice-presidents who were not really qualified to become president but did so because the president died. They did surprising things, because they were not filtered. They may become a disaster or a stunning success. Margaret Thatcher was unfiltered. John Major was filtered.[2] Nearly all great scientists are unfiltered, Einstein being a prime example.

Are you filtered or unfiltered?

Being unfiltered is more fun. It also gives you a better shot at the very top.

78   Do you have intensifiers?

'Intensifiers' are not part of your sound system, nor are they something that makes you work harder. 'Intensifiers' is Gautam Mukunda's name for extreme qualities that are often a liability, but sometimes work magic. Intensifiers are flaws that can become virtues.

Churchill's intensifiers were his patriotism. It was so extreme that he thought Gandhi was the devil for wanting a moderate amount of self-government for India. Thatcher's intensifiers were her loathing of trade unions and their leaders. Donald Trump's intensifiers are evident every time he opens his mouth: his hatred and contempt of professional politicians. Lyndon Johnson's intensifiers were his morbid fear of poverty, inherited from his childhood, which made him launch the 'Great Society'. Albert Einstein's intensifiers were his refusal to take advice or learning from any of his teachers.

If your greatest weakness is also your greatest strength, you have intensifiers.

It is far better to have intensifiers than to be an all-rounder. Nearly all great leaders, nearly all great entrepreneurs and nearly all super-high achievers, in politics, in business and in every other department of life, have intensifiers. None of them are all-rounders.

Intensifiers go with being unfiltered. The idea of intensifiers is perhaps even more helpful because it points to *how* you can evolve into greatness.

Intensifiers are part of the toolkit of 80/20 people, of extreme performers.

Do you have intensifiers?

79   Is college a way to riches?

College is a way to moderate wealth, quite possibly.

But to extreme wealth, no.

Of the Forbes 400 richest people, 58 dropped out of college or never went. The average net worth of the 58 was $4.8 billion. The average net worth of the other 342 people – those who went to college and graduated – was $1.3 billion. The dropouts and people who 'never went' made 3.7 times what college grads made.[3] That's pretty conclusive proof that college subtracted a huge amount of value from the people who went. The return on time and money is hugely negative. Going to college is, in purely financial terms, a disaster.

Nearly all colleges produce people who are quite knowledgeable but cannot think independently. They are told what to think by their lecturers or professors.

This is fatal for originality. Thinking for yourself, from first principles, is increasingly rare.

Entrepreneurs are forced to think from first principles, and to invent new products, new customers or new ways of operating from scratch. If they can't do this, natural selection ensures they will fail.

If you can enter a university that teaches you how to think, seize the opportunity with both hands. Otherwise, college may be nothing more than a very expensive finishing school.

Did you go to college? Did you drop out or graduate? Or did you skip the whole thing? What is your take on all this?

80   Smart experimenting

Experimenting is itself smart. 'All life is an experiment.' Ralph Waldo Emerson wrote, 'The more experiments you make the better.' But the 80/20 philosophy is that there are smarter and less smart ways of experimenting.

Smart experimenting involves sampling different worlds of learning, work and other experiences – the more diversity of experimentation, particularly early in your life, the better. For example:

- different approaches to learning, such as direct institutional instruction (schools, colleges), sitting at the feet of an individual teacher, reading, watching videos, private thinking in groups or alone and working in an organization that is distinctly different from others
- doing one or more of the above, but in a different country or culture
- reading widely in a foreign language to appreciate different modes of thinking
- visual experiences such as art, fantasies, imaginary animals, comic book characters
- listening experiences, for instance sampling different genres of music

Experimenting serves three generic functions:

- It broadens your mind, so you appreciate different ways of thinking and feeling.
- It expands your imagination and empathy with different experiences.
- It helps you to identify a specific area of interest that you want to explore in greater depth – this is the highest and most original form of experimenting, the ultimate destination of 'more from less'.

Have you experimented too little, or possibly too much? What is the trade-off for you of range versus depth?

81   Smart job-hopping

Smart job-hopping accelerates your learning and development of new skills, while also accelerating your earnings trajectory.

Research proves that, on average, job-hopping increases your earnings and promotion prospects.[4] Because job-hopping compounds your opportunities, it is most valuable early in your career.

The best job-hopping involves moving to a group:

- where you like the people there, and are like them;
- that knows something valuable that no other group knows as well, or at all;
- that is growing faster than its peers;
- that pays you substantially more than you earn now, and offers more scope for personal growth and promotion;
- that changes you, ideally transforming you.

Have you job-hopped enough? Smartly enough?

82   Limited objectives, high output

The danger with work and all other aspects of life today is that you bite off more than you can chew.

80/20 provides the solution. If you only do the 20 per cent of things that are most important, that are of greatest value to you and the people around you, you will perform far better than if you try to do everything.

Paradoxically, the route to high output is limited objectives.

If you don't do the 80 per cent, you will have more time.

If you don't do the 80 per cent, you will have more energy.

If you don't do the 80 per cent, you will have more enjoyment.

Limit your objectives. Ruthlessly cut out everything that is not essential, and everything that is not very valuable.

Try it today. Only do the top 20 per cent.

It works. It will make you more productive and happier.

CHAPTER 12

THE THEORY OF PERSONAL MONOPOLY

The Grateful Dead musician Jerry Garcia said,
'Don't be the best at what you do, be the only one.'
How did a 67-year-old ex-prisoner save his country?
By being the only one. Be yourself, be authentic,
be different. You are the only one who is you.
Make the most of that and turn it into your monopoly.

83   The 80/20 theory of personal monopoly

Monopolies are wonderful.

The ultimate objective for a company is to build very high relative market share – to be many, many times bigger in its niche than its number two rival. It is even better if the company is infinitely bigger – that is, it has no rival making similar products or providing services at a similar price.

The same principle applies to individuals.

Jerry Garcia said, 'You do not merely want to be considered the best of the best. You want to be considered the *only* one that does what you do.'

For bands and individuals alike, monopoly is nirvana. Whether you are a musician, a singer, a songwriter, a poet, a painter, a writer, a comedian, a footballer, a tennis player, a baseball hitter, a talk-show host, a manager, an entrepreneur or an investor, an inimitable trademark means you have hit the ranks of the great. One Shakespeare. One McEnroe. One van Gogh. One Agatha Christie. One Madonna. One Steve Jobs. One Springsteen. One Ted Williams. One Warren Buffett. And, even though he can't sing, there is only one Bob Dylan.

In many ways, your weaknesses are your strengths. If Princess Diana had been more mature and less vulnerable, would she have become 'the people's princess'? Perfection is undesirable. Sainthood is passé. Talent is sometimes optional. *Authenticity is everything.*

Ultimately, the world is a crowded place. To stand out, you have to specialize to the nth degree. To adapt Garcia, *you must be the only one in your segment.* You are the segment and the segment is you.

You probably do not want to be famous. I, for one, would hate it. But there are millions of possible segments for you to create and personify. Some may be very small and obscure. However tiny your segment, there is great fulfilment in doing your own totally unique thing.

What could be yours?

84   Bill Gates' personal monopoly (from age 20)

When he was a young teenager, in 1968, Gates was one of the first school-kids in the world to have access to computers and write computer programs. When he was 17, he formed a joint venture with schoolmate Paul Allen, and when Gates was barely 20, they founded Micro-Soft as a computer software venture, dropping the hyphen within a year. Their big break came in 1978, when IBM agreed to use their software as the operating system for the first IBM personal computer. In his most pivotal business decision, Gates refused to give IBM exclusivity, correctly reckoning that other firms would clone the IBM PC and need the same software.

From then until 2007, Gates effectively ran Microsoft, consistently making the right commercial decisions and becoming, for many years, the world's richest person. From the mid-1990s, after some initial scepticism, Gates became one of the most influential promoters of the internet, helping to make it a successful 'alternative reality' in business and all other aspects of human life.

From 1994 onward, Gates has become the world's foremost philanthropist, with many outstanding achievements, including the virtual eradication of polio as a killer disease of millions of children.

Gates is no saint, but when he dies, he will be remembered as the father of commercial software (one personal monopoly) and the world's greatest philanthropist since Andrew Carnegie and John D. Rockefeller (another personal monopoly). I hope, after many more years of good works and tennis playing, that he dies happy.

What is, or could be, your personal monopoly?

85   Nelson Mandela's personal monopoly (from age 67)

I was a frequent visitor to South Africa in the mid-1980s. I enjoyed it enormously – the sunshine, the sheer beauty of the country, the astonishing cheerfulness of most of the people (regardless of race) and the sense of being on the 'edge', living through a period in history. But one thing was profoundly depressing. Nobody believed that there was a solution to the unspeakable issue – how to avoid civil war. I met nobody who believed a peaceful solution would emerge; the only issue was the date of the apocalypse.

The solution was a 67-year-old prisoner who had been incarcerated on a ghastly rocky island outside Cape Town from 1964 until 1982, before being transferred to a much less unpleasant jail in Cape Town itself. In 1985, Nelson Mandela was the only possible bridge between the ANC, the anti-apartheid liberation movement and the white supremacist, stubborn and benighted Nationalist government. Why was Mandela uniquely qualified to bridge the chasm between the two sides?

First, because he believed he could and should do it. Second, his time in jail had only enhanced his charisma, moral stature and reputation among those South Africans ready for change. Third, he alone among the ANC leaders was available as a negotiator – the others were all in hiding or exile. Fourth, he was prepared to compromise, something no other ANC leader contemplated. These factors constituted Mandela's personal monopoly.

The deal Mandela offered to his captors was simple – they must agree to democracy: one person one vote and an end to apartheid; in exchange, Mandela offered peace and prosperity – no socialism, no communism, no retribution for the evils of the past and all the freedoms of a liberal state. He charmed his enemies, and they believed he could deliver the deal. In the end, it was irresistible.

Could you mediate and bring two opposing sides together, and find a solution acceptable to both?

CHAPTER 13

80/20 AND THE BOSS

Until you 'fire' him or her, your boss is probably more important to your happiness and success than the company you work for, or even you and your talents.

Choosing your ideal boss is a key 80/20 skill. It's not too hard and the rewards are great. You will see how here.

86   80/20 and finding the perfect boss

One of the 'vital few' causes of success and happiness at work is your boss. Pay as much attention to this issue as you can, because almost nothing is more vital.

How do you find the perfect boss for you?

Start by asking your friends to score their boss out of 10. If the boss rates a 9 or a 10, put the boss on your shortlist. Of course, you have to want to work for their company and have a chance of doing so, but the boss is often more important than the company for your happiness and success, so start with him or her.

If you can meet the saintly boss casually in a group including your friend, do so. Say almost nothing. Listen carefully. Decide if you agree with your friend.

Then look on the web for anything about the boss or their company. Access financial and other information to see if the organization is growing fast. Small but growing fast is ideal. If the group the boss works with is not growing fast, cross them off the list. If the company qualifies, try to arrange another informal meeting including your friend and the boss. Express possible interest if that seems appropriate at the time.

Then get to know the boss, informally and if all goes well, request a formal interview. If there is a green light on both sides, ask to talk to *his or her boss*.

Do you have the perfect boss already? Or have you not met them yet?

87   The psychology of interviewing

The psychology is important. Most people go to interviews as the supplicant. They are nervous and desperate to make a good impression.

Bad idea. The boss is important for you, and you are important for the boss. You can help to make your boss more successful. It is a meeting of equals. Your prospective boss will be more experienced than you, but to make a success of joining his or her team, it has to be a mutually good move. On some important dimension, you are probably better than your boss, or will become better with experience. Visualize what this may be. If you can see it, the boss may too.

Approach the boss as one human being talking to another human being. Be natural. Be yourself. Is there positive energy and a connection between you?

If you enjoy the meeting, the other person will probably enjoy it too.

Are you the right side of the psychology of interviewing?

By the way, do you like your current boss? If you don't, that's a good reason to find one that you do, inside or outside your current group.

88   Is your prospective new boss like you?

The ideal is that the boss is like you – and therefore you are like your boss – and the boss is like the rest of their group. If you are like your boss, the chances are that you will also like your co-workers. This is just as important as being like the boss, but you may not need to work it out in advance. Take it on trust for the moment but ask to speak to a group of co-workers too, if you can do this naturally.

What does it mean to be like your boss? It helps if you think along similar lines, use similar language, like the same things in life, are at the same level of intelligence and feel empathy with each other. Of course, diversity is important as well, but not in everything. Unless there is a basic 'I'm OK, you're OK' feeling between you, diverse thinking or attributes will never get a genuine chance to come into play.

Ask yourself: if I had been older or more experienced than the boss, could I imagine the roles being reversed? Could I imagine myself in his or her role, and them in mine? Would that also have been a good move for both of you?

It's also worth asking – *are you like your current boss?*

89   Is your boss going places?

If your future boss is on a fast track to promotion and greater responsibilities, either in their existing firm or potentially in another, this is good news for you. *If you and the new boss achieve things together, he or she is likely to take you with them.*

How do you assess if the new boss is on a fast track?

- Compare the boss's age to their level in the company. Are they young, average or a bit long in the tooth? See how fast they have already arrived in their current job.

- How long have they been in that role? If they have just arrived in it, rapid internal promotion is unlikely.

- Have they job-hopped? This is often a fast track: People who have benefited from job-hopping before are more likely to do it again.

- Do you get a sense from talking to them that they are wedded to their current position, or that they are super-ambitious and always looking for new opportunities?

- Ask to talk to *their* boss 'to get a broader picture of the organization's path and future'. Obviously, don't ask anything about the super-boss's view of the boss, but listen – if you have ears to hear, there will be subtle hints.

If you decide to work for the new boss, use 80/20 to see how you can help make them look good and deserve promotion. *Ask yourself, if I was the boss, how would I use 80/20 – and help the boss to think in this way too.*

Perhaps you could do that for your current boss also?

90   Should you 'fire' your boss?

It's a good 80/20 plan to think at least once a year whether you should 'fire' your boss. I've put 'fire' in quotes because clearly you can't literally fire him or her from the company. But you can, and perhaps should, fire the boss from your life; that is, find a better boss.

A better boss:

- understands and uses 80/20;
- works for a faster growing and smaller company;
- is ambitious, competent and going places;
- likes you and whom you like;
- is like you;

- develops and extends your skills and thinking;
- delegates part of their job and leaves you to do it without interfering;
- has a relaxed and confident manner and is available to help you;
- will take you with them when they move to a bigger job or start their own venture.

Do you think enough about who you work for?

91   Should you have a boss at all?

Should you have a boss at all, or should you become self-employed or start a new venture?

Here are some possible reasons for going it alone:

- Autonomy
- Being captain of your own ship – autonomy does not necessarily mean having a ship
- Being able to do the things that you are best at, and dumping everything else
- Working with a team of people you know and like, and not with anyone else
- Fulfilling your ambition or destiny
- Working the hours you want
- Making more money

Rank these objectives – what are the top three?

How motivating are they to you?

CHAPTER 14

FANTASY MENTORS, FAILURES, WINNERS AND SEX

We look at why a fantasy mentor can be better than a real one, why we should praise failure and why winners should multiply themselves.

92   Select a fantasy mentor

When he was still 19, Bob Dylan arrived in Manhattan, unheralded and unknown, yet convinced that he was a unique phenomenon. In his memoir *Chronicles*, Dylan wrote, 'There were a lot of better singers and better musicians but there wasn't anybody close in nature to what I was doing. Folk songs were the way I explored the universe.'[1] Despite this incredible self-belief, he needed a mentor. He found Woody Guthrie in hospital suffering mightily from a terminal disease, and sang Guthrie's own songs at his bedside, also singing his own 'Song to Woody'. Guthrie may not have realized Dylan was there, or who he was.

Dylan adopted Guthrie as his mentor, probably without Woody knowing it. Woody was Dylan's role model – Woody dared to write *new* folk songs. He was also a guru, a philosopher and writer of protest songs. Sound familiar? Dylan assumed Guthrie's spirit, role and *authority*.[2]

My two mentors were Bruce Henderson and Bill Bain. I observed Bruce but don't think he knew who I was. It didn't matter. I imitated his approach to thinking about strategy from first principles. I did know Bill rather well, but don't think he fully appreciated how important he was to me, nor how much I modelled myself on him, with wonderful results.

Bruce was a fantasy mentor for me. Bill was part-real and part-fantasy mentor.

It is easier to find a great fantasy mentor than a great 'real' mentor, and it can be even more rewarding. Do you have a fantasy mentor?

93   Failure is wonderful

None of us welcomes failure, but all of us should.

When I was in my late 20s, I was failing gloriously. I couldn't do the heavy-duty financial analysis loved by my firm. My response to failure was to redouble my efforts, work 80 hours a week, try harder and harder, and sacrifice everything to work. The net result – two or three years of misery. All because I couldn't bear to fail. *I should have welcomed failure:*

- First, because it could, if I let it, put a quick end to my suffering.

- Second, once one is failing, the chances of repair are slight (nil in my case).

- Third, failure is instructive, telling us what kind of work (or relationship, pastime or any other circumstance) to avoid, now and forever.

- Fourth, it gives clues on how you might succeed – look for a firm, or type of work or relationship and so forth, that is radically different, or at least different on a key dimension, from the thing at which you are failing.

- Fifth, it should teach you some valuable virtues that will increase your happiness – humility, compassion for yourself and other people, respect for people who for any reason fail at something important, flexibility, imagination and ability to find new and different opportunities (they are always there) and even optimism, because you are not going to fail like this again, or if you do, you know to cut your losses quickly.

- Finally, because it makes your future success, when it comes, all the sweeter for being in marked contrast to your past failure.

Have you failed gloriously? What did you learn?

94　Winners and their sex lives

(Please note: this is metaphorical!)

Organizations, networks and leaders who are big winners should breed prolifically. Back the winners with cash and the best skills available anywhere.

Too many winners sit in monasteries and nunneries or opt for vasectomy. They while away their days pleasantly enough, serving customers the way they first stumbled across, enjoying easy orders and fat margins. Until a rival invents something new or improved.

Winners who don't have sex will die out. Winners who have a normal sex life will horribly underperform their potential. Winners have an evolutionary duty to have a superabundant sex life, growing exponentially and spawning a large number of well-equipped offspring.

This is counterintuitive. Surely those who are less successful should be trying harder to improve what they have? That is normal reasoning. 80/20 takes a different tack. When something is working super-well, it must be improved and spread, and new generations themselves improved and spread, as fast and as far as possible. 80/20 puts enormous pressure for improvement and reproduction on the organisms which are most successful to start with.

80/20 also gives winners the inbuilt mechanisms to keep winning. Use them.

Are you using all the means at your disposal to make your biggest successes even more prolific?

95   The case of Fred

I expect you know people who have been a huge hit in their careers. Not all of them, however, make good use of the special position handed to them by their success to date.

For example, my good friend … let's call him Fred. He was stunningly successful before he was 40. He made a deliberate decision not to reinvest his time and some of his money in a new venture. Instead, he dabbles in politics and philanthropy. He's also taken a few outside director positions in prestigious causes. He spends a lot of time travelling and meeting prominent people.

For sure, he's had a positive impact in all these activities. They are all worthwhile. Yet he no longer sets the world alight. He has stopped doing what he does best. He is one of the world's best technologist-inventors. Why isn't he inventing something new? I think he's retired to a rather pleasant monastery.

If you've scored a hit, by all means take a break. Recharge your batteries. Spend more time with your family.

But please, do what you do best. Do it on a massive scale. If winners don't breed prolifically, the gene pool will degrade. We'll wallow in the mediocrity of the majority.

And as for you, my friend, well, if you are like Fred, you won't have as much fun as you could do. For people like you, work is more fun than fun.

CHAPTER 15

MORE ON HAPPINESS ...
AND ROMANCE

Now we circle back to happiness, the most fundamental 80/20 theme. Here you'll discover how to become happier, how romance fits into the picture, why the 'baseline happiness' theory is too pessimistic and the 'seven secrets of high happiness'.

96   Become happier by changing the people you see

Your happiness is strongly affected by the five people you see most often – and perhaps the next five too.

Rank the top 10 people you spend most hours a week with. The top two or three will influence your happiness most. It is hard to be really happy if you don't like one of them. (This may include your boss.)

The next two or three will still be important, and the rest significant, to your happiness.

Who would you like to see more?

Who would you like to send to Siberia?

Do it!

97   Happiness, virtue and the racehorse

A racehorse needs daily gallops and frequent races to keep it fully tuned.

But what is the point of a racehorse? The point is to win races. And how does it win races? By remaining in shape and running fast every day. And what makes a racehorse happy? Remaining in shape, running fast every day and winning races.

Similarly, to do good things – in rather prissy words, to be virtuous – you need to practise virtue, to do something kind or useful every day.

What is the point of virtue?

The same thing – to do something kind or useful every day.

And what makes you happy?

The same thing.

The means and the ends are the same.

What good deed or deeds will you do today, to practise virtue and enjoy happiness?[1]

98   Happiness and romance

In a survey of extremely happy people, all of them, with one single exception, were in a romantic relationship. Martin Seligman, a distinguished psychologist, says 'Perhaps the most robust fact … is that married people are happier than anyone else.' (Seligman uses 'marriage' as shorthand for long-term romantic relationships of any kind.)[2]

There are exceptions, but there is a very high correlation between high happiness and being in a long-term relationship. To some extent, happier people are more likely to get married and make a success of it. But when the statisticians crunch their numbers, it is still highly likely that you will be happier if you are in a long-term relationship. This is one of the most important 80/20 hypotheses in this book, perhaps the single most important one.

There are many reasons. One is that the people you see most in your life have an enormous impact on your happiness. Assuming you pick and keep someone you like, seeing your partner more often than anyone else is bound to give you great opportunities for happiness.

Having a dependable mate, a solid rock permanently around, also buffers you against the sea of troubles that will undoubtedly arise in life.

A more profound reason is that true love is inherently unselfish. We have already seen that doing other people a good turn is one of the best ways to be happy. We all need a cause outside ourselves. Love for a partner, and for our family, gives inbuilt opportunities to compound happiness based on behaving nobly.

Are you in a long-term relationship? Are you making the most of it?

99   Living happily alone

Not everyone is in a long-term relationship. Nor should they be. You may be too young to be in one yet – and because the mutual selection of partner will be one of the most vital decisions of your life, it is important not to rush it. You may be experiencing the trauma of break-up in a relationship, or the death of a partner.

Or you may just not be suited to a long-term relationship. I have a good friend who told me, 'I have been twice married and twice divorced, and now I am happier than I have ever been.'

This case is instructive. Her happiness is based on three wonderful assets. One is her unfailing cheerfulness and wish to help other people. Then there is her work, which is creative and demonstrably useful to her clients, and well paid – she is absorbed in her work and loves it. Finally, she is very close to the families of a brother and a sister, as well as to half a dozen other long-term friends whom she sees frequently. In a sense, she has eight or nine very close relationships which have the three main benefits of a successful romantic relationship – enjoyment of company, a rock (or series of rocks) to depend on in adversity and the opportunity to display genuine love for people she cares for.

If you are living alone, for whatever reason, you can be as happy as some-one in a great romantic relationship, and for some of the same reasons. Living alone also raises the stakes for having a job you love.

If you are fortunate enough to have a great partner, consider developing a close friendship with a single person you both like, who perhaps needs one or two additional friends.

100   Sexual attraction and 80/20

Sexual attraction is one of the great and most joyous mysteries of the universe. It clearly fulfils in the most central way our biological imperative to fill the earth. Sexual desire also demonstrates an extreme form of 80/20 – the chemistry of love can occur in fleeting seconds, so that you feel 99 per cent of the attraction in 1 per cent of the time, and you know at once and with absolute certainty that this is the person for you!

Beware! Both fulfilling the biological imperative, and the intensity of an 80/20 feeling, should put you on your guard. Danger and wasted happiness could lie ahead. There are many people with whom you could, in theory, bond; your uncontrollable hormones will ensure that this rush of blood to the head or the heart will happen again. Enjoy the sex but do not automatically draw a conclusion that may well be wrong.

There are a few other 80/20 considerations:

- Is your partner inherently happy?
- Will you both accept each other as you are, warts and all?
- Will you commit to each other for the long term?
- Do you share broadly the same values?
- Will you be close friends throughout life?
- Will you be substantially 'equal', or else cheerfully accept certain inequalities?

The 80/20 view of selecting a life partner is blunt – this may be the most important decision of your life.

101   Is your partner inherently happy?

If you have not yet selected a partner, note that your happiness will be greatly affected by the happiness of your partner. For your happiness and for love, you will want to make him or her happy. But this is a lot easier if, to start with, your partner has a happy temperament and/or consciously adopts a pro-happiness daily regime.

Team up with an unhappy person and the odds are that you will end up less happy, or positively unhappy. However much mutual love abounds, people with low self-esteem and poor happiness habits are a nightmare to live with. Two unhappy people, even in love, will drive each other nuts.

If you want to be happy, choose a happy partner!

Of course, you may already have a partner who is not happy. We have already seen several ways to become happier. It should be a major project for both of you to make your partner happy.

Happiness needs to be worked at. Anyone in love will want to make their mate happier, and there are 80/20 ways in these pages that show how to do this to great effect.

102   Can you accept your partner as they are?

Warts and all.

John Gottman has the world's largest 'love lab', devoted to identifying the causes of marital breakdown and success. He is a meticulous and insightful researcher.

One conclusion he draws particularly resonates with me. One of the very few reasons why long-term partnerships founder is because one or both of the people involved attempts to change the other one.

The reasons are often trivial. Jane may complain that her husband John doesn't do his fair share of housework. Based on her early observation of him, did she really expect him to?

Stuart gets upset because Fiona parks their car badly, never fills it with fuel and takes it 'without permission'. She also drives badly and refuses to drive at night. Did he marry her because she was a model driver?

For better, for worse.

Take the time to realistically assess your prospective partner's worst attributes (we all have them). And your ability or inability to accept them.

If you can't accept someone's flaws cheerfully – even affectionately – don't get involved with them.

If your partnership is failing because you are criticizing your mate over trivial issues, the fault is yours, mate. Love turns a blind eye.

There are just a few reasons why relationships fail. Avoid the reasons. It should not be hard.

103   Committed to being committed?

I have had five serious relationships.

Three of them failed for the same reason, and it was my fault.

Everything went well for the first few years. None went badly. But after a while, I began to wonder whether there might not be an even better partner available. I grasped the existing relationship by the roots, examined it, and never gave it a chance to grow deeper and deeper.

I was not committed to being committed. And it was not fair, because most of my partners were more committed than me.

It is important that there is symmetry in a relationship. It is fundamentally vulnerable if one partner is more committed.

Check this. Then commit mutually. This may not involve a wedding, but with or without a public commitment, there must be agreement about the timescale you both envisage. And you must *work* to make the relationship last at least that long, perhaps forever. Love is not an emotion. It is hard work. Don't put your hardest work into your job or anything else. Put it into your relationship and, therefore, into your happiness.

By definition (we hope), a lifetime relationship lasts a long time. All kinds of difficulties and roadblocks *will* emerge.

Do you have your ideal partner?

If so, commit to him or her. Whatever happens.

Commit to being committed. Quash doubts. Do not think for a moment about alternatives. Work to make it work. This is not a dress-rehearsal. It is the real thing.

104 Live beautiful days

I love this sentence from Friedman and Rosenman, 'If you are to live a beautiful life, you first must begin to live beautiful days.'[3] Their concept of a beautiful day involves beautiful things and events.

Write down – in the next 10 minutes – 20 things you want to do, which are possible in the next month, and don't require serious money.

And the sillier, the better.

For example, laugh with friends, play a board game, walk in the sun, play table tennis, have a pub lunch, cook a meal for friends, tell someone you like them, go for a swim, get a tan, play with a dog or a child, see a movie, call a long-lost friend, have a picnic, go to a sporting event …

Choose a day, arrange whatever you want to do with friends and pile at least five things you really enjoy into the day. Now do the same for a day you want to spend on your own.

And choose another day when you will do at least a couple of things you want to do, that you have never yet done.

Make sure you have a beautiful day every week.

It takes a little planning and imagination, as well as some self-indulgence, but if you have more beautiful days, you will have a happier life.

Design your next beautiful day NOW!

105   Pleasure versus flourishing

Happiness is not so much a <u>state</u>, as a <u>process</u>.

Happiness is not primarily the *state of pleasure*, but rather the *process of flourishing*.

Pleasures are nice, and not to be undervalued, but it is hard to live a life that just includes pleasures. We need a sense of personal progress and adventure. Flourishing is even nicer than pleasure, and can be a continuous process, throughout your whole life.

Flourishing is a process of self-expansion, of becoming more this month than last month, more this year than last year.

Pleasures are basically external, like the effects of sunshine, a good meal, an exhilarating ride on a motorbike or a warm bath.

Flourishing is internal, related to you and not transient external circumstances. You flourish by becoming more than you used to be. You flourish by expanding your mind, your sympathy and oneness with other people and the world, your body and its facilities, your prowess in sport or any other skill, your personality and your humanity.

Flourishing is personal progress over time. There are so many dimensions to flourishing that you will never run out of ways to continue flourishing.

The best way to become happier for longer is to continually flourish.

How will you flourish, today, next week, next year?

106   Defeat the 'baseline happiness' concept

Psychologists claim that we have a 'baseline happiness level' to which we revert after any exceptional positive or negative events. There is some sense behind it, and even some comfort. If you are seriously incapacitated, you may suffer severe regret for your decreased mobility and the things you can no longer do. But sooner or later, having adjusted your expectations, you may revert to your baseline happiness.

A common view of psychologists is that if you have exceptionally good fortune, you may be euphoric for a time, but slowly but surely, the psychologists posit, you are likely to revert to your 'real' happiness level.

The example they always choose is lottery winners, who, they say, may end up no happier than before their big win. This is a contentious claim. Not only is the evidence distinctly mixed, but it is an extreme, atypical example. Lottery winners tend not to have experience of large sums of money, and often don't use it wisely.

Though many people may revert to a previous level of happiness, this is by no means inevitable. People can and do become permanently happier. We have already seen several ways to increase your permanent level of happiness, of which one of the very best is to *increase your level of optimism*.

Optimists tend to have happier and more fulfilling lives than pessimists. And your optimism, like your alleged baseline happiness, can be permanently upgraded.

107   Summary: the seven secrets of high happiness

1. Choose the right romantic partner.
   - Choose slowly and carefully.
   - Sex is great, but chemistry, mutual admiration and friendship are far more important and durable.
   - Choose a happy partner.
   - View life together as an adventure.
   - Discuss any potential problems or different views before you commit.
   - Have equal power or cheerful acceptance of inequality.
2. Be committed to being committed to your partner.
3. Love your work.
4. Use money to gain freedom.
5. Cultivate a few great friends.
6. Be true to yourself and follow your conscience.
7. Become steadily more optimistic.

Are any of these a challenge? Which of these would increase your happiness the most?

CHAPTER 16

A SHORT COURSE ON SELF-LOVE

Before you can truly love other people or do good deeds, you must first cultivate a deep appreciation for yourself and your positive attributes. Here's where you start.

108   Self-love

Love, like charity, begins at home.

Before you can truly love anyone else, you must love yourself.

How can you do any good, unless you see goodness in yourself? Otherwise, doing good is a cynical exercise in manipulation and building a false reputation.

There is good and bad in everyone. Your job in life is to nurture and expand the good in yourself, and the results such goodness can engender in the world. To fulfil your destiny, you must identify your '20 per cent goodness spike' – the best in yourself. Love yourself for your best attributes and figure out how to deploy them to help both the people you care about and the world at large.

Good attributes, magnified and adroitly deployed, drive out bad. If you are gratified by the good you do, you will expand its scope and effects. Loving yourself becomes a virtuous circle, the most pleasurable duty you have throughout your life.

Too much self-regard is, well, too much, but too little helps nobody.

Do you have enough?

109   Self-compassion

Being compassionate to yourself is as important as self-love; perhaps more so.

Self-compassion means going easy on yourself – forgiving yourself when you make mistakes or do something wrong, not being hard on yourself when you feel depleted or overwhelmed, not driving yourself relentlessly to perform or achieve, not feeling that you always need to prove yourself. Self-compassion is being gentle with yourself, realizing that there is nothing wrong with being fully human, fallible and vulnerable.

Will self-compassion blunt your edge or tempt you into lower standards?

No! When you take responsibility for some failure, you are open to admitting your frailty, that you have fallen short of high standards. Taking responsibility means putting your hand up and saying, 'I failed.'

Implicit in taking responsibility is recognizing that you need to do better in the future, to put right what has been wrong or poor.

Self-compassion raises happiness and lowers anxiety. And it makes you more compassionate to other people.

Are you sometimes too hard on yourself?

110   Avoid your snake pits

There are certain situations with which I cope badly. You, too, are likely to have your pressure points. But what should we do – learn to cope better with these situations? Or avoid them as much as possible?

I lean towards the second solution. I've never seen the point in training people not to be afraid of snakes. The more sensible action is to avoid the jungle (or the pet shop).

I can't abide pointless bureaucracy, lawyers, crowds, traffic jams, people who make excuses and lack of sunshine. I've restructured my life to largely avoid these problems.

Write down *your* bêtes-noires. What solutions could minimize exposure to them? The cumulative effect on your happiness and stress levels (in opposite directions) should not be underestimated.

Small victories can have great effects.

What are your snake pits? How will you avoid them?

CHAPTER 17

MONEY AND HAPPINESS

Surprisingly, studies show that greater wealth *does*, in general, increase happiness. But it is not automatic. Money buys you the *opportunity* to be happy – it depends on how you use it. The best use of money is to buy freedom – and to be generous.

111   Can money buy happiness?

Studies show a strong correlation between wealth and happiness. Of course, there are happy poor people and miserable millionaires, but in general, the more money people have, the more likely they are to say they are happy or very happy.

Psychology professor and happiness researcher Ed Diener reports 'individuals who are well-off are on average happier than poor people.'[1]

After extensive research, Betsey Stevenson and Justin Wolfers said definitively, 'Many scholars have argued that once "basic needs" have been met, higher income is no longer associated with higher wellbeing' but 'we find no support for this claim.' There is, they say, 'no evidence of a saturation point' beyond which more wealth does not lead to more happiness.[2]

So, a crude but basically correct conclusion is that *more money can, and usually does, buy more happiness.*

Does your plan to increase your happiness include becoming richer?

112   It depends on what you buy

Money can buy happiness, but it is not automatic.

Money buys the *opportunity* to be happy.

Although rich people tend to be happier, there is a lot of difference between how happy rich people are. It depends on how they use their wealth.

The best use of money is to buy freedom: the freedom *from* work or activities you find boring or frustrating, and the freedom *to* do what you enjoy or find worthwhile.

Using wealth wisely is an art. It does not come naturally to many people. It is an 80/20 art, the art of using your time to generate happiness.

Do you have this art? Do you know how valuable your time could be, when you can spend it just as you want? Are you ready to be rich?

113   The happiest use of money

The happiest use of money is to give it away.

To do this, even on a small scale, is highly gratifying – so long as you know the recipient personally.

Giving to a charity is much less likely to generate happiness.

If you become one of the super-rich – if you have far more money than you can intelligently spend – the disposition of your wealth becomes one of your very few vital activities. If you are ever in this position – and why not try to be? – take the responsibility seriously.

If you were super-rich, who would benefit and how?

CHAPTER 18

FRIENDS

Who are your top friends? Do you spend the right
amount of time with them? Do you admire them?

114   What is your attitude to friendship?

Imagine your life without friends, or the possibility of friendship.

It doesn't bear thinking about.

But we often have a casual attitude towards friendships. This is not wholly bad. Some of our deepest friendships arise serendipitously. You might be studying something alongside a stranger and the stranger becomes one of your best friends. A friend introduces you to one of their friends who ends up becoming one of your best friends. You bump into an acquaintance from long ago in the street, start talking and discover a deep common interest. Endless accidental contacts make the lottery of life pregnant with possibility.

80/20 asks three possibly inconvenient questions about your friendships:

- Who are your five best friends?

- How many _really close_ friends do you have?

- How important are these top five relative to all the others?

115   Your top 20 friends

List your 20 best friends.

As a matter of interest, where did your lover/partner come on the list? Above or below your parents and children? (But destroy the list once you have finished this exercise.)

Now allocate a total of 100 points between the relationships, in terms of their importance to you.

A typical 80/20 pattern would be:

- The top four relationships – 20 per cent of the total – would score most of the points (maybe 80).

- There would tend to be a constant relationship between each number and the next one down. For instance, number two may be two-thirds or half as important as number one; number three may be two-thirds or half as important as number two …

If number two is half as important as number one, and so on, number six is only about 3 per cent as important as number one – that is, not very.

How much time do you actively spend with each person on the list (watching television or any other passive activity does not count)?

Are you spending enough time with your few vital friends?

116   The village theory

Anthropologists say that the number of exhilarating personal relationships that we can establish is limited. Typically, we might have two important childhood friends, two significant very close adult friends with whom we share everything and two doctors or other advisers. Just two sexual partners may eclipse all the others. Most commonly, you fall in love just once or twice, and there is one member of your family you love above all others.

The number of significant personal relationships is remarkably similar for everyone, regardless of location, sophistication, culture or age.

Hence, the anthropologists' 'village theory'. In an African village, all these relationships happen within a few hundred metres, often in a short period of time.

For us, the relationships may be spread out all over the planet, and over a lifetime. Still, we all have 'the village' in our heads.

Does the village theory resonate with your experience?

What are the implications?

117   Ballard's Californian rehab project

J. G. Ballard cited a rehab project for young women in California who had all mixed with criminal men. The women were young, under 21. Their experience of life had been sad.

Many of them had married when in their early teens and had their first child at 13 or 14. By the time they were 20, many had been married three times. They often had hundreds of lovers, some of them with men who were then shot or imprisoned. They'd experienced the whole gamut of human experience when in their teens.

The project introduced them to new social backgrounds in the form of middle-class volunteers, who befriended them, showed them love and attention, invited them to their homes and gave them a glimpse of a better way of living.

Do you like the sound of the project?

Would you have been willing to consider volunteering?

Do you think befriending a love-starved young person is a wonderful thing to do, and could change lives?

Read on to find out what happened.

118   Ballard's rehab project – the results

The project was a complete fiasco. Not a single success story.

The young women were incapable of forming any new friendships. The women were 'all used up'. Their relationship slots had been filled, forever.

This sad story is relevant to us all.

- 80/20 suggests that a small number of relationships typically accounts for a large proportion of the emotional value we take from friends.
- And probably the first few significant relationships we experience can be the most deep and meaningful. Once we have 'filled up our relationship slots', other relationships may be superficial and unimportant. The first truly deep relationships occur first; after them, diminishing returns increasingly set in.

Fill your friendship and relationship slots slowly and very carefully.

119   Are your friends admirable?

We've already seen that your happiness increases if you spend more time with people whose company you enjoy.

But there is a further consideration. How admirable are your friends?

It is entirely possible to like a friend whom you regard as a bit of a rogue. But if you spend a lot of time with your wayward friend, what may happen? Yes, you may become a bit like him or her.

Perhaps you should become closest friends with those you admire.

Who are the friends whom you love seeing and also most admire?

CHAPTER 19

MORE ON OPTIMISM AND OPPORTUNITY

We will explore: optimism and pessimism down the ages
and their impact on history; how to become more optimistic;
and how to find extraordinary opportunities.

We will see that optimism and pessimism produce vital
results from individuals, groups and society, and that
optimism leads to prosperity and happiness.

120   Optimism, happiness and virtue

Optimism and happiness are twin cherries on a single stalk. Optimism is hope, and hope concerns the future.

For Saint Paul, hope was one of the three great virtues – 'faith, hope and love'. Hope actively generates a better future.

There is no steady state of happiness. Contentment, perhaps, can be static. But genuine happiness is forward-looking. It is less a measure of the present, than an expectation of the future. 'It is better to travel hopefully than to arrive.'

Our objective circumstances may not be pleasant, but if we have hope and a confident expectation that things will improve, that we can make things improve, we can still be happy.

If we become more optimistic, we can become happier. As we feel happier, we also become more optimistic. This is a virtuous circle, in two senses. Optimism and happiness are virtues and they feed on each other.

Are you happier than you used to be? More optimistic? Do you agree that they move together?

121   Optimism and Jewish–Christian beliefs

In the six centuries before Christ, Hebrew prophets such as Ezekiel, Hosea and the two known as Isaiah, preached a view of personal responsibility and self-improvement, incorporating ideals of social justice, mercy and love. The world could improve itself – they saw the hand of God helping humans to become better and therefore change the course of history.

In ancient and modern times, Jews, despite all that has happened to them, never let go of their optimism, activism and mission to the world, leading to results far disproportionate to their numbers.

If we have to single out one single Jewish prophet who preached a gospel composed of equal parts of love, progress and optimism, we can do no better than study the enigmatic and much misunderstood character known as Jesus Christ.

In the Gospel of Thomas, he says, 'The kingdom of God is spread out in the whole world, and men do not see it.'[1] The early Christians believed that Christ had changed the whole course of history, enabling everyone, of whatever nationality, gender or social status, to perform works of wonderful goodness and effectiveness, and to enjoy life after death.

It is hard to imagine a more optimistic philosophy.

In my opinion, the early Christians of the first and second centuries created the most attractive philosophy or religion ever.

Do you agree or disagree that optimism is most attractive and effective when linked to personal self-improvement?

122   The Renaissance and optimism

The Renaissance in Florence and other parts of Italy is generally dated to very few years: 1480–1520. In a single generation, Leonardo, Michelangelo and Raphael revolutionized the arts, Columbus sailed to America, Luther started the Reformation and Copernicus initiated the Scientific Revolution.

The roots of the Renaissance lie in the previous three centuries. Byzantine and Islamic cultures rediscovered ancient Greek and Roman philosophy, mathematics and science. Reviving Greek and Roman culture generated a new wave of optimism about humanity and its future. Humanist philosophers believed that God wanted humans to control the world by understanding His mathematical and physical laws. As in early Christianity, humanity was elevated to near-divine status.

In the Middle Ages, life was suffering – an endless succession of plagues, famines, wars and social, racial and religious oppression. The only way to become richer was to exploit other people. God was not in favour of progress. He had arranged the world; it was not a playground for human rearrangement.[2]

From the Renaissance onward, even as wars and oppression continued, the possibility of human progress led to irrevocable progress in human wealth and welfare, and eventually a kinder, gentler view of everything from the family to the importance of human liberty.

Human creativity changed everything. It is hard to argue that we are better people than in the Middle Ages, but our creativity has made, and continues to make, a hugely better world. At the heart of the 80/20 philosophy lies progress, and at the heart of progress lies effective, results-oriented creativity.

Progress follows belief in progress.

123   The Industrial Revolution and optimism

The late eighteenth century brought two overlapping revolutions – one economic, the other political and social. They also followed on from earlier progress; yet marked a great discontinuity in human experience. The future began to arrive.

The first revolution, which started in England and Scotland around 1760, was industrial. The main impetus was inventions such as the first economically useful steam engine, and the industrial, machine-based system organized in mills and factories. Innovation proliferated as optimistic entrepreneurs experimented and got rich.

At first, the Industrial Revolution had a bad press, epitomized by the 'dark Satanic mills' of William Blake's magnificent hymn 'Jerusalem'. Early industry was ugly, regimented, harsh and, by modern standards, inhumane.

Yet the Industrial Revolution made humankind, for the first time, a biological success. Throughout all previous history, population expansion had inevitably run up against the barriers of plague, warfare, malnutrition and famine. Life, a century before Darwin, was truly Darwinian, a miserable and fruitless struggle for existence.

After 1771, it was different. The machine age arrived. Enormous cotton mills, using water and steam power, sprouted up – by 1787 England had nearly 150. England's population tripled between 1750 and 1850.

Industrial growth became self-propelling. Economic space – city space – generated economic value vastly greater than agricultural space, and as cities increasingly predominated, living standards soared, doubling every generation.

124   Political revolution and optimism

The second revolution was intellectual and political. The 'Enlightenment' philosophers of France, England and Scotland believed in reason rather than superstition; some of them even believed that humans could be made perfect. Hence, the American Revolution of 1776, and the French one of 1789–94, which preached liberty, equality and fraternity (although this involved chopping off heads of aristocrats, priests and revolutionaries themselves if they were not sufficiently extreme).

Despite the excesses of the French Revolution, the political philosophy of the Enlightenment was profoundly optimistic and favoured 'the people'. In the nineteenth century, small revolutions erupted, but fizzled out as living standards improved. By the last third of that century, even conservative statesmen such as Otto von Bismarck in Germany and Benjamin Disraeli in the UK decided to 'trust the people' and increased the numbers who could vote in elections. The ultimate destination was twentieth-century democracy.

The philosophers of ancient Greece and Rome were highly innovative, but their societies were highly stratified, with a very few people at the top who were able to become creative, and a large slave class who were treated more like animals than people.

The glory of our many civilizations today is the democratization of personal potential. Our societies, though deeply flawed in many ways, allow for the possibility that most people can become creative and autonomous and improve their lives, not least through optimism.

By 1900, the world had seen seven centuries of fantastic economic, political and social progress.

Do you think it could last?

125   1900–45: when optimism nearly died

The first half of the twentieth century was a time that intellectuals and other opinion-formers deserted the flag of optimism. It's no coincidence that it was also a time of global disaster.

The rot started in 1900 with Freud's dark fantasies about the unconscious mind, or perhaps earlier with Nietzsche's nihilistic philosophy, the bombs of the Russian anarchists, the art of the early Expressionists and the violent antisemitism of Russian, Austrian and German nationalists.

The tragic blunder of the 'Great War' of 1914–18, itself partly caused by extreme German nationalism, set the scene for the malevolent triumphs of Lenin in 1917 and Hitler in 1933 and, therefore, the world war of 1939–45. Most influential European intellectuals became communists or fascists, opponents of individualism, liberalism, human decency – and optimism.

Communists and the Nazis had negative and hateful philosophies; nothing creative or helpful to humanity could grow there. From 1917 to 1989, even the survival of optimism and other Western values was in doubt.

Pessimism is dangerous. It can threaten freedom, happiness and human decency.

126   Baby boomers and optimism

'Whether you were born in 1945 or 1950 or 1955, things got better every year for the first 18 years of your life, *and it had nothing to do with you.*' So writes Peter Thiel in his wonderful book *Zero to One.*[3]

The backcloth of the 1930s and 1940s was the Great Crash of 1929 and the ensuing Great Depression, Hitler, Stalin, total war and the devastation of Europe. Pessimism aided and abetted these phenomena.

What is remarkable is how, in the US and Western Europe at least, younger people in the 1950s and 1960s threw off pessimism, even in the face of possible nuclear war. The change from pessimism to optimism had more to it than the European economic miracles of the 1950s and the extra options added by prosperity and large-scale university education. Study the lyrics of pop music and for every doleful song such as 'Eve of Destruction' there were hundreds of songs about love, peace and parties.

Optimism did not flow from prosperity; it was the other way round. A new libertarian generation threw caution and deference to the winds. After seven centuries of progress and optimism, and half a century of diabolical destruction and pessimism, we were back on track.

If you can avoid news media and look around, the world since 1945 has become better and better. Incomes are higher, houses and city centres are more attractive, healthcare and life expectancy have improved, there is far more choice, opportunity, freedom and international travel. Products are lighter, cheaper, more colourful, useful and convenient, and the best of them, such as the internet and smartphones, did not exist 30 years ago.

Optimism works. What can you personally do to increase the optimism around you?

127   Optimism and cyberspace

Inspired science fiction can be amazingly predictive.

A decade before the internet took off, William Gibson, a computer illiterate, banged away on an ancient typewriter and invented 'cyberspace':

'A consensual hallucination experienced daily by billions in every nation ... a graphic representation of data abstracted from every computer in the human system. Lines of light ranged in the non-space of the mind, clusters and constellations of data. Like city lights, receding ...'[4]

This brave new world is comparable in its impact on the economy and society to Europeans' discovery of the New World and the resulting influx of precious metals. Over four centuries, that discovery changed the world, giving a huge boost to optimism. Cyberspace may do the same in a few decades.

We take the internet for granted, but it marks a qualitative change in human experience. 80/20 matters here. Much time spent online is wasted or has only trivial results. The trick is to use cyberspace selectively and wisely to learn and create new experiences.

Could you halve your time online, yet double its value to you?

128 Change and optimism

You are optimistic when you believe that things will change for the better. But there is a paradox here. Most, perhaps all, of us have some fear of the unknown, some hesitation to go beyond the familiar. Mark Twain summed it up: 'I'm all for progress; it's change I don't like.' We all have a bit of this attitude.

Optimism, hope, trust in life, fellow humans and the universe – these are the emotions which can overcome our fear of change. And if it is true that 'once bitten, twice shy', the converse can apply as well. Once we go with hope into a new world and find it welcoming rather than intimidating – partly because of the welcome induced by our positive attitude – we can learn to accept and even relish change and risk. *Change is the price of progress. Learning to welcome change is the essence of optimism.*

Progress and change – in ourselves, in our relationships, in our groups, in our societies and in the world – are inseparable. Hope is the lubricant that eases our fear of change and turns it into progress.

What's your honest view of change? Are you good at stoking up your personal sense of hope to conquer fear, shyness and the dislocations of progress?

Do you believe that change can greatly increase your opportunities? How?

129 How to become more optimistic

Tests purport to sort optimists from pessimists. Can the tests capture such an elusive attribute? It's like trying to pin down a butterfly, and about as much use. But even if reliable, the tests are beside the point.

The point is – you can shed large elements of your pessimism. You can *learn* to be more optimistic. What could be more 80/20? Celebrated psychologist Martin Seligman, in his book *Learned Optimism*, shows how. Here is my brief summary:

- We all have an explanatory style, a way of explaining to ourselves the causes of good or bad events.

- Pessimists 'catastrophize' whereas optimists are more generous to themselves.

- Pessimists assume bad things are permanent. Optimists think they are temporary.

- Pessimists think bad things are universal. Optimists think bad things are specific.

- Pessimists think bad things are their fault. Optimists blame them on others.

Are you an optimist or a pessimist?

Could you shift to the optimistic way of explaining events?

130   When bad things happen

- **Pessimists** think the causes are **permanent**. I do badly on a test and conclude that I will always do badly. I give up. An **optimist** will assume the bad thing is **temporary** – 'I had a bad day because I was tired.'

- **Pessimists** assume causes are **pervasive**. I go to a new city and get mugged. I avoid that city because it is dangerous. An **optimist** thinks 'I should choose a better part of the city'.

- **Pessimists** internalize the bad fortune, thinking the causes are **personal**. I have a bad relationship and assume it was my fault. **Optimists** think 'I chose the wrong person. It was all their fault.' They externalize the responsibility.

When bad things happen to you:

- If you think they are *permanent*, ask whether they could be *temporary*. Since life is long, they probably could be. If in doubt, assume that.

- If you think they might be *pervasive*, ask whether they might be *specific* to particular circumstances. This is usually quite plausible.

- If you think they are *your fault*, ask whether someone else might not be partly to blame. Or perhaps nobody is really to blame; it was just bad luck or unfortunate circumstances.

Be like the optimists!

131 When good things happen

Optimists think:

- The causes are **permanent**. I have good luck; that's natural – I always tend to have good luck.

- The causes are **universal**. I do well; that is because I am smart and good at tests.

- The causes are **internal**. Our team came up with the best presentation; that was largely due to me.

These are explanations *to yourself*. Don't go broadcasting them to your friends and colleagues, as this may make you sound big-headed and make you unpopular!

Optimists expect and look for good outcomes and take advantage of opportunities. Pessimists look for bad outcomes and tend to dismiss good outcomes as flukes, temporary, specific or due to other people.

We tend to see and find what we expect to see and find.

Expect the best. Think that it was in some way your doing – even if it was pure chance!

Can you learn to take bad events in your stride and not brood on them?

Can you learn to interpret good events as part of your charmed life, making you grateful but also self-confident?

132   Internal versus external opportunity

External opportunity is everything that happens in the world around you.

Internal opportunity is everything that happens in your head.

Internal opportunity must necessarily come first. You cannot grasp an external opportunity without having an appropriate internal sense of opportunity.

Internal opportunity is knowing what will take you to the next level of life, and being ready to take the opportunity when it arises.

External opportunity is what life provides; believing that it may provide what you want; constantly scanning the environment for that; and pouncing when the current of events gives you the ghost of a chance.

You can change the extent of **external opportunity** by deliberately putting yourself in the stream of events that is most likely to give you the chance you want. Go where the external opportunity is likely to be greatest.

Opportunity is infinitely expandable by what you do to be ready and by being alert to possible opportunity.

Are you fully prepared to create and notice opportunities?

133   How to find hidden opportunities

- Work for a small but fast-growth organization that knows something nobody else knows.
- Team up with a brilliant person who is also searching for (and may have found) a mega-opportunity.
- Go and live in a foreign country – the contrast with your own experience may enable you to see something nobody there can see.
- Go and live in a city or small region which is the 'capital' of a new trend or idea just taking off.
- Find a hot idea and apply it in a new context.
- Imagine doing something great that nobody has yet done but you could do.

How will <u>you</u> find your big break?

134   Your muffled opportunity

The great nineteenth-century statesman Bismarck said, 'Man cannot create the current of events. He can only float with it and steer.' Bismarck steered the current of events so successfully that he won three short wars, united Germany and avoided war in Europe for another 20 years.

He had definite objectives from the start. He was also very impatient. Yet he forced himself to wait until the right moment, the right opportunity, came sailing along. It took a nearly a decade.

Then wham! He pounced immediately and events played into his hands.

This is the essence of hearing and acting on muffled opportunity:

- *Be sure what you want to achieve* in life, or at least in the next 10 to 15 years. What will move you from one level of existence to a higher one? It could be a relationship, a job or career, a definite goal, a desired lifestyle or an opportunity to change the world in some way that pleases you.

- *Every day, reflect for a few moments on your big objective.* Write it down (in code if necessary) and put it on your desk, kitchen table or bedside table. Say it to yourself before you go to sleep.

- *Be patient.* Be ready for it to take years or decades.

- *Wait* for the faintest possible intimation, the slightest gap in circumstances, that might allow an opening for your objective.

- *Pounce. Act quickly and decisively.*

If you want to spot a muffled opportunity, put these steps into place now.

135   The time of your life

There are one or two occasions in any lifetime when the stars line up to give you a terrific opportunity. It may be fleeting. You may not notice it. Or it evaporates before you do anything. Or someone beats you to it.

You cannot manufacture opportunity by willpower. It comes along, unbidden, in unexpected shapes, often in completely unforeseen circumstances. It can come from a conversation with a friend or acquaintance, from something you read, from observing something similar in a foreign country, or from a flash of insight courtesy of your subconscious mind.

By definition, very few of these potential opportunities will prove to be the one or two that can best transform your life and impact on the world. Also by definition, the top one or two potential opportunities will at some stage float past you, whether recognized or not. I think the difference between people who grasp great opportunities is partly the quality of their search for them, but mainly the ability to recognize them when they turn up, and the ability to tell a great opportunity from a merely good one.

When your stars line up for your jackpot, don't walk on by!

Are you ready?

CHAPTER 20

THE TIME TRIAD

The Protestant work ethic: how to overthrow it
and spark your time revolution!

136   The time triad

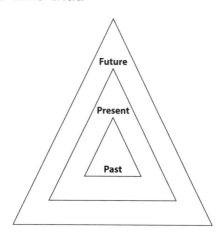

The Western view of time is linear, going from left to right. This view is apparent in all business graphs of time, for example. A more Eastern view of time is shown above. The past is embedded in the present and the present is embedded in the future.

The future is a dimension of the present and the past, giving us the opportunity to create something better.

How can you use your past and present assets and creativity to create a better future?

137   Time is the benign link between past, present and future

Time is a synchronizing and cyclical device, as illustrated by a round clock. Time keeps coming round, bringing with it opportunities to learn, to deepen a few valued relationships, to produce a better product or outcome and to add more value to life. We do not exist just in the present – we spring from the past and have a treasure trove of past associations and experiences.

Our future, like our past, is already inherent in the present.

And our future will be brighter and more wonderful if we make use of the very best that we already have in the present. The best skills, the best ideas, the best relationships and the best opportunities that lie within or just beyond our current grasp.

Thinking about time this way highlights the imperative to carry with us, throughout our lives, the *most precious 20 per cent of what we already have* – our best personalities, abilities, friendships and mental and physical assets – and ensure that these are nurtured, developed, extended and deepened.

The future can always be better than the past. You are not losing time – you are building on time.

How can you build on your past and present to create a better future?

138   Time revolution requires being radical

There is no point tinkering around the edges. You are not aiming to make your use of time a little bit more efficient. Unless what you propose to do is really radical – a big departure from what you normally do – it is unlikely to be a time revolution with great results.

It is not necessary to think big. This *may* be the answer. But equally, or more likely, you should *think small*.

What is it that only takes a very small amount of your time but generates terrific results? Whatever it is, could you do it on a much greater scale?

The answer may well be a *decision* you make, or a seemingly *wacky idea* that may work fantastically well. If the latter, cut your losses if it doesn't work very soon and go on to the next wacky idea.

What revolutionary step could just work out fantastically well for you?

139   Overthrow the Protestant work ethic

The belief that hard work is virtuous is so deeply engrained in everyone, of all religions and none, that we must make a conscious effort to expel it from our minds.

Hard work is a fool's philosophy. It leads to low returns. High returns come from hard thinking, from insight and from doing what we most want to do.

Whenever I am tempted to do too much, I recall Ronald Reagan and Warren Buffett.

'It's true hard work never killed anyone,' Reagan mused, 'but I figure, why take the risk?'

Buffett attributes his legendary success as an investor to an approach which he says 'borders on lethargy'. He thinks very hard about which stocks to buy. He buys very few of them. He holds them for a very long time. If he worked harder, he wouldn't be so rich.

Time will be kind to you if you are kind to time.

Take your time.

Will you?

140   Give up guilt

In relation to time, giving up guilt means jettisoning hard work. *Do what you enjoy.*

People who achieve the most necessarily have to enjoy what they do. It is only by fulfilling ourselves that we create extraordinary value.

This does not necessarily mean limiting your work, only limiting work you do not enjoy. Picasso was a one-man art factory long before Andy Warhol. Picasso enjoyed life to the full. It was not hard work. Intense though it was, his painting was not hard.

Other artists work differently. Leonardo da Vinci painted very little, constantly revised his work and left many works unfinished. It did not matter. If he had only produced *The Last Supper* and the *Mona Lisa* – the most famous paintings in history – his reputation would still have been secured for all time.

Time is there for you to use it how you want, for work and play. Whatever you do, as long as you enjoy it, there is no cause for regret.

Have you rid yourself of guilt, of the sense that you have to produce, produce, produce? Are you taking the time to be great? Or to be happy and spread happiness around? Either way, be like Edith Piaf. *No, no regrets; no guilt.*

141   Control your time

It is a fair bet that when 80 per cent of time yields a meagre 20 per cent of results, that work is undertaken at the behest of others.

The 20 per cent of people who are great achievers work for themselves, or behave as if they do.

It's hard to make good use of your time if you don't control it.

Of course, you will always have obligations to other people. This is good for all kinds of reasons. You have partners, employees, people who depend on you, a rich network of contacts, from whom nothing can be expected if nothing is given.

Give generously.

Ultimately, however, only you can design and execute your very best work. Only you can craft the best possible life for yourself.

Be uncompromising here.

Control your time.

Do you?

142   Be eccentric with your time

It's unlikely that the most valuable 20 per cent of your time will come from being a good soldier, in doing what is expected of you, in attending meetings and in doing what most of your peers do.

So do as little of this as you can get away with.

Instead, work out the most unconventional ways in which you could spend your time, without being thrown out of your world.

Who amongst your acquaintances is both effective and eccentric? How do they spend their time?

You may want to copy them, both in what they do and what they don't do.

143   Achievement islands

Remember happiness islands? The 20 per cent of your time when you are happiest during a day, a week or a longer period.

Now we come on to achievement islands. Identify the short periods when you achieve a much higher ratio of value to time during the rest of the day, week, month, year or life!

What were you doing during those achievement islands – what type of work or other activity? For example, were you coming up with an idea, writing something, persuading someone, providing leadership to a team or doing something else of incredibly high value?

Identify, as far as you can, the common characteristics of your achievement islands. *Do more, if possible <u>much</u> more, of this type of activity.*

Separately, list your achievement *desert* islands – your periods of greatest sterility and lowest productivity. What do they have in common?

Stop doing these things!

144   Multiply the 20 per cent of your time that gives you 80 per cent

When you have identified your happiness and achievement islands, you will want to spend more time on these and similar activities.

A short-term objective – usually feasible – is to take the 20 per cent of time on high-value activities up to 40 per cent within a year.

This one act will raise your happiness and value by between 60 and 80 per cent.

Ideally, move the time spent on high-value stuff up from 20 to 100 per cent. This may only be possible by changing your career and/or lifestyle.

But why not do that?

Why not do what you are meant to be doing – being as happy and useful to other people as possible?

145   The top 10 low-value uses of time

1. Things other people want you to do

2. Things that have always been done this way

3. Things you're not especially good at

4. Things you don't enjoy

5. Things that are always interrupted

6. Things you can't share with at least one other friend

7. Things that have already taken twice as long as expected

8. Things with collaborators who are unreliable or low quality

9. Things that have a predictable cycle, repeated over and over

10. Zoom calls

Which item on the list do you most resent? How can you stop doing this?

146   The top 10 best uses of time

1. Things that advance your overall purpose and meaning in life

2. Things you have always wanted to do (but never done yet)

3. Things already in the 20/80 relationship of time to results

4. Innovative ways of doing things that will slash the time required or multiply the quality of results

5. Things other people say can't be done

6. Things other people have done successfully in a different arena

7. Things which allow you to use your personal creativity

8. Worthwhile things you can easily delegate

9. Activities with great partners who use time eccentrically and effectively

10. Things where it is 'now or never'

Choose one of these to do today!

CHAPTER 21

MORE ON CREATIVITY AND HOW TO INVENT VIRGIN TERRITORY

Creativity is essential for success. The 80/20 way to creativity is to invent your own virgin territory – and the *easiest* and *best* way to do this is to take super successful ideas and adapt them to a new field. Cherish solitude and embrace idleness so that your greatest ideas emerge.

147   How BCG invented business strategy

In the mid-1960s, the Boston Consulting Group (BCG) was casting around for new ideas to define its consulting practice. Bruce Henderson, BCG's founder, had some vague idea that competition between different firms in an industry might have some rules that he could discover.

He fused together two venerable but quite separate disciplines – **financial analysis** and **market analysis**. He called the combined new approach 'strategy'. He posited that larger firms in a competitive system would have an advantage over smaller ones, because greater scale and experience in a particular product would give lower costs. Analysis proved that this was generally true, and that was the link between financial analysis, which looks at company profits, and market analysis, which generally had not realized the importance of market share.

Henderson's thesis was that high market share would lead to high return on capital. He further found that the relationship was proportional to the relative size of each company in a product or market 'segment'. From this starting-point, BCG developed elegant theories which could be empirically verified.

BCG also invented two simple, explosively useful charts – the experience curve, and the growth-share matrix of cash cows, dogs, question-marks and stars.

BCG took the commanding heights of business strategy, a field which has grown massively ever since. Business strategy is many times more valuable and high margin than either financial or market analysis, and much more fun too.

Could you put together a new territory which you could own, by combining two different disciplines which together are far more valuable?

148   How Bain & Company created virgin territory

In 1973, Bill Bain deserted Bruce Henderson and his very successful company, BCG, to found Bain & Company. This might have seemed quixotic. BCG 'owned' the territory of business strategy. Bain & Company's only hope was to develop its own territory. And that it did, with devastating originality.

Bill liked BCG's concepts – indeed, he had a major hand in developing them. But whereas Bruce wanted to change the way the world thought about strategy, Bill wanted to make mountains of money, for his clients, his firm and himself. Bain & Company focused on virgin territory – the *process* of consulting and the way it could add to the market value of their clients.

Bill believed that a novel partnership between the client organization and his consulting firm was the way to multiply the value of both.

In 1980, I left BCG and joined Bain & Company. The two firms used the same concepts but could not have been more different in every other way. BCG wanted the right answer; Bain & Company wanted financial results. In doing so, Bain created new territory, which the company still owns.

What proven ideas could you use in a totally different way?

149   How LEK stumbled across its own territory

In 1983, Jim Lawrence, Iain Evans and I left Bain & Company to start LEK Consulting. We started as a pale imitation of Bain & Company. That didn't work too well. We used the common heritage of BCG's concepts and Bain's way of working with clients, but we took a while to create our own product.

We had a lucky accident. We found it hard to attract business school graduates, but easy to hire 'research associates' ('RAs') direct from top universities. One year in and we had a *bizarre* bottom-heavy staff structure – 3 partners, only 4 consultants with MBAs and 30 RAs. The researchers initially knew nothing about business or strategy.

How could we use all those young people? What they could do very well was information gathering and analysis of our clients' competitors. LEK's 20 per cent spike was intensive data-gathering and quantitative analysis. So, we had what marketing experts had said since the 1950s was the wrong strategy – we made what we could produce very well, rather than what the market said it wanted.

Yet we had an ace up our sleeve – Einstein's dirty little secret. We knew we must find a new application for the powerful ideas we had absorbed from BCG and Bain. Through trial and error, we invented the 'mergers and acquisitions strategy consulting product'. The 1980s were a great time for better-performing, well-managed companies to make acquisitions, particularly outside their own industry. For this they needed what we could provide – detailed information and analysis of acquisition targets. We ended up doubling our size every year and had the highest profit margins in consulting.

Why not stake out your own valuable territory? It's not rocket science. It *is* fun. And you just might make a fortune.

150   Gravitate to the expertize hot spots

It is remarkable how 80/20 operates in Creativity – there are certain times and places, tiny proportions of time and geography, which produce incredible creativity. Ancient Greece in the fifth century BC. Southern Spain under Islamic rule in the twelfth and thirteenth centuries. Amsterdam and Venice for art since the fourteenth century. Florence and the Renaissance, heavily crushed into the period 1470–1550. Paris in 1852–70. New York in the 1920s and 1950–70. Silicon Valley from the 1950s. Silicon Valley–Seattle and its counterparts in other countries today.

And there are *hot spots* too for specific industries. Germany and Italy for music and opera in the eighteenth and nineteenth centuries. More recently, Liverpool, London, New York and LA for music. LA for cartoons and movies since the 1920s. Paris and Milan for fashion. Tokyo and Munich for electronic consumer goods since 1960.

There are also *micro-hot spots* known only to industry insiders, such as Boston for strategy consulting since 1963. In the 1960s and 1970s Boston housed the majority of all strategy consultants worldwide. (Lucky Boston! Lucky strategy consultants!)

Nobody really knows how these centres of creativity arise. Yet, once critical mass is reached, *the attraction of other creative people becomes irresistible*. It is so much easier to be creative when there are examples of creative people and their work everywhere you look.

Where should you move to?

Go there as early as possible.

151   Cherish solitude

Creative people can be extroverts or introverts, or quite unusually often, both in different settings. Science is quite a gregarious business, and creativity requires being able to exchange ideas and get excited by them.

But creative people also appreciate solitude. To be able to paint, sculpt, write anything creative, work on mathematical problems or work in a laboratory, you must like your own company for hours on end.

Some people, particularly young people, just cannot do this. Being left in a quiet room with a book for company is torture. Yet if you are truly excited by something abstract or conceptual, you can grow to love solitude. Walk alone in the mountains. Stay at a monastery.

Distractions are an ever-present temptation.

Lock your studio door. Hide in the library or a hut in the garden. Send your children on a treat. Go for a long, solitary walk (dogs allowed). Hide your phone. If you are working online, close all other programs, notifications and apps.

When, and where, will be your next period of creative solitude?

152   Feed your creative juices

I have studied many highly creative people, dead and alive – artists, writers, poets, musicians, scientists and entrepreneurs. They all have a varied life. They recreate themselves from many sources, such as:

- going to beautiful places – cities, mountain ranges, rivers and ravines or beautiful countryside;
- extending their reading beyond their own territory;
- attending seminars and lectures, and talking to other creative people;
- taking up hobbies outside their field;
- going to the cinema, theatre or concerts; taking part in lively activities such as dancing, singing or sports;

- visiting historic buildings, museums, art galleries, botanical gardens and the like;
- *working at night*, when their subconscious mind wakes them up with the solution to a problem that has been baffling them.

The 'tortured genius locked in an attic' is passé. Creative people today may be relaxed, self-indulgent, quietly eccentric, mobile geographically and sometimes affluent from their creativity.

Are you delivering enough grist to your creativity mill?

153   Be idle

Most creative people do not work long hours.

They may take frequent breaks.

Shakespeare had long rests between plays.

Charles Darwin went for long walks. He had a leisurely breakfast and finished work before lunch.

Churchill, a great writer as well as leader, drank, painted, read and talked incessantly.

Idleness is crucial for creativity. *Its seat is our subconscious mind.*

Ideas have to simmer just below the surface of the conscious mind, before the subconscious can tie them all together and push them to the surface. If we act, we may block our thoughts. If we work too hard, we may weary of the problem and give up.

Being idle gives the subconscious much-needed breathing space.

Do you want to be more creative?

Then work less.

154   Throw most of your ideas away

Creative people have lots of ideas. But they cheerfully throw most of them away. All but the very best.

80/20 applies to ideas. Very few are great.

Treasure these precious few.

Incubate them.

Hatch them.

Nurture them.

Polish them.

Test them.

Progress the single best idea.

Promulgate it with force and brio.

What will be your great idea?

CHAPTER 22

GROWTH AND HOW TO COMPOUND YOURSELF

All of the positive (and negative aspects) of your personality can be compounded over time through small, consistent efforts, so be sure to define and focus on specific areas for compounding. Alternatively, you can just leapfrog the process by unexpectedly landing a top role or starting your own venture!

155   How to compound yourself

Everything good about you – your brainpower, your knowledge, your particular skills, your interpersonal competence, your ability to collaborate, your wealth, your generosity, your insight, your friendships, your love and your value to yourself and to other people – can be compounded. Small amounts of growth compounded over a lifetime add up to a huge amount of total growth.

But everything bad about you can be compounded too. Over a lifetime, the results can be crippling.

Compounding yourself when you are young – and very young – is hugely important. This is one reason why parents do the most important job of anyone.

Parenting can also be done very well or very badly.

If you had bad parents, I hope you escaped their influence as early as practicable. And found good friends, as opposed to bad ones.

Compounding has the biggest effect if you can make a small – even an extremely small – improvement every week, for many years.

80/20 also teaches us, however, that our life-energy, however great, is finite. To be truly productive and influential, we not only need to compound over a long period, but also focus our energy on limited areas and objectives.

The biggest decision you can make in your life is *where to compound yourself* – along which dimensions, and ideally in a life-segment where you are unique and have no rivals – *in your wholly-owned territory*.

Do you know what that is?

It may take a long time to define your territory but the sooner you do, the earlier you can start compounding your unique skills.

Compounding is often started or accelerated by founding or joining a fast-growth venture that itself finds unique territory.

156   How Helena Rubinstein compounded herself

The founder of the Helena Rubinstein cosmetics empire was born on Christmas Day, 1872, in the Jewish quarter of Kraków, Poland. To pay household bills, her mother wanted to marry her off and collect a fat dowry. Helena had other ideas. She immediately left home. When she was 24, she emigrated, on her own, to Australia, taking with her, so the story goes, 12 little pots of her mother's homemade face cream.

Helena became a domestic servant, hated it, and made her way to Melbourne, where she became a waitress. Pretty, diminutive and vivacious, she became friends with four customers who changed her life. The four were all friends who met regularly at a smart café. One was a wine merchant, one a painter, one a printer and one a major tea importer called John Thompson. She told them of her plan to open a beauty salon. The friends took her seriously and helped her with money and advice. The artist drew her a logo based on an Egyptian motif and designed her brochure, which the printer produced. Thompson taught her how to display, market and advertise her wares.

The salon opened around 1903 and was an instant sensation. Helena fabricated a legend about her mid-European heritage, wooed wealthy clients and journalists, sold treatments, invented new cosmetics and charged a small fortune for them. From then on, Helena Rubinstein was on a roll. She went on television in the US to promote her brand, and had the time of her life in Paris, where she mixed with everyone rich, beautiful or famous, serving them champagne in gold goblets and canapes on gold platters. She patronised and promoted Dior, Jean Cocteau, Truman Capote and many others. She was friends with Gary Cooper, the Gabor sisters, Gore Vidal, Salvador Dalí and other self-publicists; she met President Roosevelt and was guest of honour for David Ben-Gurion. She was sketched by Picasso and painted by a roll call of famous artists, including Graham Sutherland. *She had compounded herself to fame and fortune.*

What would your dream life look like?

157 How Marie Curie compounded herself

Marie Curie was one of the most brilliant scientists of her generation, and her discoveries related to radioactivity (a term she coined) probably saved more lives than any other contemporary breakthrough. She was the first woman to win a Nobel Prize and the only one to win two: one for physics and one for chemistry.

Her compounding came in successive waves. Born in Poland in 1867, she was barred from university by the country's Russian rulers, simply because she was a woman. She worked as a governess to save enough money to go to university in Paris, where she lived in a sixth-floor garret with no heat, lighting, water or kitchen, 'living on air' and often not eating for days. She was happy to study intensely, graduating top of her class in physics in 1893, and second in mathematics the following year. She fell in love with Pierre Curie, a professor, married him and formed a working partnership with him.

Marie further compounded herself by becoming the premier researcher in the hot new area of radioactivity, discovering how it was generated. She also discovered two new chemical elements, one of which, radium, she identified, isolated and proved to be 900 times more radioactive than uranium, the only element previously known to be radioactive.

During the First World War she ran a fleet of mobile X-ray units, saving the lives of an estimated one million wounded soldiers. Her intellectual curiosity and innovative experiments meant that she knew more about radium and radioactivity than anyone else in the world. Her fortitude and dedication in difficult circumstances were exemplary. Her lesson for anyone fascinated by an intellectual problem is clear – go first and deep into an exciting new field, and experiment creatively until you understand exactly how it works.

Can you identify a field – of any kind – where you can be the first and foremost investigator?

158   How Albert Einstein compounded himself

This career is easy to understand. Although initially an indifferent student – he hated being taught and was quietly rebellious – *Einstein lived 'in his head'*. His whole life revolved around problems in physics and quantum mechanics, many of which he solved. But there were always intriguing new problems and questions, which fascinated, frustrated and challenged Albert. His love and family life always took a distant second place to his intellectual life. His relationships failed. This does not appear to have bothered him greatly.

Einstein continually and progressively compounded himself, getting deeper and deeper into the strange doings of the micro-world, of atoms and particles and all that incomprehensible stuff – barely comprehensible even to Einstein and, one suspects, to God too.

Albert's life moved up a few thousand feet in 1905, his annus mirabilis. The crowning glory was his special theory of relativity, which subverted everything physics had believed since Isaac Newton. Einstein's five theoretical papers of 1905 – including the one on relativity – are an object lesson in 80/20. He wrote all five epochal papers in a frenzied 'flow' of just four months, between March and June. Immediately, classic physics was dead. In a tiny amount of time, through the mind of one person, our understanding of the universe was transformed.

Einstein's reputation grew and grew. The mediocre high school and polytechnic student assumed the mantle of genius. The general theory of relativity in 1916 was another fantastic landmark. Yet there was no sense of anti-climax in his mind. To the end of his days, Einstein wrestled with this – did God play dice with the universe? Einstein said no. Most of his intellectual peers said yes. Can you imagine being fascinated by this issue for decades? Einstein was, very happily.

Do you have an Einstein-like fascination with any important puzzle? If so, you will die happy.

159   How Nelson Mandela compounded himself

Nelson Mandela had to endure a version of hell before he began compounding to a most remarkable degree. Mandela's hell was a tiny cell on Robben Island, a rocky, desolate and ugly place, from which he could glimpse the unattainable heaven of Cape Town, forever denied to him by the life sentence handed down in 1964.

Yet Nelson believed in the impossible, not for selfish reasons, for what he deemed to be right. About 1980, he pondered the future of South Africa. The ANC, to which he belonged, was making the country ungovernable. In response, the Nationalist government was clamping down with ever-increasing repression. Mandela came to believe in two positive but unlikely ideas – that peaceful transition to democracy was possible; and that he, sealed up as he was, was *the person to lead it*. Many eminent people began to visit him in his cell and he signalled to them, and therefore to the outside world – to the Commonwealth, to liberal South Africans, to his ANC comrades and, especially, to Margaret Thatcher's government and his Nationalist oppressors – that he was willing to compromise and that a bloody revolution could be averted. *No other ANC leader had this vision.* Using his unique blend of charm and iron resolve, he challenged P. W. Botha, the 'great crocodile' of apartheid, to work with him to avoid civil war. He insisted on one person one vote – giving black South Africans the large majority – but personally guaranteed there would be no bloodbath, no communism, no socialism, just democracy.[1]

He began secret negotiations in 1985. By 1994, he was president, popular in all sections of the community. There are few fairy tales in recent politics. This is the most heart-warming of all.

Even in politics, the right thing is sometimes possible, with happy results for millions. What can 'doing the right thing' be in your life?

160   How Jeff Bezos compounded himself

Jeff Bezos was always super-bright and super-ambitious – his teenage girlfriend said he wanted a fortune 'to get to outer space'. In the 1980s, where did a gifted American go to make money? Wall Street. But Bezos hated the formality and pointlessness – the whole *mores* – of the Street. His compounding began at age 26 when he met David Shaw, a computer science professor who had founded D. E. Shaw & Company (DESCO) in 1988, to specialize in quantitative investment management. Bezos and Shaw became soul-mates – both unbelievably bright, ambitious and creative.

Shaw was one of the very first true believers in the commercial potential of the internet. He and Bezos worked on a project to set up an online 'everything store', which became the blueprint for Amazon. Both men believed in only hiring the very best people, and wanted to build the store into the planet's most customer-centric organization. Together they hatched the idea that customer ratings and reviews would be posted on the site.

Shaw intended to start the business within DESCO. But Bezos wanted to do it himself and asked Shaw's permission. With extraordinary generosity, Shaw agreed. On 5 April 1994 Bezos started Amazon in his garage.

Bezos compounded himself by demanding high standards in everything – unbeatable prices, customer service, delivery and innovation. Bezos sacrificed short- and medium-term profits to gain market share. Being an Amazon worker, supplier or contractor cannot be easy, but the share price of Amazon has compounded very nicely.

Is there anything Bezos did that can help you compound yourself?

161   How J. K. Rowling compounded herself

When she was 24 years old, with an ordinary job, Joanne Rowling was sitting on a delayed train, staring aimlessly out of the window. Suddenly she had a vision of a little boy on a train heading for a special boarding school for wizards. She received a kind of 'download' of the boy, scrawny, black-haired, bespectacled and ordinary-looking, but somehow endowed with magical qualities. She was hugely excited by writing his story and started that evening.

But the book about Harry Potter took seven hard years to write and get published. In between Joanne experienced some difficult times and ended up coping with financial hardship and depression. The two things that really pulled her through were her infant daughter Jessica and her story about Harry Potter. She struggled, but persevered, writing longhand in Edinburgh cafés, nursing a single coffee for hours while she watched over Jessica, determined to finish *Harry Potter and the Philosopher's Stone* if it was the last thing she wrote.

Of course, it wasn't. The book was published in 1997, firing the imagination of millions of children throughout the world. She wrote six more Harry Potter books, sold more than 600 million copies, and earned an estimated £1.2 billion from them and Hollywood film rights. She has since moved into adult detective novels under the pen name of Robert Galbraith, inventing Cormoran Strike, a disabled war veteran turned ace sleuth, as the main character in a series (so far) of seven gripping and bestselling books. Rowling has also become a generous philanthropist, supporting women and children at-risk and other causes. She continues to rejoice in her good fortune and is still compounding herself every year.

However bleak your life, find inspiration and hope in the moving story of J. K. Rowling. We are all endowed with imaginative powers beyond our reckoning.

162   Is your career compounding nicely?

Jeff Bezos, Marie Curie, Albert Einstein, Helena Rubinstein, J. K. Rowling and Nelson Mandela all compounded their careers on their own. Bezos got his head start from David Shaw, but his career really took off with his solo launch of Amazon. Marie Curie got her big break from the Sorbonne, University of Paris, but she arrived there purely on her own merits, without any sponsorship or external funding. Her career was built on intellectual curiosity, creative experimentation and pushing the boundaries of science. Einstein had the same qualities and required no academic credentials to shatter two centuries of physics. Rubinstein was helped by rich friends but succeeded due to her superb entrepreneurship and imagination, like a peasant-princess from a fable. Rowling triumphed due to *her* imagination and character invention, and a natural ability to write well. Mandela swapped a terrible life sentence for eternal glory.

Which all raises a thought-provoking question – is it possible to compound your career inside a company or institution you do not control? You may rise to the top of the pyramid, but can you create something of enormous value that did not exist before? I do not say that it is impossible, just that it is unlikely. No great example springs to my mind; does it to yours? It is certainly easier to enrich the world your way, with unconstrained originality. Even from a high-security jail.

There are some organizations in which you can continue to double your learning year after year – conceivably Apple is one, perhaps Google or Space X are others – but I rather doubt it. When it gets down to the ranks of mere successful rather than world-beating companies, or any firm that has been going for more than 10 years and has well-defined patterns of success, it is near-impossible to compound original results. For that you need your own vehicle, and the ability to continually import and make absurd demands on young people who are even more creative and untrammelled than you.

Don't get bogged down in the slough of mediocrity. Break free!

163   Define and limit what you want to compound

You want to compound yourself – to make your career or your life something that *reaches new heights every year*.

80/20 says that this is either unlikely-verging-on-impossible, or else relatively easy.

It is difficult or impossible if it is too ambitious *for you*, if you have bitten off more than you can chew. It is difficult because you are one of the 80 per cent, not one of the 20. You are not a natural at it, you are not effective at it. It is above your pay grade.

It is relatively easy if you are good at the task, or if you have discovered some knowledge, some secret shortcut. Then you are one of the 20 per cent who achieve 80 per cent. So do what is relatively easy for you.

What makes the difference, usually, are two things – the fit of the task with your skills, knowledge and contacts; and focus. The first of these is obvious – do things you are uniquely good at. *Focus is not so obvious, but it is essential.*

Focus means thinking small, not big. It means thinking hard about what you want to compound.

None of us can do too many things. It's hard to be a great parent and also change the world or look after a country. Perhaps Steve Jobs, Nelson Mandela, Queen Elizabeth II, Margaret Thatcher, Winston Churchill and Albert Einstein illustrate this. You can't be laser-focused on making money and also be Mother Theresa. Husband and wife – or husband and husband, wife and wife – can focus on different dimensions of achievement, or the same one, but it must be clear which it is.

Are you compounding what you are already good at?

164   Hills and mountains

Anyone who achieves anything worthwhile in a career knows what it is like to climb a hill or a series of hills. You start with an objective – to reach the top of the 'hill' or a more distant or taller hill. It might be to pass an examination or gain a qualification, to join a particularly intriguing organization, to gain a promotion, to become self-employed and reach a certain level of earnings, to make enough money to be able to spend your time as you please, to start a business which can become profitable or to start a social business or charity which gains traction and sufficient funds to do some good in the world.

But what happens when you reach the top of your hill? If you are incurably ambitious or curious, you glimpse yonder mountain, glinting in the sunlight, taunting you to climb it.

When you were concerned with reaching the top of the hill, you didn't realize the mountain was there, or if you did, you thought it was well out of your league. But now it is different. The hill is climbed. The mountain is next.

You acquire a valuable skill – reach the top of your hill – and then you think, how could this become ten, a hundred, a thousand times more valuable, by starting a business or a network? You become a member of parliament or Congress, and then think about becoming a secretary of state. You become a secretary of state, and then think, could I possibly become prime minister or president? Your business is viable and profitable within a certain country, but could it be global?

Why can you see the mountain which was previously invisible or irrelevant? Because you are a different person – more qualified, more confident, with more rare knowledge, and with greater contacts and relationships. Because you are a different team. Because you can think differently – you are aware of how opportunities appear or disappear; you are more creative; *you know how to create your own opportunities out of thin air.*

Have you climbed your hill? Where is your mountain?

165   The footnote theory

There is a good metaphor for hills and mountains. I call it 'The Footnote Theory'.

The entrepreneur Sam Altman – who was president of Y Combinator and is currently head of OpenAI – says he always wants his next project to be one that, if successful, makes what he has achieved already a mere footnote to his career.

So far, he has succeeded.

What new project could, if it works, dwarf anything you have achieved so far in life?

166   The leapfrog alternative to compounding

When I was at school, the headmaster once caused a sensation by handing out, in assembly, a promotion to school prefect to someone who had not previously been a house prefect. I don't know whether it was a mistake or a reproach to the housemaster for not having made the boy a house prefect. Either way, it broke all precedent. But it gave me hope, because I wasn't a house prefect either and thought I should be a school prefect.

I never made those giddy heights, being too non-conformist to be prefect material. But it seems to me that in life, as opposed to school, it is possible, and perhaps *not that unusual*, to leapfrog the process of compounding, by unexpectedly landing in a top role without going through the normal progression, or after spectacular failure.

Lenin, Hitler and Churchill all spring to mind. So, in a roundabout way, does Steve Jobs. He was the head of Apple, the company he started, but was then kicked out of – for quite good reasons. After a decade in the wilderness, he came back in triumph in 1997, reinstated as the only alternative, so the Board thought, to impending bankruptcy. He then proceeded to make Apple a fabulously successful and valuable company, something he had not done the first time around.

If you really are talented enough, or clever enough at spotting an opportunity not noticed by anyone else, you can always put two fingers up to power and start your own thing. It is often *easier and quicker* to get some financial backing, or use your own money, *to start a venture, than to get promoted* through the ranks in an existing company.

Could you do something like this?

CHAPTER 23

HOW TO INCREASE YOUR EFFECTIVENESS WITH LESS EFFORT

You can't be 'intelligent and lazy' and achieve high success without 'leverage' – you need other people to do most of the hard work! In this chapter, you'll find seven different ways to high leverage and success without you working harder than you really want.

167   Avoid hard work through leverage

I've argued passionately throughout this book that the best way to live is to be intelligent and lazy – to aim at very high achievement, but to limit your hours of work to a reasonable level.

What is reasonable? If your work is so enjoyable that it merges nicely with your leisure, or you prefer working to doing other things, then you are extremely lucky. And rare. Once you stop enjoying your work, stop. Whether you end up working 20 hours a week, or 30, or 50, or 5 is up to you. So it should be. You should not be a slave to convention, or to other people.

I am assuming that you can do this, because you work for yourself rather than other people. If you still work for someone else and are intelligent, you must and you will find a way to stop that. Maybe you will still formally be on someone else's payroll, but if you control your time and effectively have no boss, you are working for yourself. That is how it should be, after you have served your 'apprenticeship' and defined and mastered your territory.

If you work for yourself, you need never be stressed, except by yourself. That is enough stress in this life. To take stress from other people is not in the job description of anyone sane and intelligent.

There is, however, a 'but', and it's a big one:

To be lazy and still achieve great things, you need other people to do things for you.

You need leverage.

You'll discover various forms of leverage in the following pages.

Pick the one that best suits you and your mission.

But do get leverage. You are very unlikely to achieve great things without it.

Have you worked out how to get your leverage? If not, please pay close attention.

168   Disciples

Over the next few pages, we will look at *six* ways of increasing personal leverage. You can choose one or more of these to multiply your power and influence, and thus achieve more impact with less time and toil personally.

First up are 'disciples'. Chief executives and leaders generally are frequently the 'bottleneck' in an organization, especially if they insist on working very hard and being involved in all important decisions and initiatives. The more they do, the less the organization can do, and the longer it takes, because the top person is the bottleneck.

One excellent way to do more with less is to find and train trusted disciples. It worked for Jesus and it can work for you too. The point about disciples is that you train them to do what you can do. They are a personal extension of you. You must tell them everything you know – and make sure they really understand it – and are good communicators. They must be lively individuals, confident, self-starters and ambitious. Once they can do what you do, but better, you send them out into the world and hey presto! – *you have multiplied your reach and influence*. Even better, you can stop doing all the things you do now, and just do the things (or preferably, thing) at which you are supremely good and most enjoy.

Disciples should be young. Ideally, decades younger than you. They will have more energy, be more grateful and obedient to you, and be cheaper. Obedience and loyalty are vital. Disciples will carry your brand, your message, your authority. There can be no scope for heresy or self-glorification (that is your prerogative).

Have you been a disciple? Do you have disciples? Would you like to?

169   The pyramid

The second way to increase personal leverage is called the pyramid. If you are near the top of a pyramid or could start your own, this is worth considering.

There are many definitions of a pyramid. Mine is as follows:

- It involves clear differentiation between roles and experience levels – at least three different levels, but not normally more than five.

- It is *not* bureaucratic at all. Nor is it hierarchical for the sake of it. It merely means that the top echelon delegates *as much as possible* to the next level down; the second echelon delegates to the third one, etc.
- It has three advantages over a more traditional structure:
  - It enables the top echelon person to concentrate exclusively on high-value tasks, which are usually the most rewarding and fun.
  - It enables lower echelon people to reach up to do as much of the work of the higher echelon person, thus learning as much as possible, doing more interesting work and, perhaps, demonstrating their credentials to move up the pyramid.
  - It is more cost-effective, thus enabling the firm to lower prices and gain market share, and/or increase profit margins.

Have you ever worked in this kind of pyramid firm?

Do you like the sound of it?

170 How does a pyramid work in practice?

The idea is that you should never do something yourself if a lower cost resource – that is, a person paid less than you – could do it themselves. You get someone who is less experienced, less expensive and less demanding to do the stuff you don't want to do and that they can.

Now, obviously they will not do it as well as you to start with. They might not do it as quickly. But the difference in cost between you doing it and them doing it can be so great that it's economically worthwhile. And it certainly trains them to move up. It's an extreme but intelligent form of delegation.

Clearly it has its attractions for the person who delegates.

It's different from having disciples, because the disciple is in charge of his or her time, an autonomous unit imitating the guru. The pyramid is more continuous; it sets up the organization so that it reduces activity at the upper levels and therefore produces more with less. There is more time for creative thinking, which is the highest value activity.

Who or what is at the top of a pyramid? Nothing, just a point in space. The chief executive exists, and is therefore a smidgeon below the apex, but does very little except think, inspire, issue orders and decide rewards. I repeat, he or she *does* almost nothing, except think! Action *cannot* drive out thought, because there is virtually no action.

This is 80/20 at its purest. Pure magic.

Get the idea? Could you join or start a pyramid?

171 Clone yourself

The closest you can get to cloning yourself is to get someone to impersonate, shadow and imitate you so that they appear to be the same as you. This is only worthwhile, of course, if they are less expensive or less busy than you. If so, cloning is more with less: less cost or less (of your) time.

Here are a couple of examples:

- A famous person writes their memoirs, or another book. The clone ghosts the draft. The clone may actually do this better than the famous person, as well as costing less.

- Your Executive Assistant drafts your letters and you just scan through them before signing. Or the EA signs them as well, without you having to.

I have a friend who charges a lot of money for executives to belong to his club, where one of the main benefits is a frequent 16-page newsletter. This is mainly written by another – lower paid – person. The quality of the newsletter is consistently high and it is impossible even for someone who knows both of them to tell who has written what. The weird thing is that the friend actually tells his clients that this system exists. As far as I know, nobody has complained.

Could you clone, or be a clone?

172   Increasing personal leverage: 80/20

If you can identify where 80/20 is operating, you can achieve a tremendous amount with almost no work, except a little thinking – and some analysis, which you can easily delegate at little cost.

For example, the CEO of one online trading business I know asked his people to calculate the true value of all his customers. It transpired that *17 per cent of customers resulted in 164 per cent of true value.* Some customers made losses. With this information, it was easy to raise prices to the loss-making customers and to 'fire' those who refused to pay more; to try to sell more to the 17 per cent of good customers and to recruit more customers like them.

In the case of Filofax, when my syndicate controlled it, we found that just 4 per cent of products produced 93 per cent of sales, 142 per cent of profits and 190 per cent of cash generation. We stopped production of the loss-making 96 per cent of products, increased sales of the profitable 4 per cent and increased the value of the business seven times in seven years.

If you just investigate the profitability of your products and customers, which takes very little time or money, the results can be astonishing!

Have you done customer and product line profitability analysis?

173   Automate

Henry Ford was the first person to automate car-making, by standardizing the product – the famous Ford Model T, available in any colour so long as it was black – and using a moving assembly line to take production to workers doing each specialized task. As a result, between 1908, just before he started mass production, and 1920, the number of cars he made each year went from 6,000 to 1,250,000 and the price fell by 63 per cent. Naturally, profits soared more than 200 times.[1]

Brothers Dick and Mac McDonald designed the first assembly line of food and Ray Kroc rolled it out across the US. Today the firm has more than 35,000 restaurants worldwide.[2]

From a standing start in the early 1970s, Ingvar Kamprad automated furniture production and retailing. He designed and retailed the products: IKEA now has sales in excess of €30 billion and is estimated to be worth around €50 billion. IKEA is 10 times the size of its nearest rival. The furniture industry has grown by only 2 per cent annually, but IKEA's growth has been 14 per cent.[3]

Even service firms can be automated. When I was at the LEK consultancy around 1986, we invented three automated products which came to comprise most of our sales, and increased sales and profits dramatically.

When I and two colleagues started Belgo, the London-based Belgian restaurant in 1992, we provided the first upmarket automated eatery. We sold it six years later, making more than 20 times our money.[4]

Can you make a fortune by automating a product or service?

174   Hiring better people

One pivotal lesson learned by nearly all super-influential people, from CEOs to political leaders to entrepreneurs to anyone who makes the world a better place, is to hire or collaborate with people who are better.

Better than the people you already have in your camp.

And most of all, better than <u>you</u>.

Bill Bain knew this. Bill never wanted to do any consulting. It was not his thing. Working out an unbeatable formula for his firm, yes, dramatically yes. Mentoring, motivating and controlling his lieutenants, yes. Making oodles of money, yes. He ran by far the most successful consulting firm of the 1980s worldwide. But actually *doing* consulting? He could think about it better than anyone else. But doing it? Nah!

So when, in the early days of his firm, a new client asked him personally to work on the assignment, this is what he would do. He would schedule a meeting for himself and, say, Ralph Willard, one of his top five people, with the new client, the head of a huge company. The client had come to know and like Bill, but had never met Ralph. Bill would engage in a few pleasantries with the CEO, possibly about the weather but probably about last night's sporting event, then stand up, shake the hand of his startled host and say, 'I'll leave you with Ralph. You'll like him. He's better than me.' Then Bill would walk out and fly back to Boston.

The client might say, 'Well, Ralph, are you really better than Bill?' And Ralph might reply, 'Bill certainly thinks so and I'm told he has excellent judgment about people.' And they would laugh uproariously and the chemistry was settled.

You can do anything in life if you co-opt people who are better than you.

Have you done this? Will you?

175   Your formula

If you rely on disciples or other excellent people, you need a great formula for your enterprise. Unless you have your own proprietary formula, which is going to make the people underneath you heroes, you have not really started.

Which makes it imperative that you design a great formula. If any human endeavour is not prospering, ten to one it is because the formula is wrong. It is not usually because there is anything wrong with you or your people, not because the marketing is bad, nor because you face a fiendishly clever rival. *It is because your formula is not clever enough.*

It is always possible to think of a better formula.

If you look at any high growth professional service firm, behind its inexorable rise in people and profits you will find a unique formula, systematically rolled out. The same is true behind any business to consumer firm – high growth and profits rest on market-leading products in high growth markets or niches.[5]

80/20 is your go-to of course but there are other formulas like the star principle, something derived from one or both of them, or a totally different economic principle that works. Whatever you use, attracting brilliant colleagues relies on a consistent, repeatable formula.

Do you have one yet?

CHAPTER 24

THE ART OF 80/20 THINKING

Here's a primer on 'thinking the 80/20 way'. The basic idea is to identify the very few things that give fantastic results for relatively little effort, and to *only* do these things. You'll also see that the 80/20 Thinking is reflective, hedonistic, progressive and non-linear. Aim to do something every day that is both highly valuable but not unpleasant, unduly arduous, stressful or too time-consuming.

176   Do you think?

The natural response to the impertinent question 'Do you think?' is 'Of course I do! What is Richard on about?' Yet it may be the most important question anyone has asked you for a long time.

You see, your success and happiness – whether you really thrive or not – depends far more on how carefully and strategically you think about what you are doing in life. It is not so much *what you think*, but *how you think* and, most of the time, *whether you think*.

Ideas rule the world. Thinking is humans' secret weapon in the biological war of species, and the one thing that gives meaning to an otherwise random universe.

Not everyone really thinks much, nor should everyone. Original thinking is a gift from the gods. So too is the ability to act, to get things done, to move and shake, lead a team of high-energy doers and conquer the world. Only a tiny number of remarkable people can both think and do extremely well.

The great majority of high achievers are either extraordinary thinkers or extraordinary doers, not both.

Which are you? Or are you one of the very few people with the potential to do both?

177   Thinking is hard, but more fun than hard work

I am biased. I prefer thinking to doing, and episodic work to long, hard hours of work.

Here's the case for hard thinking. Thinkers may work many fewer hours than doers, and it's not just because they are lazy. It is hard work being a thinker. Thinking may actually be more difficult, as well as being more valuable, than being a hard-working doer for 10 hours a day.

How do humans progress? By thinking more and doing less. Take agriculture. If you go back 300 years, 98 per cent of people worked on the land and they worked incredibly hard. It was a horrid, back-breaking existence and they didn't have any combine harvesters. At the very most, the peasant would have an ox or a mule. Peasants worked very hard, yet always suffered malnutrition or the spectre of starvation. Now we have only 2 per cent of people in agriculture, not 98 per cent, and they produce vastly more because they are using better techniques and all these machines. Should we feel guilty about having combine harvesters instead of mules and peasants in the fields? Of course not. Society progresses through thinking and not hard labour.

On the other hand, there are some people who would run a mile from hard thinking and are glad to spend their life working hard instead. I was once at a seminar in Chicago and a participant reported what people often said to him – 'My head would explode with all the fear and stress of the decisions that thinkers have to make. They are happy with working hard and they express fear, loathing and contempt for having to do a thinking job.'

Not everyone wants to be a pampered thinker. Nor can everyone work limited hours. Some highly skilled and valued roles require 'being there' – surgeons and airline pilots, for example.

But for those who like mental exercise, it is exhilarating, and keeps you fit and young. It certainly gets my vote.

Does it get yours?

178   How to think 80/20

80/20 observes that there is an inbuilt imbalance between causes and results, inputs and outputs, and effort and reward. Causes, inputs and effort divide into two starkly different categories:

- *The majority*, which make little impact (the '80 per cent') versus:
- *A small minority*, which produce major, dominant results (the '20 per cent').

A lot of effort goes into producing little. A little effort produces most results.

The art of 80/20 is to look for the small inputs or causes which produce the biggest results.

In business, what are the few products, customers or uses of time which lead to high customer satisfaction and high profits?

In life, what takes you relatively little effort for a great reward – achieving high customer-satisfaction levels, for example, with a natural ability to please other people – leading, therefore, to those most elusive things we all want: *success and happiness*?

You can approach 80/20 from either end. One way is to look at which products, uses of time or activities have great results. So, you conduct analysis and look at the results – the results *fall out* of the analysis.

The other way is to guess – a more respectable word is *hypothesize* – what is important and then measure its impact.

Either way, you find the small things that give you great results. They always exist, because 80/20 is everywhere. All you have to do is to find them.

It is a great game, and the best, most efficient way to think about anything.

Have you joined the game yet?

179   How 80/20 launched me at university

I had one of the best times of my life, aged 18 to 20, during my three years at Oxford University. But early on, I faced a common dilemma of undergrads. *There was so much to do*: so many extra-curricular activities, sport, talking about life to friends, drinking, sexual adventures and, in my case, staying up all night to play poker, which was not only fun but also essential to fund my studies. Yet I was also ambitious and wanted to get a top degree. How could I do that without being stuck in the library all day?

Ironically, my salvation came one day when I was in the Bodleian Library, a beautiful domed building which looked far nicer from the outside than the inside. It is a copyright library, so you can request any book you like from the underground 'stacks'. One day, tipped off by a friend, I ordered a book by Italian economist Vilfredo Pareto, published in 1896–97, called *Cours d'économie politique*. I was fascinated by the section in which he described how incomes and wealth, in all countries and in all centuries, followed almost exactly the same very unequal pattern. Pareto never used the phrase '80/20', but that was what he was describing.

And then I had a brainwave. *Could I use this in my final examinations?* You see, there were 11 papers I had to write, answering three or four questions. I ordered up all the exam questions for the last 20 years. There was a bewildering number and variety of questions on each paper, but I had the idea that there would be some questions always asked in one form or another. And there they were! Always a question on the causes of the French Revolution, the First World War, the Russian Revolution and the rise of Hitler, for example. For each paper I chose the six most popular questions and confined my studying to those subjects, gambling that they would come up again. And they did! Bingo! A top degree without much studying, heavily focused on the key questions.

When I got my results, I resolved to make 80/20 my best friend in life.

Why don't you do the same?

180   More examples of 80/20 Thinking

Was I using 80/20 Analysis or 80/20 Thinking when I looked at previous exam papers to find the subjects which cropped up the most? This is a borderline case, because there was a tiny bit of analysis, but actually just sifting through the exam papers gave me the answers without actually having to add up the numbers – the popular questions stood out a mile.

Was it 80/20 Analysis or 80/20 Thinking when I decided that opportunities would be greatest in high growth industries? It was 80/20 Thinking. I never undertook any analysis; the idea seemed so intuitive and obvious. I still haven't done any analysis – I don't think it is necessary. Either you get the idea or you don't. And proving 'opportunity' is a pretty nebulous thing. Still, I am sure it is true. *I know it is true*, because I have made a fortune many times over by investing in high growth firms, even when they were tiny at the time (Betfair is a prime example).

My erstwhile business partner, the great Iain Evans, was a brilliant analyst and one of his most profound *dicta* was: 'This may not be statistically significant, but I can tell you that it is significant.' What he meant was that it was so obviously true that analysis was redundant.

If you had to analyse something to believe it, you would fail to do many useful things, such as falling in love.

If you want a better life, do a lot of 80/20 Thinking!

181   The hypothesis is the answer

Marshall McLuhan famously said, 'The Medium is the Message.' He meant that the dominant communication medium of the time was more important than what it communicated. The alphabet changed human life – words and the meaning of words made children think and act automatically in certain ways. Visual and aural information was downgraded; the printed word and books upgraded. This process was hugely magnified when Gutenberg invented movable type printing. Books which could be printed, rather than copied by hand by a scribe, provided the first uniformly repeatable commodity, leading logically (although not for a few centuries) to the assembly line and mass production. Similarly, electric and electronic technology have downgraded books and analysis, and upgraded visual learning and imagination – the internet being the best case in point. With 24/7/365 news, we now live, sadly, in a global village.[1]

'The medium is the message' sounds glib but is actually profound.

At the risk of sounding and being glib rather than profound, I propose that, when it comes to 80/20, *'the hypothesis is the answer'*.

Very often, the hypothesis is more valuable than the analysis, and can render analysis unnecessary. It may be better to guess the answer and, if you are confident it is true, act decisively on it, than to gather voluminous data. Data gathering takes time and money. Not only can this be expensive and/or wasteful, but it can actually be harmful. In business, and often in life, there is such a thing as competition. If you don't do something – buy a company, hire a brilliant person, collaborate with a genius, propose marriage, become someone's best friend, buy a house, get to the hospital on time – someone else may, and very often will.

On important matters, get in the habit of forming accurate hypotheses quickly.

182 Become an 80/20 Thinker

I may have thought and written more than anyone else in the world about 80/20, but in the hurly-burly of life I know how easy it is to fall back on traditional ways of thinking and doing. It is:

- easy to think about everything, to be comprehensive, not selective;
- easy to charge ahead and get on with the day's tasks, rather than consider whether they are exceptionally useful to anyone and could be left undone;
- easy to do what everyone else does – for example, work hard, do things that do not move the dial, waste time yet feel desperately short of it – which can be summarized as 'action without thought';
- easy to think we are average, when, at our best, on the things we do best, we are quite exceptional little angels;
- easy to settle for the best that has been achieved in anything, rather than raise our eyes to something wonderful which we can imagine, but which has not so far been done;
- easy to go a whole day without thinking about 80/20, even though it hovers at our elbow, ready to serve us in so many ways.

I don't know about you, but I find that my sweetest days are when *I think about 80/20 morning, noon and night*. When I relax, smile and laugh the most.

Try it!

183 80/20 Thinking is reflective

The aim of 80/20 Thinking is to generate action that does not take enormous effort yet makes marked improvements in your life and that of others. Actions like that require insight. Insight requires reflection and introspection. Sometimes insight requires more information, but not always, not usually. *Your brain already has much more information than you can imagine.*

Most thinking today is rushed, opportunistic and incrementalist. It is also mainly linear – for example, here is something good or bad, what caused it? Causes are often impenetrable, coming in inextricable or obscure bundles, and heavily coloured by your background, experience and carefully cultivated blinkers. It is often easier, quicker and more peaceful to remove problems rather than identify their culprits. This often requires counter-cultural thought, and tolerance of ambiguity and paradox.

Traditional thinking is rational and analytical. 80/20 Thinking is intuitive and comes from your subconscious mind.

Genuine reflection is rare because of our impatience and compulsion to go faster and faster. **Slow down.** Reflect. Look at an issue from top to bottom, inside and outside, as through the eyes of a child. Turn what everyone else is saying on its side, on its head. Your mission as an 80/20 Thinker is to leave action behind, do some tranquil contemplation and mine a few precious insights. Then and only then, to act, cautiously and selectively, on a few objectives and a narrow front; begin by acting experimentally and then with increasing certainty and confidence, decisively and impressively, to produce breath-taking results with as little energy and heavy-lifting as possible.

You can be reflective. But how often do you actually engage your reflective gear?

184 80/20 Thinking is hedonistic

80/20 Thinking seeks pleasure. Thinking should be fun. Thinking gives you options nicer and more rewarding than following your instincts. 80/20 Thinking also believes that life should be enjoyed. It believes that most achievement is a by-product of interest, joy, pleasure in our skill and the desire for future happiness.

Most of us fall into some of the following traps. We spend a lot of time with people we don't much like. We do jobs we are not enthusiastic about. We use most of our 'free time' – an inherently anti-hedonistic concept – on activities we don't much enjoy.

Conversely, we don't spend most time with friends we like best. We don't pursue the career we would like the most. Most of us are not great optimists, and even the optimists amongst us do not plan carefully to make our future better.

All this is the triumph of guilt over glee, of our genes over our intelligence, of fate over choice and, ultimately, of death over life.

Hedonism is often held to imply selfishness or lack of seriousness. This is a smear. Hedonism and happiness are necessary conditions for really helping others and for achievement. It is hard, and always wasteful, to achieve something great without enjoying it. If people were more hedonistic, the world would be much better and richer.

Should you be more hedonistic?

185   80/20 Thinking praises progress

For the past three thousand years there has been a sharp difference of opinion on whether history demonstrates a jagged upward path or something less hopeful. Against the idea of progress range Plato, Aristotle, Seneca, Horace, Saint Augustine and most living philosophers. In favour of progress stand nearly all the eighteenth-century Enlightenment thinkers, and most nineteenth-century scientists and thinkers, including Marx and Darwin.

Team captain for progress must be the oddball historian Edward Gibbon, who invited us to join 'in the pleasing conclusion that every age of the world has increased, and still increases, the real wealth, the happiness, the knowledge, and perhaps the virtue, of the human race.'

The debate can never be resolved. Belief in progress has to be an act of faith, even a duty, because only a belief in progress can create it.

80/20 Thinking is inherently optimistic. This is paradoxical. 80/20 reveals a state of affairs that is seriously below where it should be. Yet this gives scope and hope for progress. Only 20 per cent of resources truly achieve great results. The large majority are just marking time. Therefore, give more power to the 20 per cent, get the 80 per cent up to a reasonable level, and we can reach a much higher level. Even at this level, there will still be a warped distribution of inputs and outputs. So, you can progress again to a much higher level. Humans have to act stupidly to stop this. Einstein said that the difference between genius and stupidity is that genius has its limits. Still, let's vote for 80/20 and progress.

The progress of business and science vindicates 80/20. There is no end in sight to such progress. Now apply the same principle to other provinces of life. We might even prove Gibbon right – real wealth, happiness, knowledge and, just possibly, virtue, can be constantly increased.

Optimism creates progress. Please think likewise.

186   80/20 Thinking is non-linear

Traditional thinking is linear. Linear means 'of or in a line', something existing in only one dimension. For example, in thinking about causes, A leads to B, B causes C, and Y is the inevitable consequence of X. You made me unhappy because you let me down. My poor schooling led to my job flipping burgers. I have been successful because I am clever. My firm cannot grow because the industry is declining.

Linear thinking is attractive because it is simple, cut and dried. But it is a poor description of the world and even worse preparation for changing it. Scientists and historians long ago abandoned linear thinking. Why should you cling to it?

80/20 Thinking offers you a life raft. Nothing flows from one simple cause. Nothing is inevitable. Nothing is ever in equilibrium or unchangeable. No undesired state of affairs need endure. Nothing desirable need be unobtainable. The balance of circumstances can be shifted in a major way by a minor action, by a minor accident or by a tiny shift in several dimensions simultaneously.

Only a few decisions really matter. Those that do, matter a great deal. Choice can always be exercised. Decisions and choice need not be linear – they can involve many dimensions and options.

Growth is always important. Be attracted to growth opportunities – growth firms, growth trends. *Personal* growth is important. Growth, however, is usually linear – that is, slow and predictable. But the strongest and best growth is 'exponential' rather than linear. Exponential growth is accelerating, becoming more and more rapid. (It means growth raised to a power, an exponent. For example, if growth is raised to a power such as a square, it means the thing that grows is squared; that is, doubled each time period, such as a year.) *Go for exponential growth personally, in your work and career, as much as possible.*

80/20 Thinking is dynamic and multi-dimensional, not linear. Are you thinking about the rare things in life exhibiting exponential growth?

187   Should you *ever* work extremely hard?

Yes and No.

There is a case for working – or at least *thinking* – very hard, when you are in the early stages of a career and still learning the ropes. If you are the apprentice and you have found a brilliant master to work for, he or she may require you to work extremely hard as the price for sitting at their feet, especially if they themselves work like blazes.

And to get promotion in a firm where the culture is intense, you may need to fall in with the prevailing ethos. Early promotion leads to faster learning, so it is a price worth paying.

Even so, if you can to some extent choose a boss, try to find that rare beast, an 80/20 boss, who will teach you how to think and work super productively with great economy of effort.

Your career is likely to take off faster, and be far more enjoyable, once you get beyond the stage of having a boss. When you are self-employed, or able to act as if you are, you can control your time. It is only then that you can revel in the 80/20 life, combining great achievement with relatively little stress and time expended.

Be intelligent, be lazy and be ultra-successful, in whatever terms matter to you.

Have you reached this stage yet? If not, how can you reach it quickly?

188   Do something valuable every day

The night before each day, or first thing every morning, you might want to decide just *one thing* you will do which will add considerable value – in your work, for you personally or for a friend.

For example:

- A specific work task which will have excellent results.
- An important favour or surprise which will make someone happy.
- Some exercise or change to your diet to make you healthier.

- A break in your routine to recharge your batteries and increase your creativity.

- An enjoyable event for you and friends.

- At least two uninterrupted hours reading a good book.

Use 80/20 in thinking what to do. Make the benefit as great as you can with as much enjoyment as possible, or at least avoiding pain and stress.

Can you do something valuable today, tomorrow and every day?

189   Ignore your flaws, accentuate your virtues

The well-rounded person is either a delusion or a menace. A delusion because modern life has so many dimensions and specializations that to be OK at everything means to be excellent at nothing. A menace because even *trying* to be competent at most things will decrease your pleasure and skill at the few things you do best.

Be aware of your flaws, but do not brood on them or beat yourself up about them. A person's flaws add greatly to your friends' amusement and the gaiety of nations. Your flaws make you fully human and less intimidating. Laugh at your flaws and draw attention to them.

Be excellent at very few things, perhaps just one thing. Practise them daily. Hone them remorselessly.

For your flaws, find someone to clear up their negative fallout. Someone who is a good friend who has your back. Ideally, fall in love with this person!

How good are you at ignoring your flaws and accentuating your virtues?

CHAPTER 25

DECISIONS

Decisions are a human monopoly. We decide far too much, when no more than around a dozen decisions made in our lives will really matter. We'll see how to reduce the number of decisions we make. Less choice is better.

190   Humans and decisions

All other creatures on the face of the earth rely on instinct. Their genes dictate. The glory and danger of humans is that we can make decisions. We can defy our genes, conventions and instincts. We don't run on tramlines. We can soar up, up and away … or down to our private hell. Either way, <u>we</u> are responsible. We decide. Nobody else, not God, not Fate, not our genes, not our friends and advisers. We. Me. You. Alone. We are gods. Our weapon is decisions.

Decisions are levers to a different path. To freedom. To perdition. To our own private heaven.

Decisions are tricky.

Two or three centuries ago, 99 per cent of people didn't make many important decisions. Perhaps none of any great moment in their whole lifetime. They couldn't, because of poverty, conditioning or lack of imagination or precedent and role models. They might decide to murder, commit suicide or disappear. There were few other decisions available.

Now it is different. Now we are – in theory or in practice, as we choose – free to make decisions as individuals with a huge, incalculably large, number of options. We can decide.

You might think, therefore, given the existential and historically unprecedented extent of our freedom to decide, that decisions would be studied scientifically and there would be great help available in making decisions.

You would be disappointed.

But as always, 80/20 is a great guide.

When did you last make a vitally important decision? How did you decide?

191   Less choice is more

Psychologist Barry Schwartz gives a trivial but telling vignette – one group of students was given a box of six chocolates to evaluate; another one of 30. The first group liked the chocolates more. *Choice had negative value.*

Schwartz says that the number of choices we have to make today has accelerated well beyond our ability to make informed decisions. As technology gets more complex, we find it harder to sift through all the options. Every decision in life offers more choice than a generation ago, but there are three problems. Each decision is harder. We are more likely to make mistakes. And more likely to regret them.[1]

Back in the 1950s, economist Herbert Simon divided people into 'satisficers' and 'maximizers'. The satisficers merely want a good solution. But maximizers go to great lengths to get the best solution. Simon concluded that given the cost of investigating the options and the perils of making the wrong decision, the satisficers would nearly always end up happier.

Schwartz came up with this great insight – we are likely to be happier if we make our decisions permanent and irreversible, and if we appreciate life as we have it. If you can't have the one you love, love the one you have.

Are you a satisficer or a maximizer? Have you made the right choice?

192   Only a dozen decisions in your life really matter

We face a huge number of decisions in our lives. *Probably no more than around a dozen matter.* Here are some examples.

- Who to love?
- Whether to have a family?
- Where to live?
- What is your ambition?
- Which work to love?
- Which one or two people to collaborate with most closely?
- Which causes to support?
- How to be happiest?
- What the meaning of life is for you?

Which of these decisions have you made?

Which remain to be decided?

193   Make fewer decisions

All decisions have a cost. Even fairly trivial decisions, such as deciding which route to take on a long journey, or which microwave to buy, take time and mental energy. It gets worse. Decisions have proliferated on a wave of greater and greater choice, greater competition (which brings new suppliers and options) and ever greater expectations. Even where the trends are benign, the explosion of choices is at best an unpleasant side-effect, at worst a paralyzing source of stress, creating a sense that we are bound to make mistakes we will regret.

80/20, however, teaches you something even more distressing. *Trivial decisions drive out important decisions, even vital decisions.* How can you think about what matters in life and the long-term decisions which will affect your happiness and influence, when your mind is flooded by a torrent of inconsequential but insistent, apparently urgent decisions?

The number of decisions we make has increased, is increasing, and ought to be diminished.

One of the more useful decisions you can make is how to reduce the number of decisions you make.

Think for a minute or two about how you can reduce the number of decisions you make. Give your less important decisions the chop.

194   Coin analysis

'Coin analysis' can help you reduce the number of decisions you ponder. Coin analysis is simple, fast and has no cost, unless the coin rolls away under some furniture and you lose it. It also guarantees no angst, because it is the coin and not you that makes the decision.

Yes, you've guessed it. The next time you have to make a relatively unimportant decision, toss a coin.

If you accept the decision, depending on whether the coin turns up heads or tails, you have made the decision effortlessly. You have thumbed your nose at the absurdity of modern life, where many people will construct a spreadsheet to decide something that does not matter. You have also washed your hands of responsibility, should anything go wrong. True, you decided to toss the coin, but you can make this a default category for *all* relatively unimportant decisions. Some of those decisions will work out better than others, but who is to say that you would have made better decisions on average from more complex analysis?

What cannot be known cannot be a source of regret.

There is one final benefit that may come from any single decision via coin analysis. When it has come up heads, you may experience a momentary pang of regret – you wanted tails! Then you have the freedom to overrule the coin and do what you really wanted, what your instincts said was the right decision. A small victory for a painless and quick decision, and for life as you want it.

Will you adopt coin analysis as a fun way to make all unimportant decisions?

195   Reducing the number of decisions through trust

Trust is an essential weapon in the 80/20 armoury. Whether for your personal life or work, trust is a great simplifying mechanism, reducing stress, increasing pleasantness, and removing cost and complexity.

If you trust someone to have your interests at heart, to be truthful and to be competent, you can get more of your objectives fulfilled with less time and trouble. Trust simplifies. Trust requires less explanation of what you want; the other person knows that already. Trust eliminates all the shadow-boxing that must take place before you truly trust someone – the checking that they want to help you, the 'negotiation' on the benefits to and obligations of both parties, and any careful and tedious 'de-coding' of what they tell you, any reading between the lines, costly supervision of any particular task on which you collaborate, and understanding the terms of reciprocity between you.

Here are three useful rules for generating trust. One is to *trust someone as much as you reasonably can from the start of a relationship*; only pulling back when trust has been forfeited.

A second rule is to *be totally honest and transparent*, revealing your vulnerabilities and fears as well as your hopes and goals.

Third, *demonstrate increasing trust* as the relationship evolves.

The decision to trust someone <u>totally</u> is a big one. You can't, and shouldn't, trust everyone. It is a privilege to trust and be trusted. It has big risks as well as big rewards. It is better to trust fewer people but select them carefully and trust them totally, so that they become a key part of your life and work. Over time, the relationship cements itself and is a source of ever greater value and joy.

If you trust someone totally, you need to do far less work and make far fewer decisions yourself.

Whom do you trust totally? Should the number increase?

196   Reducing the number of decisions through conscience

This is a good old-fashioned way to cut the number of decisions you need to make in life and work. We often evaluate decisions, especially business decisions, by what is expedient – what will put you in the best position, what will make you the most money. There is another way worth contemplating:

What is the right thing to do?

There are hidden benefits to following your conscience. It makes you feel good. It increases the trust that other people are likely to put in you. And it is a way of reducing the horribly escalating number of decisions you feel you have to make every day.

A moment's thought will tell you that you should take account of: the benefits not just to yourself, but also to your partners, collaborators and workmates, and to the firm or any other group to which you belong; the good of your customers or clients; the good of the local, national and global economy; the good of our planet; and the impact of any decision on your reputation.

How can you possibly work out all the interests and trade-offs between all these different interests and constituencies, some of which will conflict with each other?

Amazingly, you have a computer in your mind which can work all this out instantly, without any need for spreadsheets or even rational calculation.

Just follow your conscience.

Could you make most decisions by following your conscience? Are you doing that already?

197 Outsource activities and decisions

For three or four decades, organizations have progressively outsourced (contracted out) more and more of their work to outside suppliers, in order to concentrate just on their – horrid jargon alert – *core competencies*, the things they do best. But this is an effective strategy not only for big outfits, but also for you and me as individuals. And not only for activities, but also for decisions.

Activities you can outsource include: secretarial and research; shopping; house management, maintenance, painting and cleaning; arranging travel and accommodation; interior design; banking, cash management and insurance; tax returns, payments and other accounting needs; driving; cooking and catering; entertaining; gardening; learning languages and other skills; negotiating; childcare and education; pet care and sitting; and all your computing and technology needs and adjuncts.

Why outsource anything? For the same reason organizations do – to concentrate on the things you do best and enjoy the most. If a lower-paid person can do something and you can earn or enjoy life more, it makes sense. But do not outsource human and family needs, especially responsibility for loved ones.

In outsourcing any activity, you automatically outsource the decisions necessary. If you outsource the shopping, for example, you don't need to decide which shops to go to, and you will probably use a standard weekly list, cutting down the need for (and temptation of) frequent discretionary additional purchases.

Outsourcing simplifies and reduces your range of activities and decisions.

Do you outsource enough (or too much)?

198   The most vital decisions – those not made

Although we make far too many decisions, it is the decisions we _don't_ make that damage our lives most. And often, the multiplicity of decisions we make stops us from making the few decisions we should. *Trivial decisions drive out vital ones.*

Decisions not made fall into two categories – missed opportunities and missed escapes. A missed opportunity involves *not* deciding to do something – a love affair not started or aborted; a product idea that you don't pursue, which might pop up later from someone else; a job opening or change of career not followed up; a trip mooted but never made.

Examples of missed escapes are: a failure to leave your home town for greener pastures; a failure to end a toxic relationship or friendship; a failure to escape an addiction; a failure to become optimistic and cajole yourself into greater happiness; a failure to escape mental limitations and believe in yourself.

These are the warning signals indicating that your failure to decide is a mistake, possibly even a tragedy:

- Failure to stop something making you stressed or unhappy
- Failure to live up to the potential you know you possess
- Failure to get close to individuals who have greater kindness or vision
- Any shortage of nerve, courage or imagination
- Any decisive failure to become a better and more useful person
- Any failure condemning you to a smaller or less hopeful life
- Any failure to help a friend in need

Are there any missed opportunities or missed escapes in your life so far? Are there any looming currently?

199   Contrarian decisions are great

You should always make decisions that appear to have 80/20 characteristics – that is, big results for small means, and also that are contrarian; that is, go against the crowd.

The biggest contrarian decision advocated in this book is that you decide to be highly ambitious but refuse to work long hours. By all means be intense and extreme in your ideas, your self-belief and the results you target, but get other people to do the hard work for you. The great insight of my mentors was that you could aim to change the world – and succeed – but do progressively little work personally, and only the work you massively enjoy.

Another contrarian decision is to exercise for at least an hour a day *but only an exercise you genuinely enjoy*, whether it's walking, cycling, swimming, tennis or (much less likely) gym. The health benefit will be enormous if you do this year after year, and you will also enjoy it and release nice chemicals into your bloodstream. Why is this contrarian? Don't lots of people go to the gym – or at least belong to it? They do, but generally they exercise through gritted teeth. *The contrarian element is insisting on exercise you enjoy.* And also doing it every day, year after year, forever. Not many people do that, but those who do are happier, healthier and live longer.

What other contrarian 80/20 decisions have you made? Or could you make?

200   Genuinely new decisions are great

There is nothing new under the sun, except when there is. Language, writing, the wheel, paper, agriculture, gunpowder, eyeglasses, printing, canals, the steam engine, steamships, railways, steel, bicycles, cars, planes, plastics, aircraft, semiconductors, nuclear bombs and power, computers, the web, artificial intelligence … what next?

Whether in business, arts and popular culture, or in life generally, the most interesting and rewarding decisions are unprecedented. The first mass-bottled carbonated soft drink. The first car for the middle- and working-classes. The first automated restaurant without waiting staff. The first low-price, high-quality paperbacks. The first budget airline. The first easy-to-operate PC. The first quality alternatives to taxis and hotels. The first paintings with perspective and the first secular art. The first opera. The first photographs. The first impressionist art, abstract art and surreal art. The first folk music. The first jazz. The first cartoons. The first antibiotics. The first talking movies. The first electric rock.

Some of these 'firsts' had no acknowledged individual innovator, but most of them did. Most were conscious decisions. Most involved doing something *opposite* to the prevailing practice and/or *using new technology in a different application.*

Have you ever done anything unprecedented? Would you like to make an unprecedented decision?

There is nothing stopping you.

201   Brave decisions are great

Sometimes it is right to stand alone. During the 1930s in Britain there was almost unanimity amongst the political and literary–academic establishment that Germany could not be disarmed forever, and that Hitler was a reasonable, pragmatic politician whose word could be trusted. The historian Arnold Toynbee said Hitler was 'sincere'. Lloyd George, Britain's leader during the First World War, met Hitler in the 1930s and said he was 'the Greatest German of the age'. Labour Party leader George Lansbury, a pacifist, said 'Germany needs peace … Nobody understands this better than Herr Hitler' and his party endorsed a 'constructive policy of appeasement.' In October 1938 the British prime minister, Neville Chamberlain met Hitler in Munich and they signed the Munich Agreement, under the terms of which Hitler promised not to invade any more countries. Chamberlain said that Hitler could be trusted to keep his word, and when he landed at Croydon Airport in England, he told cheering crowds that this meant 'peace in our time'.

In 1932, even before Hitler came to power, Winston Churchill made a brave decision. He had been to Germany and seen the young Nazis with their murderous hatred of Jews, communists and foreigners and heard Hitler stoking up the Nazis' hatred. From then on, Churchill denounced Hitler and said that unless France and Britain stood up to him, he would bring 'calamity and tribulation' to the world. Churchill's decision cost him dearly. His Conservative colleagues excluded him from office and disregarded all his warnings. He was almost alone in the political wilderness.

In March 1939 Hitler tore up his commitments to peace by invading Czechoslovakia. In May 1940, when Hitler was poised to invade Britain, the King, the Conservative party and the Labour party, who all still distrusted Churchill, knew in their hearts they had to make him prime minister – nobody else fit the bill.

Brave decisions are a gamble. They are 80/20 decisions because they go against the crowd and are important. If you know you are right, make your brave decision and damn the consequences.

202   Vital decisions: there are always multiple options

One of the great mistakes we all make about decisions is to assume that there are two options, A or B. For vital decisions, this is never true and always dangerous.

The 80/20 decision-maker knows there are always multiple options.

On any vital decision there are always far more options than you consider. Somehow, we seem to have the urge to reduce everything to A or B, X or Y. With enough imagination, there are more options than letters in the alphabet.

The next time you have to make a crucial decision about anything *widen your options, expand the frame of your vision.* Surprise yourself by making a list of a dozen or more options that could make you happy.

Have you ever limited yourself to a binary option? Are you sure you will avoid it in future?

203   Make vital decisions from 30,000 feet

You don't have to jump on an aeroplane to make a vital decision, but it could help. What you need is the detachment and view from above that a plane ride or mountain climb can give. When you look from high above, you see tiny people the size of insects. They are going about their business without the perspective, superior vision and objectivity you enjoy. You know nothing about their circumstances or their emotional biases. You can see further than they can because, paradoxically, you know less than they do.

Imagine from your plane you see a couple walking near the edge of a dense forest. They are moving round in circles. It occurs to you, they're lost! You want to shout to them, 'Just go to your left and keep going and you'll be out of the forest in five minutes.' You can see the way out, but they can't see the wood for the trees.

This is what happens to you when you try to decide something important and get affected by your emotions. Decades ago, I was pondering leaving my partner of many years. Our relationship had grown increasingly stormy and neither of us was happy. Yet every time I thought of breaking up, I was assailed by memories of good times, strong affection for my mate and fear of being alone. I only broke the logjam by asking my best friend what to do. She said without hesitation, 'Richard, you should leave.'

There is psychological evidence that you may make what is obviously the wrong decision, because emotion clouds your reason, but if you are asked what you would advise a friend in that situation, you give the correct answer.[2]

If you need distance and objectivity on hard decisions, ask a friend. Have you had a similar experience, either as the undecided person or the friend?

204   Question your treasured assumptions

My business is making venture capital investments. Venture capitalists usually believe the following:

- Nothing is so important as the quality of the management team.
- The management team must be balanced and experienced.
- Before making an investment, very detailed due diligence is necessary.

My own experience may be atypical, but this is what more than three decades of high returns have demonstrated:

- Two of my most successful investments, Belgo and Betfair, came from the least experienced and most unbalanced management teams.

- The creativity of one or two entrepreneurs dwarfs the need for balance in the team overall.

- Detailed due diligence is often unnecessary and may be misleading.

- 80/20 Analysis of our returns demonstrates that the two best indicators of high performance are (1) which source the investment idea came from and (2) the growth rate of the business immediately before investing. All the high return investments came from long-standing personal networks. All the high growth businesses made high investment returns.

Rigorous questioning of common assumptions at work or in life usually pays off handsomely. Some stellar businesses have been built on doing the opposite of standard practice.

205   How to question your assumptions on vital decisions

Whether at work or in life, questioning your most basic assumptions is a costly and often painful process. It is only worth doing for life-changing decisions but is essential for these.

Here are two ideas which I have used in my life, both drawn from the admirable book *Decisive* by Chip Heath and Dan Heath.[3]

First, ask yourself, a friend or (in business) an executive or small team, to try to prove the _opposite_ *of your most important assumptions.* Lay the assumptions bare and gather all the evidence, objective and subjective, which contradicts the assumptions or indicates better assumptions.

In imagining the opposite of what you assume, you may find a new life or a new business for yourself.

Do *not* collect any evidence or findings which validates your initial assumptions. Just consider the opposite.

Second, Roger Martin, dean of the Rotman School of Business, asks this question of any decision: What would have to be true for this decision to be the right answer? The question is best asked of several different options. By examining the assumptions necessary, it is possible to decide which has the greatest chance of being the solution.

You can only be open-minded by answering the 'Roger Martin question' fairly for each option.

Have you ever used one of these methods of making crucial decisions? Would you like to try one or both of the methods the next time you face a vital decision?

206   The repeat decision delusion

The Chief Executive of Quaker, William Smithburg, made an astute decision in 1983 to acquire the Gatorade brand for $220 million, 'because he liked the taste of the product'. By putting hefty marketing behind the brand, it became worth some $3 billion.

So far so good. In 1994, Smithburg decided to buy another niche brand, Snapple, for $1.8 billion. Neither Smithburg nor any of the Quaker board directors were dismayed when analysts queried the acquisition, with some saying the price was $1 billion too high. They saw it as a repeat of the Gatorade success.

It wasn't. Snapple required different distribution and its authentic image suffered from being acquired by a large corporation. In 1997, it was sold for $300 million, a loss of $1.5 billion.[4]

If you have had a big hit with an investment or any other success, beware of thinking that the next one to come along is similar. It will be what it is.

CHAPTER 26

NETWORKS

We will explore: why networks are the best way to achieve dramatic growth, why networks boost the power and reach of 80/20 and why networks become much more valuable when they are bigger.

207   Networks and 80/20 rule OK

In the last 30 years, more and more attention has been paid to the phenomenon of networks. They have grown so much and become so powerful that the brilliant Spanish sociologist Manuel Castells says, 'network society represents a qualitative change in the human experience.'

Examples of networks include social media, football teams and their fans, the internet, cryptocurrencies and all app-based organizations and platforms.

The distinguishing economic benefit of networks, for those spending time in them and for their investors, is that they can grow fast without either top-down direction or lots of marketing money.

Networks exhibit 80/20 qualities – more from less.

How can you benefit from networks? Possibly from working in a high growth network or starting your own.

Have you thought much about networks?

Can you think of examples of networks in which you already participate?

208   Why has 80/20 become much more prevalent and powerful?

Over the years, 80/20 has become more powerful, but why is that? Perhaps it just seems more important and prevalent because it has gained a great deal more publicity – an old and dusty law of the universe, known only to economists and folks who went to business school, is now being used by millions of people. Perhaps also, my reinterpretation of the principle for use in ordinary life as a tool of personal achievement without extraordinary work or angst has had an influence.

But now something is happening in society which means that 80/20 is becoming vastly more powerful, and it has absolutely nothing to do with me or my publishers.

The 'something' is the burgeoning power of networks, which grew slowly up to around 1970 but have taken off since. Hierarchies have declined, as networks – which are easier to run, easier to scale and much more profitable – have proliferated. All networks follow the 80/20 pattern, often in an exaggerated, extremely lopsided way. More networks, more 80/20 phenomena.

This is very good news for you. Because there are many more networks, there are more ways for you to get more from less.

Where do you think networks that you could join or start are most abundant and growing fastest?

209   Cyberspace, networks and 80/20

Networks are growing fastest in cyberspace, which itself is expanding exponentially.

One paradox of cyberspace is that it is open to everyone and without barriers, yet it results in extreme forms of 80/20 – often 90/10 or 99/1. Cyberspace proliferates niche monopolies.

Eric Schmidt, chairman of Google's parent Alphabet, explains:

'I would like to tell you that the internet has created such a level playing field that the long tail is absolutely the place to be. Unfortunately, that's not the case.

What really happens is something like a power law. A small number of things are very highly concentrated and most other things have relatively little volume. Virtually all the new network markets follow this law … the vast majority of revenue remains in the head …

It's probable that the internet will lead to larger blockbusters and more concentration of brands … when you get everyone together, they still like to have one superstar … a global superstar.'[1]

Market share concentration allows networks to achieve their greatest depth and reach.

What are the implications for you? Paradoxically, they are good, if you want to start something on the internet, whether for profit or not. If you want to have influence, you must start something totally novel, in a new niche you create, and see if it spreads like wildfire. If it doesn't, give up and try something else new. If it does, push it as far and as fast as possible.

210   What exactly is a network?

Kevin Kelly, former editor of *Wired*, says it well: 'The network is the least structured organization that can be said to have any structure at all.'[2]

Facebook and Twitter are networks; so are terrorist organizations, criminal gangs, political groups, sports teams, the internet, the United Nations, a group of friends and the world's financial system. Nearly all the web- or app-based organizations that have burst upon the scene and built extraordinary wealth – such as Apple, Google (Alphabet), PayPal, Uber, Amazon, Netflix and Airbnb – are either networks or have networks nestled in their ecosystems.

How are networks different from traditional top-down organizations?

One defining difference is that all traditional organizations, whether state bureaucracies, armies or all the business and social organizations before the internet, depend on initiative from the top of those organizations. They cannot grow without intricate planning from the top. It used to take a long time and huge manpower, coordination and money to grow to their full size.

Networks are different – their growth comes not from inside the organization (if there is one) but from inside the network. The network grows as a result of initiative and actions by the network members, usually without any payment. If the network is owned by a business, the 'members' of the network are also 'customers' or potential customers. The network grows from its own internal dynamics; it is in the interests of network members that there should be as many members as possible. So, internet-based networks which are also businesses can grow to be huge and become very valuable in short order.

Does this encourage you to consider starting a network?

211　Network growth – the Betfair example

I invested in Betfair in 2001, a few months after it started. Betfair was a new beast – a 'betting exchange', an electronic market for betting which did not need the intervention of the ancient enemy of punters – bookmakers, taking 10–20 per cent profit on each betting event. At that stage Betfair was valued at £15 million – which I thought was much less than it was worth. Of course, it was risky. It was tiny and almost all industry observers thought it would never take off. The UK legislation on betting exchanges did not exist as it was a new phenomenon, and the bookmakers lobbied hard and long to have it made illegal. Yet what attracted me to Betfair was its astonishing growth rate – 10, 20, 30, sometimes even 50 per cent *each month*.

Where did this growth come from? It didn't come from any sales and marketing effort by Betfair, which was virtually nil. The growth came from the network itself – Betfair customers, who liked it so much they told their friends to join. The customers wanted the network to get bigger so they could place bigger bets and get them matched by someone on the other side of the transaction.

All networks are like this. The people in the network itself want it to get bigger, because bigger means more useful and value rises exponentially with the number of users.

This is wonderful for the owners of networks. It explains why their value can grow so rapidly, with modest cash expenditure on the part of the owners. It is also good for workers in the companies that own networks. The growth in the company vastly increases opportunities. It also makes it possible to pay more to the workers and to give valuable share options.

Do you work for a network? Do you want to?

Could you invest in a relatively new and fast-growing network?

212   Why do networks become more valuable when they get bigger?

Network firms are different from traditional organizations in two ways – because the network itself generates most of the growth in the size of the network; and because bigger is better, not just for the firm itself, but also for its customers. If a traditional firm such as Heinz or Gillette doubles in size, that doesn't make things better for Heinz or Gillette customers. The can of soup doesn't taste better. The razor is not sharper.

But if a network doubles in size, it becomes more than twice as valuable. The increase in value to the customers is great, and it is geometric rather than linear.

Imagine a dating platform in your country with 1,000 members, all potentially interested in a date with you. Would you join it? Nah, it would be too small. But if the size doubles to 2,000? Well, the value of the network goes up about four times. The possible number of permutations of members of the network grows from 499,500 to 1,999,000. You might still think it is too small, but that increase in potential dates might change your mind.

Networks also thrive and proliferate because the fuel driving their growth is information. As information technology expands its reach and capabilities, so networks multiply, becoming denser and more useful to their members. For instance, app-based giant firms such as Uber and Airbnb could not have existed without the smartphone. Whatever comes after the smartphone will expand the power and reach of networks almost immeasurably.

Information technology is the part of the economy which is most 80/20-like, though of course it is more similar to 99/1. In his excellent book *Zero to One*, Peter Thiel argues that in recent times technology has not advanced much, with the exception of information technology. Even if Thiel is right, this may not matter too much. It is logical that technology advances most where it is most valuable.

Are you converted to the new 'religion' of networks?

213   The strangest innovation in our lifetime requires a personal 80/20 audit

The term 'cyberspace' was invented by science-fiction writer William Gibson, appropriately enough in 1984. 'I was trying,' he said, 'to describe an unthinkable present. Science-fiction's best use is the exploration of contemporary reality.' Cyberspace, he said, was 'a consensual hallucination experienced daily by billions in every nation … unthinkable complexity. Lines of light ranged in the non-space of the mind, clusters and constellations of data.'

Whether or not Gibson helped to invent the internet, it is worth pondering its strangeness. We take it for granted now, but it *is* weird in the extreme – a different country, really a different planet, which we can all connect to and experience something as revolutionary and habit-changing as Gutenberg's invention of printed books. It has changed our lives. You never used to see people below a certain age bending reverentially over their phones, as though they are prayer books with a hotline to God. Just as Gutenberg changed the world both immediately and gradually over centuries, I suspect we will see the same thing with the internet and whatever it develops into.

The internet is definitely the most important 80/20 innovation of our lifetime. The medium is the message. As always, however, there are many layers of 80/20 nestled in the internet. It is vital to retain perspective. Some applications of the internet can change your life for immense good, and some can do immense harm – for example, to your eyesight, your extraversion and your social life.

Use the internet super-selectively – intensely for a few applications, such as focused knowledge acquisition. Do not use it for trivial or self-destructive purposes. The extent and volume of trivia on the web exceeds even the enormous quantity of trivia on television.

Which applications are vital for you? And which are trivial or worse?

214   Cyberspace and popular bars

The most popular sites in cyberspace are like hugely fashionable bars in the real world. Trendy bars are popular simply because they are popular. You go there because you know you will meet lots of people – your sort of people – there. Within their category, everyone wants to be where everyone else is.

Liquidity and depth of market attract more members, more liquidity, more depth of market. Networks are attractive in proportion – nay, in super-proportion – to their size in the category. At least for a season, the bar owner who is the largest in the category has the good fortune to be the winner who takes all.

Nice work. The real-world bar owner, however, won't become a billionaire. But his counterparts in cyberspace may well do so, maybe even worth tens or hundreds of billions. The sky is the limit and the sky keeps getting higher.

Cyberspace segments are natural monopolies. With each passing year they and their owners (if there are any) become ridiculously wealthier.

It seems silly, but if you can't beat them, join them, by starting a new cyber-space segment and dominating it.

Are you attracted to this idea? Do you plan to do something about it?

215   The extraordinary growth in cities

Not all burgeoning networks are online. One prime example is cities.

Ever since humans decided some ten thousand years ago to settle down in one place rather than be nomads, cities have become massively important networks, steadily increasing their size and importance, adding to wealth and increasing the exchange of knowledge, culture, inventions and innovations, and goods and services, as well as providing the infrastructure of government.

Parag Khanna, who calls himself a 'global strategist', says that 'cities are mankind's most enduring and stable modes of social organization, outlast-ing all empires and nations.'[3]

In 1500, only 1 per cent of people in the world lived in cities. By 1800, the proportion had tripled to 3 per cent. In 1900, one seventh of humanity. Today more people live in cities than don't.

The steady advance in wealth in Europe – and later the rest of the world – which began in 1450, and made humans a biological success, depended on the growth in the number and power of cities. They were centres of ideas, trade and commerce, run by a very small but vital new middle class of burghers, neither peasants nor nobles. Cities were growing incubators of wealth, tiny 80/20 islands springing up within the vast and zero-growth sea of feudal rural estates.

It is 80/20 all the way. Today the world's 20 richest cities are magnets for talent, knowledge and money. Seventy-five per cent of the world's big companies are based in these 20 cities, comprising far less than half of 1 per cent of the number of cities – to the nearest whole number, a 75/0 relationship.

Do you live in a city? Do you want to? Do you think cities are passé or the wave of the future?

216   Cities and their network effects

As the network – the city – gets bigger and denser, the advantages of living in a city multiply (as do some disadvantages). Opportunities to meet other people with complementary knowledge and skills increase exponentially. Big cities continue to expand, which argues that for most people the benefits exceed the drawbacks.

But again, there is 80/20. Not all cities grow. Many in the US and other developed countries are struggling. Low rents and property prices in New Orleans and Detroit are symptoms of decline – they do not make the cities attractive. As always, network effects display 80/20 – or more like 99/1 – selectivity. Vibrant cities with good networks get even bigger and more vibrant, despite the rising cost of living there. Other cities decline further, some irretrievably.

Cities are melting pots. They attract ambitious, talented and extravert people from less successful cities and countries around the globe. As Jane Jacobs, the great writer about cities and the value of diversity in them showed, the degree of variety and differences between people tends to increase, resulting in faster and more varied innovations, and mushrooming opportunities.

From the 1970s, many futurists preached that information technology and the internet would encourage more people to live in the countryside, and that medium-sized cities would grow faster than big ones. It hasn't happened. A better bet is that by the end of this decade, more than 70 per cent of the world's people will live in cities, most no more than 50 miles from the sea. And more and more of the inhabitants of big cities will be immigrants to them.

How do you feel about these trends? Do you give sufficient weight to the network effects driving big cities?

217   Languages and their network effects

The invention of language was a turning-point for humanity. If everyone can speak a language – any language – that someone around them can understand, humans are connected in a new way. As communication advances and the world shrinks, there is a natural tendency for already-popular languages to advance and for languages few people can speak to retreat.

The best estimate is that there were 15,000 languages 10,000 years ago; today only 6,000. 'Language death' expert Michael Krauss predicts that in a hundred years there will only be 600. What is more important is the growth of the leading languages in the last 300 years. Before the French Revolution in 1789, more French people spoke local languages than French. Today, some 885 million people speak Mandarin Chinese, 600 million Hindi, 375 million English, and 350 million Spanish as their native language. In terms of communication, however, about one and a half billion people speak enough English to have a conversation, while no other language even approaches a billion speakers.

Demographic growth will probably push Spanish ahead of English as the third most spoken native language, yet the lead English already has as a 'super-connecting' language is likely to propel it further ahead in this regard. What probably matters even more is the number of people in the world who can communicate beyond their native tongue, and this will (barring an apocalypse) surely rise and rise, increasing the flow of ideas and more rapid innovation, together with greater wealth creation and, conceivably, greater peace as well as plenty. *Opportunities for individuals clearly increase when they can speak more than one language, and this network effect will become more important over time.*

Do you give enough priority to learning a foreign language? Which one is most likely to increase your opportunities and pleasure?

218   Transport network effects

You could make the case that the network effects that have connected more people more richly since 1492 are transport networks. In the hundred years after Columbus connected Europe and the Americas other explorers circumnavigated the planet, shrinking the world into one place. In the eighteenth century, road and canal networks expanded mightily. The nineteenth century saw railways, the penny post, the telegraph, steamships, the motorcar and mass migration across continents. Then came aircraft, telephones, high speed rail, new bridge and tunnels, maritime transport corridors, radio, television, oil and gas pipelines, cheap international travel, connected computer systems, the transport container, mobile phones, videoconferencing, fibre-optic cables, the internet and the smartphone. All of these network phenomena make the world smaller and economies larger and more interlinked; they all connect more people in more and more ways at higher quality standards and ever-lower cost.

In short, trade, industrialization, travel, communications, digitalization and networks of things and people have increased, are increasing, and ought to be further increased. Despite hiccups and crises, they almost certainly will continue increasing in myriad ways. The shrinking of the world comes with drawbacks, of course, of which the most serious are probably ecological and the disappearance of mystery as the planet becomes increasingly homogenized, but these networks have almost certainly advanced human wellbeing immeasurably. Networks and innovations operate in virtuous and ever-expanding and ever more linked circles.

Are you contributing to these advances, or making full use of them in your own life?

219   Is a more structured society also more connected?

Which society would you expect to be more connected – a less structured society or a highly structured one? Perhaps a less structured society would also be less connected, there being a price for personal autonomy in the absence of connections. If everyone does their own thing, doesn't connection go by the board?

The surprise of network society, both in theory and in practice, is that the less structured a society or the world becomes, the more connected it becomes. When free or local institutions disappear, so too does a complex web of spontaneous connections between hubs, and between hubs and individuals. If you think about it, structure equals hierarchy and hierarchy reduces lateral connections. History provides corroboration. Greater hierarchy leads to more isolation and less variety of views and practices. Why else would totalitarian states use propaganda to engender a sense of common identity between citizens, who are not encouraged or allowed to create their own spontaneous and individual sense of identity and connection?[4]

The great thing about network society is that it offers greater autonomy for citizens as well as greater connections between them. Free and spontaneous connections are always more gratifying and effective than those dictated by authority.

Do you treasure all the connections that you can freely and spontaneously make with other people? How could you increase those connections?

CHAPTER 27

TERRITORY, HIERARCHY AND HOW TO THRIVE IN THE BRAVE NEW WORLD

We will now look at the difference between territory and hierarchy, how Apple finally made it and three inescapable trends.

220   The difference between territory and hierarchy

Author Steven Pressfield has highlighted the difference *at a personal level* in how we define ourselves. In his delightful little book, *The War of Art*, he says that our definition can be 'hierarchy' or 'territory'.[1]

We are trained to think hierarchically and most of us don't shake this off. We know that we fit into a pecking order and where we are in it.

Defining ourselves by our territory is psychological. It is *our* territory. It's what we are good at, where we feel at home. Stevie Wonder has his piano; Arnold Schwarzenegger his gym; Bill Gates has Microsoft; Pressfield his writing desk.

If we're in a pecking order, we worry about what other people think and want. If we are territorial, we worry about what we want and the quality of our work *in our own eyes*. This is what artists do. They create something because they want to. They don't do it for money, fame or professional recognition.

This is brilliant. It suits our individual orientation to work, but also our view of society. In a network society we carve out our own territory. In a hierarchy we know our place, defined by authority. For me, it's obvious which is preferable. But, as Pressfield says, the hierarchical orientation is wired into our genes and sanctified by aeons of time.

Every time an individual rejects his or her place in the pecking order and stops defining self-worth by money or external opinions, hierarchical society recedes a notch, and network society advances a notch. The artist, the inventor, the innovator, the entrepreneur, the self-employed person, someone intelligent and lazy – all belong in network society. They define their own territory and like it. *Yet in making a personal decision, they benefit everyone else too.*

Do you define yourself by hierarchy or territory?

221   Why is hierarchy so hard to escape?

We have lived in hierarchies since the world began. Eve was subordinate to Adam. Every tribe had its elders and dominant personalities. Everyone knew their place.

Every class system has been a hierarchy.

Historically, the only people to escape hierarchy have been artists of one kind or another. Leonardo da Vinci may have had to suck up a little to the Duke of Milan, and Michelangelo no doubt deferred to the Pope, but essentially they were autonomous.

Later on, from the seventeenth century, Europe's top scientists and musicians enjoyed the same independence and status, as, increasingly, did all manner of other professionals – poets, inventors, engineers, entrepreneurs, architects, storytellers, actors, dancers, singers, songwriters, film-makers, advertisers and those skilled in the dark arts of marketing; even top-rank comedians such as Charlie Chaplin. Originally a very thin crust of independent individuals, artists of one stripe or another now comprise a sizeable slice of society.

By definition, artists must carve out their own territory. If they are in a pecking order, their artistry is fatally compromised. For the rest of us, though, until very recently, it has been hard to avoid being in hierarchies, unless and until we are financially independent.

Network society offers the possibility of avoiding hierarchy. Anyone can use the platforms provided to independent producers or owners by Apple, YouTube, Airbnb and many others.

If you have your own territory, you can evade hierarchy and enjoy autonomy.

Does that appeal to you?

222 Mobile phone market upended

In 2007, the mobile phone market was placid, predictable and unremarkable, typical of the 80/20 world. There were a large number of mobile phone makers, but five of them – Nokia, Samsung, Motorola, Sony Ericsson and LG – captured about 90 per cent of worldwide profits. They still lived in a world defined by hierarchy.

Today it is totally different. The market and its profit pool are very much larger. And between 2007 and 2015 a new firm entered the market and zoomed from zero market share to 92 per cent of the profit pool, leaving the other players to fight for the crumbs. The new winner, of course, was Apple and its iPhone.

The short version is that 80/20 became 90/10. But this understates the revolutionary nature of what happened. Never before in a large and highly profitable global market had a newcomer achieved such a transformation in market shares and profits so quickly. What happened was that a market defined by hierarchy became defined instead by territory. The territory belonged to Apple and it was based on crafting a new network.

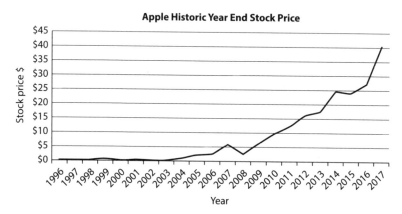

Did you buy Apple shares during this period? Would you have liked to have done?

223   The Apple iPhone story is a network story

The mobile phone market predated the internet. When the internet came along mobile phone makers were jubilant. The market exploded. More phones! More sales! And, especially, more profits! What was not to like?

What Nokia and the other major mobile phone makers did not see was the danger.

The danger was the transformation of a pre-network market into a network market.

Steve Jobs didn't just want to sell phones to customers, the way Nokia and its rivals did.

Jobs wanted to connect app developers with app users.

The app developers don't need to know who the customers are or to recruit them, because Apple had already found all the potential app customers – the iPhone users.

Jobs wanted to create a new network.

For whose benefit? Well, obviously for that of the phone users and the app developers.

Oh, and also for Apple's benefit.

Would you like to create a new network? Think of one that does not exist. Could you create it?

224   The network and the platform

If you want to create a new network market and business, you need a 'platform'.

Apple has a platform. It is the phone itself and all its associated intellectual property.

A platform can generate huge growth, profits and stock market value for the platform owner.

The platform owner can also dictate the rules for the new network business. Apple decides who – that is, which app developers – are allowed onto the platform and how app developers and app users interact.

Apple's platform could not have been created without the technological marvel of the iPhone.

But many other new networks – for example those created by Betfair, Uber and especially Airbnb – required much more modest technological innovation, which was relatively easily gained either internally or by outsourcing.

Can you think of a new network and platform that you could create, which does not require you to be a technological genius?

They exist. It is a matter of imagination, not personal expertize, to create them.

225   The story of Apple shares: up, up and away!

The rewards from creating a new network business are evident from the story of Apple's share price from 1997 to 2023. At the end of 1997 – the year of Steve Jobs' 'second coming' as CEO of Apple – the shares were 10 US cents. By the end of 2003 they had risen to 32 cents. By the end of 2006, to $2.58, 26 times the 1997 level.

Then came the years, 2007 to 2015, when Apple introduced the iPhone and made it dominant in the mobile phone market worldwide. In the year 2015 the shares fell marginally to $24.02, but still showed a 9.3 times increase since 2006. As I write the Apple share price is now at $186.68, up another 7.8 times since 2015, 1,867 times the level at the end of 1997. If you had invested $10,000 in Apple at the end of 1997, you would now (as I write) have more than $18.6 million.

Hindsight is a wonderful thing and I have no idea where Apple shares will be when you read this or in the future. Yet I think it is safe to say that the Apple platform created by the iPhone and other Apple devices of the 'noughties' (2000–9) paid off rather well.

Apple is not alone in using platforms to great effect – for example, depending slightly on the time period chosen, Microsoft has done almost as well as Apple. But, of course, Microsoft has its own powerful platform too.

Platforms creating network businesses can pay off extraordinarily well. By all historical comparisons, the wealth created by network firms has happened quicker than ever before. This puts the internet 'bubble' of 1999 in perspective. Apple shares are now 239 times higher than at the end of 1999, which at the time was unquestionably a bubble.

Have you worked out your network venture yet?

226   Does e-commerce equal network business?

Is e-commerce a network business? No.

It's important to understand the huge opportunity of networks, and therefore to understand what *is* and *is not* a network business.

The distinction between e-commerce and network business is often muddied. Be clear – networks and the online world are not the same thing.

There are many important examples of networks which are not online, like cities, languages and transportation networks. Two further examples of networks which long predated the internet are:

- Classified ads in newspapers and magazines which match buyers and sellers – the network effect is that the ads are more valuable when the network expands. The magazine or newspaper is the 'platform'. The best example is *Auto Trader* for buying and selling second-hand cars.
- Similarly, shopping centres are very successful networks. The shopping centre is the platform.

Equally, there are online businesses which are not networks. An online casino is a great business but does not have any network effects. The online casino is not multi-player; there is no community; and no data are supplied by customers. If it doubled in size this would have no benefit for users. On the other hand, a real-world casino such as that at Monte Carlo does have some network effects – when the casino is busy at night the fact that it is busy attracts other gamblers and browsers who may gamble a little (and lose, because they know not what they do).

Probably the best combination for high profits is an online business with strong network effects, such as Betfair, Google Search, Facebook, Instagram, Twitter, eBay, iTunes and the iPhone App Store. And yet ...

... the network you start or work in can be online or offline. Which would you prefer to start?

227   Are viral effects network effects?

If a product, service or meme 'goes viral' this is clearly good news for any associated company or cause. Because the number of users rockets, you might think that this is a network effect.

But strictly speaking, you would be wrong. A viral effect may enable a venture to grow extremely fast, but it does not improve the product or service itself. What is a little confusing is that the network may grow, and yet there is no 'network effect', which requires a benefit simply because (*ipso facto*) the network is larger. The aggregate pleasure given by the product may multiply because more people are experiencing it, and yet for any one user there is no benefit from being in a larger herd.

On the other hand, a viral effect can help to shift a market some of the way from 80/20 concentration to a much stronger 90/10 or 99/1 concentration. If there is more than one supplier of the product that has gone viral, the largest player will probably benefit most from viral effects. These will feed through to even greater economies of scale, and, hence, elevate the competitive advantage of the leading player. As Matthew's gospel states, those who are already the biggest will get bigger still.

In conclusion, the pivotal change driving greater company concentration is not the web, or viral effects, but networks and, in particular, the trend to *a few exceptionally profitable and fast-expanding network ventures that dominate their market or niche.*

How can you benefit from these super-powerful trends?

228   Three inescapable trends

The new network world – the landscape of 90/10 more than 80/20 – has three interrelated and compounding trends towards greater business concentration of activity, and especially super-profitable activity, within fewer and fewer hands.

First, the trend towards a higher proportion of activity – especially highly remunerative activity – within networks rather than traditional organizations.

Second, the trend within network markets from 80/20 to 90/10 and even more warped degrees of concentration, verging often on monopoly.

Third, within any particular network or network-based firm there will be a trend for the terms of trade to favour the network monopolist or near-monopolist. Traditional firms and everyone outside the network will diminish in importance or disappear altogether unless they can conquer their own defensible niche. Consumers and business customers of the network firm are likely to spend more with the network firm over time and as the network expands the spider at the centre of the web will grow bigger and more powerful.

For example, Uber has had an effect on traditional taxi and minicab services. Unless they are protected by city ordinances and their restrictions, these services either have to become more like Uber or fade away. With competition from Airbnb, hotels have to find a particular niche – tourism or business, for example – or face genteel decline. The network, and often new networks catalysed by them, will expand; conventional business will contract.

As a customer, an employee or an entrepreneur, you will be increasingly affected by the spread of new networks. It will become increasingly difficult to insulate yourself from them. The more you join them, the more you are likely to prosper. How do you plan to do this?

229   Practical advice for thriving in the new network world

There's a big potential advantage for everyone who identifies network ventures before they get big. If they are growing fast and are the leaders in their niche, however tiny they are today, these new networks may well become very large. If you can contrive it, work for them or become a supplier or contractor, getting in on the ground floor and growing with them. There is so much more opportunity in a fast-growing network than anywhere else.

In a low-growth economy, there is typically more talent than openings. In a fast-growth entity or economy it is the other way round. The first 20 people into Microsoft, Amazon, Google and the head offices of Uber and Airbnb are nearly all multi-millionaires or richer. Do you think this is because they happen to be amongst the hundred most talented people on the planet, an extraordinary concentration of brilliance suddenly arriving at the same place at the same time? Perhaps, just perhaps, they were very fortunate.

Therefore:

- *Search for new networks and platforms that have just started.* Make it a hobby to which you devote an hour or two at the same time each week.

- *Once you've been hired by a new network, think like an owner.* Grasp any stock options available and try to invest money in the venture. A tiny fraction of the company could make you rich. Do something that accelerates the firm's growth. Become a winner in the company, someone listened to and respected.

- *If you are an investor, focus on incipient network ventures.* Get in early before the value of the platform is evident. You may lose money a few times but with any luck you'll make out like a bandit on one of them.

Consider deciding that you will only work in small, fast-growing network firms.

230 Your place in the network future

If you understand it correctly, your place in the network future is wonderful. If you don't understand what is happening, the network future is bewildering. For most people, the network future will not be a comfy or familiar place. The new 90/10 or 99/1 world of networks can be more than a little scary.

You can no longer rely on the 'command and control' Goliaths, the huge firms of yesteryear. They cannot offer you security or the certainty of being on the winning side. You will have to hack your own individualized way through the forest of endeavour and the slough of mediocrity.

For success and fulfilment, you will either have to become a creative person able to provide unique satisfaction to your own highly focused target market; or become part of the early stages of a new network, scouting for opportunities to win in uncharted territory.

Let me summarize five ways to find your place in the future:

1. Only work in network businesses.
2. Choose a very small, very high growth group with which you can identify.
3. Only work for an 80/20 boss who is thriving in the new world.
4. Discover your own 80/20 and network idea.
5. Become joyfully and usefully unique.

This is not, and perhaps never will be, the road most travelled.

It is the best road for success and happiness.

Which road will you be on?

CHAPTER 28

WHAT IS THE SOURCE OF MEANING IN YOUR LIFE?

This chapter looks at various perspectives on the meaning of life. You'll see how to find meaning both in your past and in your future, and how to craft a purpose that is bigger than you and longer than your life.

231   The meaning of life in a concentration camp

A doctor of medicine and philosophy, and later a professor of neurology and psychiatry at the University of Vienna, Viktor Frankl, was sent to Auschwitz, Dachau and other concentration camps. On arrival at Auschwitz all his possessions were taken from him, including a coat in the lining of which he had hidden his magnum opus, a scientific manuscript.

Frankl had already been pondering the meaning of life, and he found it in the camps in two ways.

First, he imagined that he had to struggle to stay alive so that he could be reunited with his beloved wife, sent to a different camp but never out of his thoughts. On one occasion he was thinking of her intently when a bird hopped on the ground in front of him and he saw the bird as her incarnation. Thinking of the joy of their future reunion gave him a purpose to live. He was liberated in late April 1945, but it was not until August that he made it back to Vienna and learned devasting news about his wife, father, mother and brother. Only his sister had survived.

The second reason to live was to reconstruct his manuscript. He wrote what he could recall on hidden scraps of paper. He realized that to survive he had to think of the future. He imagined that he was standing at the lectern of a Viennese adult education college, giving a lecture entitled 'Psychology of the Concentration Camp' and saying what was currently in his mind. This trick worked. In March and April 1946, he gave the aforementioned lecture and two others at an adult education college in Ottakring, a working-class suburb of Vienna. This act pulled Frankl out of deep depression at the death of his family.

Can you imagine what it was like to be Frankl in the camps? How much the odds were against his survival, and yet the will he conjured up to make it through? Whatever your current circumstances, what is the better future you can imagine for yourself? Make it a reality.

232   Viktor Frankl's three ways to meaning in life

Frankl's book *Man's Search for Meaning*, first published in German in 1946, has sold 16 million copies.[1]

Frankl said that there were three ways humans could give meaning to their existence.[2]

- Firstly, through creative work – by doing something, by acting to bring a work of some kind into being.
- Secondly, by experiencing beauty, art, nature or by loving people.
- Thirdly, if by misfortune the first two ways are impossible, by accepting fate and suffering, remaining brave, dignified and unselfish even unto death.

Frankl reckoned that however hard life is, we can always give it a noble meaning. We can always find a constructive and loving way to give meaning to our lives.

How do you, or will you, find meaning in life?

233   Frankl: responsibility means saying yes to life

One of Frankl's most characteristic and joyous themes is responsibility, and specifically the responsibility of 'saying yes to Life'.

Every moment you bear responsibility for what you do in the next moment. Every moment contains thousands of possibilities – and you can only choose to actualize one of them. The inmates at Buchenwald camp sang a song containing the words 'we still want to say yes to life' – Frankl comments that by singing it and meaning it, many of them achieved it. *To say yes to life is meaningful and possible under all circumstances.*[3]

Every human has the freedom to change at any instant. Individuals remain unpredictable. We are capable of improving the world and ourselves.[4]

The uniqueness of each individual gives meaning to their existence. When this singularity is realized, the extent of your responsibility becomes apparent – nobody else can do what you can do. And conversely, realizing the uniqueness of another person highlights the responsibility an individual has to another. Realizing the responsibility a person has to someone who waits affectionately for them, the responsibility of love, calls forth meaning in life.[5]

Love is the ultimate responsibility, the only way to grasp the innermost core of someone's personality. Love is also the way to make actual the potential of one's own personality.[6] For Frankl, taking responsibility joyously is the essence of personal freedom, and therefore of personal meaning.

Do you agree that you can change yourself and the world for the better? How?

234 External or internal success?

If you think about external success, psychiatrist Viktor Frankl says, in some way or other all our lives are ultimately unsuccessful. No biological or sociological success in the world is guaranteed to outlive us or last forever.

Frankl defines inner success as the fulfilment of life's meaning, as decided by each individual. Once a person decides that their life has meaning, that has been achieved once and for always. Even if this meaning only emerges a short time before death, the meaning covers and pervades everything leading up to that point.

Inner success is therefore subject only to the approval of your own genuine conscience, and once you feel that you have achieved success as you define it, that verdict stands eternally.[7]

The internal world of experience trumps the external world of achievement.[8] If you find meaning in life, that is the supreme achievement, and nobody can say that you are wrong.

Are you seeking external success or internal success?

Which is more important?

Which is easier to attain?

Which is the 80/20 view of life?

235　Finding meaning in the future

A neglected but vital part of Viktor Frankl's message relates to finding meaning in the future. Frankl criticizes the therapy of Freud and Adler as being too retrospective and introspective. Instead of looking inside yourself and at your past, Frankl suggests looking to the future.

There are two key messages about the future. One is unashamedly optimistic. *The future can always be better than the present.* In a sense this is axiomatic. But it is also normative – *the future should be better.*

Why? Because of human freedom. You are free to make any decision you like which will create a better future for yourself and other people. What decisions should you make? Decisions that take responsibility and 'say yes to life'. Decisions that realize opportunity. *Everything in life is an opportunity.*

Frankl's second key message is that mental health depends on a healthy tension between what you have already achieved and what you still ought to accomplish – the gap between what you are and what you should become. This goes back to Aristotle's breakthrough concept of potentiality – humans should not be judged by what they are but by what they can attain. Frankl says that to make the future better than the present you have to improve yourself. This is always possible and always desirable, and a by-product of doing so is that you will become happier. *Individuals should not seek equilibrium, but rather should strive for a worthwhile goal, a task that you freely choose.*

Under these circumstances, not only *can* the future of the individual be better than the present, but the future *will definitely* be better. The decision for each individual is purely internal, so external circumstances cannot interfere with self-improvement.[9]

How can you improve yourself to make the future better?

236   Finding meaning in the past

Paradoxically, while Viktor Frankl urges us to find meaning in the future through self-improvement, he also invites us to find meaning in our past.

No good deed we have done in the past is lost – just the opposite. Everything is irrevocably stored and treasured. He talks of the 'full granaries of the past into which they have brought the harvest of their lives' – their deeds, loves and suffering borne without complaint.

Even old people who have no possibilities in the future have something even more valuable – the potentialities which they made real, the meanings they have embodied and fulfilled, the values they have fought for and realized. Nothing and no one can ever remove these assets from them. Nothing can be undone, and nothing can be done away with. And in one extraordinary piece of insight, he wrote, 'I should say, having been is the surest kind of being.'[10]

This is my commentary rather than Frankl's: you might get killed crossing the road today, but that does not take value and importance from your life. You have been, and that is enough. For just as true as the inevitability of death, having been alive and had experiences is just as certain, and far more significant.

Every one of us has 'has been' – this cannot be denied. You have lived, and this is cause for celebration, because the odds against you ever having been born are fantastically high. Try to compute the combined odds of every one of our forebears – from your mother and father, to theirs, and so on back to your ancestors – having been born and survived long enough to give you life, and you will rapidly run out of room on your calculator. It must be more than a trillion to one against. If a dear friend drops dead tomorrow, that is tragic. Yet the person who dies had the privilege and pleasure of being alive, and we have had the privilege and pleasure of knowing them.

What have you been that was a privilege and pleasure?

237   The great thing about 'having been'

I've just finished a terrific novel in which the protagonist is likeable, talented and (I will forgive him) hard-working. He grew up in Scotland but has a particular skill which helps world-class musicians in France, Russia and across the rest of Europe. Some of these brilliant musicians are nice, some are manipulative and unpleasant. He falls in love with an attractive woman. She appears to love him, but for good reasons leaves him. He fights to be able to live with her, but he dies in a distant land at the age of 36. Shortly after his death the love of his life appears, looking for him.

A terribly sad and poignant story? Well, yes, but such is the skill of the novelist – William Boyd[11] – that you realize that the protagonist has had, in many ways, a great life. It's not a conventional happy ending, but you feel – at least I felt – that the man's life had been thoroughly worthwhile. In Viktor Frankl's phrase, the man *had been* – to a marvellous degree. (You feel this with all good movies too.)

Wouldn't it be a great idea if at the start of each day you said to yourself: 'What can I do today that I will be proud to "have been" tomorrow?' Even in a small way, can you do something that is useful or fun for other people? If nothing grander, how can you be kind or helpful to the people around you?

In other words, can you enhance your 'having been-ness' today or this week, such that if you die at the end of the day or week, you 'have been' in a fuller way?

238   The existential choice: meaning or no meaning

In 1946, a year after being liberated from a Nazi concentration camp, Viktor Frankl gave three lectures to a working-class audience in Vienna. The second of these lectures concludes in a remarkable way.

He presents two major alternatives, each of which is unprovable but cannot be proved wrong.

One is to assert that life is meaningless. The universe is an accident, and so too is humanity. Our world is a tiny speck in our universe, which itself is insignificant in size and importance. We may imagine that we are in some sense significant, but this is a delusion.

The other alternative is to say that everything is not only highly meaning-ful, but so meaningful that we simply can't comprehend the meaning of the whole. Even if humanity is an accident, we can give meaning to life by actions of love and intelligence. We ourselves are the meaning and require nothing outside human civilization and the meaning we choose to give our lives to justify and savour our existence.

The choice between these two views is not logical. Both views are logical, if we start from different premises. There is no foundation to either view, yet we hover over the abyss of nothingness and stand at the horizon of ultimate meaning.

If you choose to vote for human meaning you do know one thing – if you believe in that, then this belief, like every belief, will have a creative effect. Belief brings into being that which is believed!

Since the outcome is not definite, why not believe in something that cre-ates good and love rather than something that is miserable and sterile?

The appeal of the decision is emotional, not factual.

Which way do you vote?

239   On the meaning of life: Charles Beard

In 1930, historian and philosopher Will Durant wrote to a hundred of the world's leading thinkers asking them 'What is the meaning of life?' A selec-tion of replies, and Durant's own views, were published in 1932 and repub-lished in 2005.[12]

Here I summarize the view of historian Charles Beard:

History reveals apparent chaos, tragedy and a flow of disasters, but I can detect subterranean evidence of law and plan and immense achievement of the human spirit. The world is not a mere bog of conflict. Something magnificent is taking place here and the great challenge to intelligence is to make the noblest and best in our very mixed heritage prevail.

Humans keep going. There is probably some biological force within us, a large measure of selfishness, the necessity of earning a living, mixed up with moments of exaltation where we rise above our baser motives. The historian can only observe and infer, yet there is a noble heritage which is worth treasuring and enhancing.

There was probably no grand design in the beginning of the universe, but fragments of purpose are evident, and mankind can complete the picture.

The good life is an end in itself, to be loved and enjoyed. And intelligent labour can and should be directed to make the good life prevail. That is my little philosophy, which keeps my mill of endeavour turning.

Do you find anything in Beard's philosophy which appeals to you?

If not, how would you answer Will Durant's question?

240   On the meaning of life: André Maurois

André Maurois was a distinguished and imaginative French man of letters with a strong affinity with Britain. His work included novels, biography, history, war memoirs, children's books and science fiction. He knew a whole generation of French politicians and fought with the Free French forces in the Second World War.

His contribution to Will Durant's compendium on the meaning of life was an essay in which a group of English men and women land on the moon. Communications and return flights have to be abandoned and they make the moon their home. After 10 years they are still behaving like English ladies and gentlemen, dressing for dinner and giving a loyal toast to the King on his birthday.

After 200 years on the moon, there is no communication from Earth. Young radicals throw off the English traditions, engage in unsatisfying free sex, and become bored, rebellious and unhappy. Literature is excellent.

A philosopher arises to chide the rebels. Why, he asks, search for the meaning of life outside life itself? The King of our legends, he says, may or may not exist, but 'I shall not doubt life, or the beauty of the moment, or the happiness of action'. Nothing, he goes on, exists except victory and life. We should live as if we were eternal, and not worry whether planet Earth is empty. 'You do not live on Earth,' he concludes, 'you live in yourselves.'

Does the idea of finding the meaning of life in life itself resonate with you?

What in life itself would you highlight as giving meaning to it?

241   On the meaning of life: Will Durant

The essay with which Will Durant concludes his book *On the Meaning of Life* is such a gem that, on purely 80/20 grounds, I beg you to read it. It will take maybe 30 minutes of your life. It is well worth the time. It will refresh your spirit, give you ideas and relax your feverish mind; the pleasure from reading it will ensure that you have a good day, certainly, and just possibly, a good life.[13]

Durant starts with a half-hearted defence of science and progress: the physical achievement of the former ('the steamship, the airplane and public sanitation'), and the reality of the latter ('to doubt its reality because of its end would be like calling the sun a delusion because it will set').

Then he concedes that probably life has no meaning outside of its terrestrial self, the individual has no immortality and that every civilization will decay. Durant cannot believe in a personal human-like God, even though he savours the aroma of belief's memory. Yet he mounts a beautiful and convincing exposition of the meaning of life, the simplest of which is joy, the exhilaration of experience itself and of physical wellbeing, the sheer satisfaction of muscle and sense, of palate and ear and eye. Then there are the moments of beauty and the thousand delights of Nature. Then human love, romantic love for sure, but also the attachment of mates or friends who have gone through much hell, some purgatory and a little heaven – the sense that someone is interested in you, depends on you, exaggerates your virtues and is waiting for you at the station.

His most enduring observation is that to give life a meaning requires a purpose larger than one's self and more enduring than one's life. The greatest satisfaction lies in being a cooperating part of a whole, so join a whole and work for it with all your body and mind, because though as individuals we pass away, the whole is made forever different by what we have done and been.

Which single thought here do you find most satisfying?

242   Your verdict on the meaning of life

You have heard several views on the meaning of life.

80/20 is all about what is most important in your life. Life can only have meaning if you believe it has meaning, so it is vital that you decide what that meaning is for you. You will be happier and more content once you have decided the meaning of your life. So, if you have not yet decided, do it today, ideally now. And if you have already decided, perhaps some time ago, remind yourself now, and often.

That meaning has to be specific and, however supremely important, it has to be limited in description.

One of the delights and constraints of 80/20 is that it always embodies the principle of frugality – few things matter, but they matter enormously.

Nowhere is this more vital than in deciding the meaning of your life.

Ideally, reduce the meaning of your life to one word or sentence.

Can you do that?

Your happiness, and your influence on other people that you care about, may depend on it.

CHAPTER 29

EVOLUTION'S LESSONS FOR YOU

Why variation is the key to energy and growth; ideas are stronger if they emerge from struggle; and why evolution loves failure. We'll also examine the generality to differentiation dialectic.

243   Evolution and profitable variation

Darwin's theory of natural selection and profitable variation is the corner-stone of the modern theory of evolution. *But the idea of profitable variation can apply very nicely to your life and career.*

First Darwin's theory. All organic beings reproduce at a very high rate. All creatures are in some way unique. The sum of their variations is inherited. Competition amongst siblings dictates that few will survive. In this struggle for existence, 'any being, if it vary however slightly in any profitable manner to itself ... will have a better chance of surviving, and thus be naturally selected.' Natural selection depends on variation. When there's a change in 'conditions of life', such as climate, 'this would manifestly be favourable to natural selection, by giving a better chance of profitable variations occurring'.[1]

Selection via competition applies to ideas, technologies, markets, companies, teams and products in the same way. Selection drives all material progress. But selection and profitable variation also drive personal progress.

Profitable *variation*. How are you different from your mates at school or college, your coworkers, friends, bosses and other important acquaintances? If you are using any ideas in your work or private life, how could you use them differently? If you have an ambition, how could it be different from everyone else's? The difference could be subtle but make all the difference, if it is ...

Profitable variation. Difference for its own sake is futile. Difference can also be negative. Profitable variation increases the chance of survival, success and happiness. What changes to how you run your life – perhaps even subtle changes, apparently minor improvements – could make a big positive difference to you feeling good?

As you go about your day, keep thinking 'profitable variation'. How could things be different and better?

244   Variation is the key to energy and growth

Darwin observed that profitable variation leads to better adaptation to conditions and therefore to growth. Profitable variations occur continually within species, but occasionally a mutation occurs, when an individual creature develops a new characteristic. If the variation is profitable, the mutant will thrive and leave plenty of offspring, which will also thrive. Over time, therefore, most species will evolve positively. For nearly a hundred years, scientists have studied one plot of desert in the southwestern US, photographing its changes in response to climate. They have confirmed that greater variation leads to greater growth. Ecologist Tony Burgess explains: 'If conditions are variant, the mixture of species increases 20 to 30 times. If you have a constant pattern, the beautiful desert ecology will almost always collapse into something simpler.' Research on 147 plots of Minnesota prairie showed that the greater the number of species in a plot, the more biomass and nitrogen it produced. With fewer species, nitrogen leached out of the soil and was wasted.[2]

A similar pattern emerges in cities, enterprise and life. Jane Jacobs showed in *The Death and Life of Great American Cities* that cities are more beautiful, energetic and wealthier when street lengths, building shapes and sizes and ages of buildings are more diverse.[3]

People who move to different places or experience greater diversity of cultures generally thrive on the variation. The same applies to people who job-hop to different companies and places. Change in life circumstances may not be comfortable, but it is usually productive. Variation allows greater experimentation and challenge and stimulates innovation – some of which will inevitably be profitable variation.

Is there enough variation in your life?

245   From generality to differentiation

Darwin and other nineteenth-century 'evolutionists' identified the first trend as being from generality to differentiation.

One original species leads to all others. New species are formed from an existing species.

This seems to be a universal principle.[4] In knowledge, one branch may give rise to many others, which start as subsets of the original branch. For example, history starts as one branch of knowledge and then gives rise to archaeology, biography, memoirs and histories of many subsets such as history of science, art, medicine, civil rights, individual countries or regions, women's studies and LGBTQ studies.

In the economy the same thing happens when one industry gives rise to more specialized branches, or when one firm spawns spin-offs, which each develop their own particular variations.

This presents you with two particular opportunities. One is to take a generality and invent your own differentiation or sub-branch. The other opportunity is to develop an incipient sub-branch along with other pioneers. The first opportunity, if successful, is likely to be more gratifying; the second opportunity gives only shared glory, but if the field is one you love, and the growth rate of the incipient sub-branch is high, this may also be tremendous.

Can you think of a subject you love and start a new branch, or be an early adopter of a new sub-branch?

246   The differentiation/generality dialectic over time

Nineteenth-century evolutionists (including Darwin) identified another trend on top of the one from generality to differentiation. This second trend is that, having gone from generality to differentiation, the new species formed by differentiation go on themselves to become new generalities, from which yet more differentiations arise.

If this sounds complicated, it's not really. What it means is that the branching out of new species – or in the modern world, new categories of knowledge, economics or technology – never ends. If history gives rise to new branches of history, such as biography, for example, biography may itself split into other branches, such as biographies of scientists or politicians, or historical novels featuring fictional characters or else fabrications around real people in history. Each of these genres may in turn spawn further branches, such as television, videos or podcasts of any popular branch.

Jane Jacobs says, 'a simple process, when repeated and repeated and repeated, produces staggering diversity.'[5] In evolution this may take enormous periods of time, but in modern economies and ecologies it may happen very quickly. Diversity can increase exponentially if the economy or new ecologies are supported by enough demand and money, and if human imagination builds on and multiplies existing branches.

Keep watching for new trends and branches in which you may wish to participate. There is no end to novel opportunities which arise spontaneously and incessantly from the branching of knowledge and from new facilitating mechanisms such as the internet and the smartphone.

247 The struggle for survival

One key observation made by Darwin, and an essential part of his theory of natural selection that he kept hammering home, is that the odds against the survival of individual plants or animals are very high. *Hence, the struggle for survival.*

This is true in nature, but does it also apply to human life, ideas, organizations and economics?

One answer is yes. How could it be otherwise? We humans exist wholly within nature. We are part and parcel of the natural order. The notion that we exist outside nature is bizarre and plain wrong.

On the other hand, we humans are increasingly sidestepping some of the struggle for survival. Due to the accelerating development of medical science since the nineteenth century, the survival rates of babies and average lifespans have greatly increased. There are ecological downsides to the explosion of world population, as we corner more and more of the earth's resources. Were we not also adding to nature's resources on a grand scale, and using contraception, the world might have ended already.

Despite our partial exemption from nature's grim reaper, human ideas, organizations, cultures and ways of organizing life do face a struggle for survival. Only those most fit for survival do actually survive. This is how it should be and how the 80/20 Principle, were it a sentient being, would like it done.

What are the implications for you?

Perhaps, if you want to have influential ideas, have a large number of them and only push your best ones.

If you want to start a great company, start several, as the early ones will probably die.

If you want to make a lot of money, make lots of bets at long odds and do not be upset when most of them lose.

If you want to write a bestseller, write many books.

248　The conditions of life determine survival

The great French naturalist Jean Lamarck (1744–1829) claimed that species evolved to survive, adapting to the demands of the environment. Darwin changed this in a subtle but vital way. Darwin said that species evolved naturally, but the environment decided whether or not they survived. Darwin's world was a tougher one than Lamarck's. If you like, Lamarck was an optimist and Darwin a pessimist.

But truth is important. Darwin was right. The evidence is overwhelming that species, and to an even greater degree individuals, cannot control their destiny. This is true for all species, except perhaps, under certain conditions, for Homo sapiens.

Humans can, to a degree, adapt to fit the rules of the environment or even, with enormous effort and cost, change the rules. For example, we can stop the advance of the sea onto land by building dykes. We can even reclaim land previously lost to the sea. We can turn deserts into gardens. If we are short of land, we can build skyscrapers. We can defeat the odds against infant survival with medical science. It took us the vast majority of history before we did this. But we eventually learnt how.

Likewise, individuals who are failing in their careers can sometimes change their behaviour, to fit what the organization wants. It may almost kill them, but it can be done.

Most likely, though, if your career is failing, change the environment. Resign and find an organization more suited to your skills and attitude. Darwin is probably right. *Don't try to adapt; if you can't join them, beat them.*

249   Good ideas are stronger if they have emerged from a struggle for life

Good ideas will be more likely to survive and reproduce if they have emerged from serious competition. Organizations should therefore consider and test a large number, before deciding to launch a new product or system.

There is even a case for actually launching a large number of variants of a new product. When Sony introduced the Walkman, they flooded the market with hundreds of variants, letting the market decide which few would survive.

Back in 1930, Procter & Gamble was the first large consumer goods company to allow competition between its own brands. This provided challenges that sometimes didn't exist elsewhere in the marketplace. Wasteful? Not if you believe in Darwinian competition. This worked extremely well for P&G, and yet it took almost 30 years for rival firms to copy the policy. Managers hate competition.[6]

How is this relevant to you? Well, most of us go out of our way to avoid competition, however it manifests itself. We all naturally gravitate to areas where we are the most experienced and knowledgeable. A professor in a university faculty is unlikely to recommend for promotion to assistant or associate professor someone whose field of study overlaps strongly with theirs, and whose intellect is as great or greater. Many chief executives show great reluctance to appoint people in roles beneath them who will also soon be viable candidates for the top job, even though that is exactly what they should be doing. Challenge and competition sharpen our saws and strengthen our teams. If we have fought our way up from the bottom to the top or near it, we will be more battle-hardened and self-confident.

As has been said, talent hits a target nobody else can hit. Genius hits a target nobody else can see. But nobody is consistently a genius. Even a genius needs competition to weed out their bad ideas.

Do you automatically advance your views with equal force and conviction, or save this for your few strokes of genius?

250 New variants will arrive sooner or later, whether you introduce them or not

Natural selection does not care which organism mutates or does not mutate, lives or dies. Economic selection does not care who owns the new and improved product or idea; it just wants it to arrive.

The market doesn't care whether it is the big brewers or new specialists that supply light beer, imported beer or microbrew beer, but it does want to see new product variants coming out.

When I was a consultant to big firms, we always used to warn them that if they did not cannibalize their own products, another firm would. The people gathered around the boardroom table would usually nod sagely at this point, and then forget it entirely.

Only the very best leaders took it to heart. Only they really cared about what customers wanted, about beating rather than avoiding competitors, and about the long term.

If any of us wants a quiet life, we should remember that life is difficult and bloody well should be. Life is a struggle, if not always for existence then always for excellence. The quiet life is not the richest life, nor is it life abundant.

Cannibalize <u>yourself</u>, or else somebody else will.

Develop new skills, attitudes to risk and rare knowledge before somebody else does.

There is always room at the top.

251 Scatter new breeds around your core

Remind yourself that economic selection – the economy – does not care who owns a desired product or service. Any organization that is dominant in a core product should know that this does not entitle it to be dominant in related products – unless it moves to supply this need before anyone else.

Take cola as an example. The Coca-Cola Company was first to introduce cola in the 1880s, and enjoyed dominance along with growth in sales and profits every decade up to the 1930s based simply on its one product and geographical expansion throughout the US and then Europe. Coke was available either at the fountain in drug stores or in the classic six-and-a-half ounce, hobble-skirted bottle. That was it. The first subsequent innovation was Fanta, the sparkling orange drink, which originated in Nazi Germany in the 1940s, some 60 years after Coca-Cola started.

Pepsi-Cola was declared bankrupt for the second time in 1931. It was always a follower to Coke. Yet there was an avenue for Pepsi-Cola to have a very profitable future and perhaps to eclipse Coca-Cola, if only it had taken it. By 1985, you could buy Coca-Cola, Caffeine-Free Coke, Coca-Cola Classic, Diet Coke, Caffeine-Free Diet Coke, Cherry Coke, Sprite, Diet Sprite, Tab, Caffeine-Free Tab, Mello Yello, Fanta, Fresca, Mr Phibb and others, in a great variety of sizes, in cans or bottles, in vending machines, shops, restaurants or fast-food outlets.[7]

Coke was lucky. Pepsi was even slower to scatter new breeds around the core product, filling up the potential product spaces so that new entrants couldn't move first into those niches.

What are the empty niches immediately adjacent to you and your career, and any success you have had? Fill them immediately.

252   The lesson of selection

Markets progress via selection. This necessarily requires the deselection or death of most of what is tested. Deselection operates at the product level, but also applies to companies – they may go bust or be taken over.

In nature, a failed or failing organism becomes food for more successful – that is, living – creatures. The same happens in the economy. When a company fails or is taken over its resources are freed up for more productive use by someone or something else. This is good for society.

A problem can arise in companies with many products. Failing businesses can be tolerated, especially if protected from internal or external competition. If a zoo lion escaped into the wild, it wouldn't last long – it wouldn't know how to compete for food. If divisions of large corporations are protected, they become zoo lions. Subsidy, whether from capitalist corporations to its weaker brethren or from the State, inhibits evolution and wastes resources.[8]

But, you know, the same things can happen to you, particularly if you are successful. You can subsidize your own pet projects, when they fail market tests. You can lend or give money to friends or loved ones for ventures that can't raise money from objective sources. You can protect your children from their own folly or failure. If you do any of these apparently good things, you are going against the grain of evolution and social good. You have a right to spend your money how you like, but you are doing more harm than good, not least to the people you are trying to help. *Evolution requires failure and so too do individuals. There is no learning from subsidy and no learning without failure.*

253   Evolution loves failure

Evolution proceeds via mass murder. Evolution requires the risk, and reality, of extinction. Evolution moves up by removing the unsuccessful part of the system. In short, evolution loves failure. Businesspeople do not love failure, but the company graveyard is the nutrient of progress.

In business and in other areas of human life, you can do something which is impossible under the stricter, ancient regime of evolution. You can fail and survive. This is a clear plus for you, but it has pluses and minuses for the system.

If there is too much survival and forgiveness in an economy, resources are wasted in feeding the failures. Given the failures of government and non-productive parts of the economy, and the tolerance of failure even within the productive economy, only 80/20 can explain why we can still move forward overall.

But how much of a plus is it for you if you fail and survive?

It depends. If failure is painful, it is better to get it over quickly.

But pain should not blind you to the value of failure. You cannot expect a great success without a great failure. The main value of failure is learning. What do you learn from failure? That is up to you, of course, but consider a couple of things. One is that you learn a better way to do what you were trying to do. The other is that you decide to try and succeed at something quite different.

Knowing the difference between these two is critical. Once you have defined the alternative paths, work out which one would most gratify you, and which has the greater chance of success. That should give you the answer.

Have you had a good failure? What did you learn?

CHAPTER 30

A GENETIC PERSPECTIVE ON HOW TO MAKE MORE MONEY AND HAVE MORE FUN

Darwin's theory of evolution is one of the richest and most brutal guides to how the world *really* works. In this chapter, we consider the action implications for you and your colleagues. Two of the most vital ideas are these: identify ideas ('economic genes'), which work brilliantly in one arena, and apply them to another; and consider starting a spin-off from a very successful entity.

254   Is chance at the heart of life?

There was something that Darwin couldn't explain. If traits were inherited, how did this work? He admitted, 'The laws governing inheritance are quite unknown.'

Gregor Mendel (1822–84) was a monk in the Austro-Hungarian empire. His life's work was experimenting with crossbreeding peas and other plants. He was surprised to find that traits of peas did not blend – a tall plant bred with a dwarf plant led to a tall plant, not a medium-sized one. Then if he bred these tall plants, a quarter of their offspring were dwarf. Mendel concluded that the traits were inherited, with the dominant trait determining appearance, but the 'recessive' trait lying in wait for the next-but-one generation. In the early twentieth century, it was realized that chromosomes carry genetic information. Mendel was right – inherited traits are not blended, and the actual outcome over generations is entirely random.

Genes influence our health and our actions, but they do not determine our destiny. You can transcend your life's endowment by working out what you want from life and using 80/20 to gain more of what you want with less effort, time and money.

Nevertheless, the random element implied by your genetic inheritance cannot be denied. We live in a world where sheer chance is a key part of life's operating programs. Whether you want to or not, and whether you realize it or not, you have to gamble in making your decisions. It is worth asking, therefore, what do successful gamblers do? They identify where the odds are out of sync with real probabilities. This is hard to do at the races, but much easier in real life.

Do you accept that chance is important in life? What are the implications for you?

255   Make asymmetric bets

For decades, my way of deciding whether to make venture (small, young company) investments has been to compare the downside if it goes wrong – usually the amount of money to be lost if the venture fails – with the upside if it succeeds. It is harder to know the upside, but a range of successful outcomes can be estimated. The upside has to be many times the downside for me to invest, and it also has to be plausible, even though I cannot know its probability.

This is known by investors as 'making asymmetric bets'. In plain English, the upside must be much greater than the downside. This method can ultimately be traced back to 'Pascal's wager', a theological argument of the seventeenth century.

But it is far more vital to make asymmetric bets when making decisions which affect your happiness.

Every 80/20 decision in life – the few that really matter – can be treated the same way. Every vital decision can be viewed as a bet on happiness. Will I be much happier if I make the decision one way, and it works out well? And if it doesn't pan out as I hope, will I be much less happy? And which outcome is more likely?

For example, if you are courting and considering marriage, how much happier will you be if it works out? And how much unhappier if it doesn't? The fact is, marriage is usually a good bet – married people tend to be happier. But if a marriage goes sour … So, if you do tie the knot, make it work.

If you go to work in a foreign country, what is the upside and the downside? In most cases, the upside is greater. After all, if it doesn't pan out you can usually go home. Something similar usually applies to every experiment you make. *Action is usually better than inaction.*

Does this approach appeal to you? What difference might it make?

256   Reading the odds in life

80/20 will not make you a fortune at the racetrack. Alas, I have spent a significant portion of my life trying to identify such a formula and have failed. In truth I do not expect to succeed. Why? Because bookmakers and other individuals are trying to do the same thing – to identify asymmetric bets, where the actual odds are out of whack with reality. The market at the races is not perfect, but pretty good.

I *have* been able to identify asymmetric bets somewhere other than the racetrack. The place is in venture capital investments, where I believe it is possible to identify investments which, while being high risk, have potential returns at variance with the cost. But that is a different story.[1]

The focus here is on 'life bets': actions you can take which greatly improve the odds of something desirable, at a cost that is a fraction of the benefit; or in some very happy cases, at negative cost.

Here is one example of a good, asymmetric life bet:

If you and your romantic partner genuinely like each other and you both commit to a lifetime partnership, the payoff in happiness is likely to vastly exceed the cost of commitment.

Have you made a similar or completely different life bet, where the benefit greatly exceeds the cost?

257 Some more asymmetric life bets

Asymmetric life bets are ones where the expected cost is dwarfed by the expected benefit:

- If you eat five portions of fruit or vegetables every day you are likely to enjoy better health and live longer.
- The same is probably true if you avoid stressful situations which seriously dampen your mood and happiness.
- Your happiness will be greatly increased if the five people you see most in your life are also friends.
- The same applies if you love your work.
- The same applies if you follow an optimistic religion or philosophy of life …
- And/or a very active social life …
- And/or if you believe life has real meaning for you …
- And/or if you are very generous …
- And/or if you are intelligent and lazy

Can you think of other really good asymmetric life bets?

How many of the ones above have you adopted?

258   The theory of memes

Richard Dawkins is most famous for his selfish gene theory, but I feel his greatest contribution is his theory of memes. Our species is unique, he says, in being able to pass on knowledge in the form of culture – language, customs, art, architecture, music, science. This constitutes a new form of immortality in the form of 'memes', units of cultural transmission. A meme might be a book, a play, an idea, perhaps even the seven great plots of novels, a hummable tune, catchphrases, proverbs, ways of building bridges or houses. Memes propagate themselves by leaping from brain to brain and being imitated.[2]

Memes are a human invention, but once invented they have a semi-autonomous life of their own. Memes replicate, vary, adapt and incorporate themselves in robust vehicles such as books, movies and videos. Memes may produce ever more complex entities in a similar way to genes.

The closest you can get to immortality is to deliver an idea that permanently changes humanity. If you contribute to knowledge that builds on itself, you have a fighting chance. G. H. Hardy said, 'Archimedes [mathematician] will be remembered when Aeschylus [poet] is forgotten, because languages die and mathematical ideas do not.'

Useful memes such as 80/20 can also be inculcated and spread through example and through books. And, of course, new memes can always be invented and spread.

Would you like to invent a meme or multiply its use and value? Which meme? How would you increase its velocity of circulation?

259   80/20 memes

We have seen that memes are units of cultural transmission that may be used to defeat the purposes of our selfish genes.

What, then, is an 80/20 meme? It is my term for memes that can do the greatest good in terms of increasing human happiness, comfort and creativity, with the least expenditure of blood, sweat and tears.

Defining which memes do this best is a subjective process, and one worth going through personally in order to decide which memes you want to propagate, and which memes of a similar type you might want and be able to invent. Here is my selection of a few 80/20 memes to illustrate how you might select memes according to two criteria – their value and their ease of use:

80/20 Meme	Value	Ease of Use
The 80/20 Principle	high	high (once you get the idea)
Democracy	high	high (once established)
Social equality	high	high (ditto)
Politeness	high	high (ditto)
Personal freedom	high	high (ditto)
Traffic rules	high	high (ditto)
Boston box (cows, stars …)	high (in biz)	high (in biz)
Star Principle	ditto	ditto
Time revolution	high	high (once a habit)
Healthy eating	high	high (ditto)
Daily exercise that you like	high	high (ditto)
Exclusive personal relationship	high	high (ditto)

What would be on your list?

260 My theory of economic genes

What is the DNA of business, the most fundamental unit of value? It is economic information. Units of useful information may be called 'economic genes' – similar to Richard Dawkins' word 'memes' to describe a unit of cultural transmission.

Examples of economic genes are ideas: the design behind a basic technology such as the steam engine, the internal combustion engine, telephony or computing; the script for a movie or the design of an integrated circuit; the formula for Coca-Cola or an ethical drug; or robotics and AI. An economic gene is anything intangible that comprises useful information and can be incorporated, alone or alongside other economic genes, either into a product or service, or into some vehicle providing a product or service.

Economic genes are the building blocks of knowhow, skills and technology in the broadest sense. They comprise information that needs to find a commercial vehicle before it can fulfil its role as a valuable product or service. They seek to replicate themselves as widely as possible by incorporating themselves into commercial vehicles: buildings, machines, software, factories, offices, trucks and products; but also living things such as people, teams, corporations, services and economies.

They are knowledge of how to increase wealth and wellbeing. The vehicles of these economic genes are the visible apparatus of economic activity, the moving parts, including people, teams, firms, physical assets, products and services. Vehicles are likely to attract good genes if they are the best possible vehicles for them.[3]

Could you invent, propagate or incarnate an economic gene?

261   Humans and economic genes

It is fascinating where we humans – I hope no robots are reading this – stand in relation to economic genes, ideas and units of valuable information. We can be their creators. But we can also be their vehicles and therefore use information while also being used by it.

We can propagate ideas that we did not invent. Indeed, this is the normal course of economic progress. For every human inventor of an idea, there can be hundreds – occasionally even millions – of people who use and develop it.

80/20 is a case in point. Who invented 80/20? Though he never used the phrase, Vilfredo Pareto invented the observation behind it. In 1949, Harvard professor George K. Zipf developed it into his 'principle of least effort'. Shortly after, the quality guru Joseph Moses Juran developed it as the Rule of the Vital Few. In the 1950s the phrase '80/20' slowly came into currency, and in the 1960s thousands of unsung heroes at IBM used and publicized it. Rather late in the day, in 1997, I clambered onto the bandwagon and have spent decades pushing it downhill.

Most people who become rich or unusually influential in business do so by using other people's ideas, not their own.

Henry Ford invented the idea of mass-market automobiles, but he made it work via the moving production line, which he did not invent. One great idea required another. *Using someone else's breakthrough, for a greater purpose and reward than they did, is quintessentially 80/20 – more from less.*

Which proven idea could you use to greater effect than anyone has yet?

262   A genetic perspective on economic life

The new perspective has economic genes – ideas and new ways of arranging life – driving the bus. Humans have multiple roles in the process – as creators of the genes; as users of them to create better products and services; and as consumers and customers and therefore arbiters of their survival, spread and demise.

This is a less corporatist and more entrepreneurial view of economic life. (I include in entrepreneurial anything artistic, musical, authorial, web-based or self-employed which provides highly paid services where your unique skills or personality are deployed.)

The great economist Joseph Schumpeter told us that capitalism progresses via a process of 'creative destruction'. Companies go bust all the time and this is, on balance, a good thing, ensuring the survival of the fittest. The novel element in the past 50 years is that big corporations are losing ground both to smaller and younger companies, and to their human creators.

Increasingly, the principle of economic selection tells us that someone, somewhere, will be experimenting with new products or technologies, some of which will challenge the sclerotic old firms.

The reckoning can be postponed, but not averted, and when large and previously very successful corporations eventually face innovative and appropriate competition they may quickly crumble. Think of the near-collapse of IBM. Think of the actual collapse of the Soviet Union, which at one time was, amongst other things, the world's largest corporation.

The process of killing off firms that have outlasted their usefulness will be accelerated as more and more people adopt the perspective of economic genes. Vehicles that are no longer working well should be abandoned by healthy economic genes and, increasingly, they will – sooner rather than later.

Can you adopt this new perspective?

What are the action implications for you?

263   Consider being part of a spin-off

Spin-offs are becoming more prevalent and successful.

What is a spin-off?

It's when a group of people from one organization go off and start their own business, with or without the blessing or a shareholding from the original entity.

Cadbury, the chocolate company, agreed to a buyout of its food business and retained a minority stake in the new business, Premier Foods, which was later sold to Hillsdown Holdings. Both Cadbury and the entrepreneurs behind Premier Foods benefited nicely.

It is no accident that industries which produce many spin-offs also grow faster than other industries – and also deliver faster increases in value to customers and investors. Silicon Valley is stuffed full of spin-offs. So are venture capital, management consulting, headhunting and investment banking.

In boring industries, where progress comes at the pace of an arthritic snail, and where the element of human creativity is lower, spin-offs are rare. Perhaps if there were more spin-offs, these industries would become more interesting and successful.

Natural selection predicts what happens with spin-offs. The new group takes much that is good from the old entity – it inherits the latter's good genes – while also adding new twists in terms of product, service and customers. It is a virtuous circle for the people involved and for the whole ecosystem. Nobody spins off from an unsuccessful or low-growth firm. If you want to give nature and the market a helping hand, take part in a spin-off.

Have you ever thought of starting or participating in a spin-off?

264   Team moves

Team moves are what they sound like: a team that has worked successfully together in one particular organization decides to 'sell itself' to another one in the same industry. Team moves are popular in the same high-growth industries as spin-offs – high tech, investment banking, consulting and venture capital for example. They take place for the same reason – that a group of people want to 'do their own thing' and develop their practice in new ways and for their own benefit too. Like spin-offs, team moves are rather '80/20' – they tend to involve the most ambitious and creative people in ambitious and creative industries.

Team moves are easier to do than spin-offs. Instead of needing to raise capital to start a new company, all that is required is to negotiate with the owners of a new 'home' for the team for a share of the upside created by the move. On the other hand, if the cost of a team move is lower than that of a spin-off, the upside is usually considerably lower. Conceptually, a team move is half-way between continuing to work for the original company as ordinary employees on the one hand, and spinning-off on the other. The other potential disadvantage both for the team making the move and their new home is that the chemistry between the team and the new organization cannot be guaranteed. The team will be sure of intra-team chemistry, but how the team and their new home get on will be less certain.

Have you ever come across a team move?

Would one make sense for you and your team?

265   Belong to a vibrant gene pool

The study of genes has shown why taboos on incest are well founded. The concept of inbreeding is useful in thinking about how evolution is restricted in a technology, product, company, market or nation, when there is little change in its metaphorical 'gene pool'.

Take the case of an organization. The gene pool is not just the skills of the senior executives; it comprises all the 80/20 inputs to the firm that make it different and super-productive – or not. These inputs include its history and values, usually derived from its founder or founders, what suppliers contribute by way of their products and expertize, the technologies and distribution channels used, how customers are used to help the firm improve (difficult customers are best), what investments are utilized and, in particular, all collaborative networks within and outside the company. Important collaborators for high-knowledge firms include individuals and firms within universities, and all existing employees and new recruits.

The location of the firm and its ability to access interlocking networks can be crucial. It has been convincingly argued that in some ways Silicon Valley, for example, resembles one complex ecosystem, comprising not just individual entrepreneurs and producing companies, but also the expertize of venture capitalists, headhunters, the entire 'supply chain' and all centres of knowledge and technology. Firms compete with each other, but also gain valuable expertize from the ecosystem, not least when new individuals and teams move from one organization to another. Cities can also be vibrant 'exciters' of gene pools.

'Inbreeding' occurs when the total gene pool is not sufficiently replenished, changed and stirred. High growth in industries and companies is a useful 'stirring' mechanism, as new people continually enter and enrich the gene pool. Growth and diversity cover and dissipate a multitude of sins.

How vibrant are the gene pools in which you swim? How can you increase and best tap the power of your gene pools?

266 Use the best economic genes available

Economic genes are units of economic transmission, the begetters of growth in value and, vitally, new sources of 'more from less'. A successful organization and successful individuals will use and generate a large number of economic genes. Examples include ideas and ways of working, the design behind its technology and products, and the 'script' for interacting with suppliers, customers and sources of innovation.

There are three ways to deploy such genes.[4]

One is to create them from scratch – invent a new product or service or a new business system. This is a rare event, requiring serious creativity, yet not so hard as is often imagined. Have a go.

A second way is to appropriate and use economic genes that have already proved their potency. Remember, the genes want to multiply, so they like being used. Get ahead of anyone else in using great ideas and you are away to the races. For instance, my friend Raymond Ackerman, founder of the Pick n Pay supermarket giant in South Africa, used the idea of self-service supermarkets after it was already proven in the US but before it had become so in Africa.

A third way is to take an already-successful idea and modify it slightly, tilting it to a new niche of product-customer identity.

These ways are very 80/20 – by identifying a simple personal mission you can create your own benign empire. Much more with much less.

Which of these three ways appeals to you most?

267   Make yourself an excellent vehicle for successful economic genes

As we have seen, economic genes are powerful generators of personal and company success. Economic genes are distinctive and are 80/20 ideas, and ways of working that produce more with less. Two examples of long-standing but still-unexhausted economic genes are self-service, and providing a product or service quicker than anybody else.

The easiest route to personal success is to familiarize yourself with one or more successful ideas such as these, and then innovate using them. To do this, you must further the purpose of the genes and help them multiply. This, in turn, requires you to adapt the gene to a new product or service, customer group or geography, or some permutation of these variables.

Adapting economic genes is an art. But it is not an art best confined to your studio or other private space. Expose the genes to a new environment, which is an open process and necessarily requires revealing your idea to potential competitors.

Don't seek to insulate yourself from internal or external competition, because if you do, you'll stop developing. Compete in major markets, not in backwaters. Publicize your new idea; rely on your skill in becoming the best possible vehicle for the business genes. If you understand, embody and evangelize the business gene(s) more effectively than any other individual, team or company, then you are bound to win. If you don't, you don't deserve to win. The genes would be better off multiplying through a different route.

Economic genes are best used by individuals, entrepreneurs and small groups. Beware of working in giant corporate pyramids, which insulate executives, especially senior ones, from the cutting edge of competition. Go small to go big.

Which economic genes are you going to propagate in a new context? Where and how?

268   Use the best vehicles available and drive them fast

You are central to the process of value creation. You are the user of economic information. In an important sense, you are the fundamental economic gene(s) – you provide the knowledge and skills, including the skill to collaborate with other successful ideas and their vehicles: with other individuals, with teams and with organizations. *You are the value added. You are the driving force.* The team or company you start or join, the other resources you commandeer, are vehicles for you.

The vehicles are there for you to drive. They are there for you to advance your purpose, to provide protection, to incarnate your energy. Be clear that the vehicles are just there, and the only reason to work through a vehicle is if it is the best possible vehicle around for your purposes.

Ask yourself continually – am I driving or being driven? Am I driving the right vehicle? Is there anywhere else I could add more value? Is there any other objective that I could pursue which would enrich the world more?

What vehicles are you driving? Are they the best vehicles for what you want? Are you driving or being driven?

These are hard questions. Yet they are fundamental. Take time to answer them properly.

269 Career evolution requires variation

The theory of evolution by natural selection says unambiguously that variation drives progress. As Darwin wrote, 'this preservation of favourable variations and the rejection of injurious variations, I call Natural Selection.' When the 'conditions of life' (such as climate) change, he says, 'this would manifestly be favourable to natural selection, by giving a better chance of profitable variations occurring; and unless profitable variations do occur, natural selection can do nothing.'[5]

Your career evolution will be driven by variation – a series of new jobs (with or without changing organizations) and new ways of doing the existing job. Also helpful are variations in colleagues, changes in product or service focus, changes in customer responsibilities and changes in where you work.

The more variation, the better.

But there is variation which happens to you, and variation which you seek out and cause or catalyse. Start a project. Take on a new role and responsibility. Change the furniture.

Identify new economic genes, alliances or partnerships that can provide you with fresh direction and for which you can be the best vehicle.

It is not how long you work, or how hard, but how many different experiences you have and the ideas you can use to drive forward the amount of extra value you can create for customers, co-workers, your organization and your ecosystem.

How much variation have you experienced in the past year? How much more could you generate in the next 12 months?

270 Genetics: summary of action implications

- Identify economic genes – valuable economic information, ways of working or technologies – that are under-exploited and currently have poor to mediocre vehicles (for example a company that is not providing the best possible product or service). Create the best possible vehicle.

- Fashion existing successful genes into new combinations. Provide excellent vehicles for the new combos.

- Make yourself – and colleagues if suitable – the best vehicle for a unique winning combination of genes.

- If you participate in running an organization, spread the view that its value derives from being the best possible vehicle for successful genes.

- Find ways to continually replenish the gene pool with new inflows of talent and ideas that have already proved their power.

- Create spin-offs – and spin-outs (where the original firm takes a stake in the new one) – from existing organizations. Be the person who makes spin-offs and spin-outs happen.

The perspective of economic genes is powerful, whether you are in an organization or working on your own account as an artist, writer, editor, video-maker, photographer, event organizer or other high-level service provider.

Do you get the idea and feel enthusiastic about it?

CHAPTER 31

NICHES AND BREAST-BEATING

It is plausible that our emotional responses owe much to our origins in the Stone Age. Here we look at four dangers to avoid and one different way to be very successful.

271   Gause's Principle of Survival by Differentiation: find a unique niche for yourself

Charles Darwin noted that the struggle for existence would 'almost invariably be the most severe between individuals of the same species, for they frequent the same districts, require the same food and are exposed to the same dangers' and, therefore, 'fill nearly the same place in the economy of nature'.[1]

This fits in with some intriguing experiments on small organisms by Soviet scientist G. F. Gause. He put two protozoans of the same family but different species in a glass jar with limited food. The little creatures managed to share the food and they both survived.

Then Gause put two organisms of the same species in the jar with the same amount of food as before. This time, they fought and died.

This is Gause's Principle of Survival by Differentiation, and it is highly relevant to your career. To have a definite place in what Darwin called 'the economy of nature' you must be different from all your (human) competitors. The difference(s) may be very slight, but to win you must be different on some significant dimension from everyone else. The differences may not be obvious, but they must exist.

Another charming illustration of this comes from ecologist Robert MacArthur and his observation of warbler birds in spruce trees. MacArthur noted that each type of warbler has its own bit of a spruce tree which it uses for food and its home. Each warbler has its own tiny niche.[2]

What is or are your unique niches? What is your 'home' in the world of work and life?

272   Why we still live in the Stone Age

Evolutionary psychologists have come up with a fascinating – and plausible – hypothesis which argues that our genes lag behind changes in our society. Humans emerged as hunter-gatherers about 200,000 years ago and evolved traits to suit that life. Then, a mere 7,000 to 10,000 years ago, humans gave up gathering berries and hunting wild beasts and settled down to an agricultural society, growing crops and husbanding animals. Finally, about 200–300 years ago, industry and commerce began to become much more important and dominant than agriculture, and more and more of us began living in large cities.

Each of these changes required different approaches to life. Yet a difference of 10,000 years (and certainly 300 years) is just not long enough for human evolution to produce genetic traits that match our new surroundings. Most importantly, our natural responses to challenges are still based on Stone Age psychology – for example in the way that our emotions dominate our reason. Like the Flintstones, we go by first impressions, beat our breasts and magnify our self-importance, develop small clans of followers, dislike outsiders, follow the herd, gossip and follow confident leaders unthinkingly. In many ways, we are wired to be what our genes make us – Stone Age animals.

Emotions are valuable, but often lead us astray. Think twice before reacting in a hostile way. Avoid unnecessary anger. Calculate. Behave collaboratively. Smile. Welcome strangers. Give way to others. Believe in peaceful coexistence.

Keep your Flintstone genes under control. Modern life need not be 'nasty, brutish and short' if we behave in ways consistent with our urban, interdependent and civilized existence.

273   Beware of your first impressions

The Stone Age world was threatening and complex. It was not clear which berries were good food or poison. Which regions were good for hunting? Which beasts were the least dangerous to hunt? Which strangers you could trust? Snap decisions were often necessary, and the wrong decision could be fatal. Sitting around to analyse data was not life-enhancing.

The only basis could be stereotypes based on first impressions. If a stranger looked and acted friendly, they could probably be trusted. If not, they were probably an enemy.

Today it is not so vital to decide instantly. Yet research shows that we give enormous weight to first impressions. In turn, our immediate reactions affect the confidence and empathy returned by the people we meet, which reinforce our first impressions. It is likely that we make many poor decisions, and fail to weigh evidence judiciously, because of our Stone Age programming. Yet we also waste time, because it seems rude to decide instantly. If we're going to go on first impressions, we might as well keep all meetings down to five minutes.

You will make more friends and influence more people if you are wary of first impressions, especially if they are negative. You will also avoid costly mistakes if you wait until there is evidence that someone has great qualities before you decide to collaborate with them.

Do you accept that you often go by first impressions? Why are you in such a hurry?

274   Don't beat your breast too hard

In the dangerous world of the hunter-gatherer, when life was random and terrifying, the person who appeared least terrified and most confident was likely to attract followers, food and sex. Genes for confidence were likely to proliferate and be reinforced. Confidence was rated more highly than realism.

In the Stone Age, therefore, breast-beating was not just an indulgence; it led to success.

In modern times, breast-beating still attracts followers, as many gurus and charlatans have proved. But three things are different.

First, events have become more complex and harder to call.

Second, our tools of analysis and intuition have developed and it is less necessary to decide instantly.

Third, blind confidence ain't what it used to be. Nor are egotism and breast-beating. They used to impress; now they often annoy. Our environment has changed and some of us have registered this.

Yet our genes often drag us back to the Stone Age. Today beating your breast is not only unattractive; it is often counter-productive.

Do you beat your breast too much or too little?

Is it time for a change of personal style?

275   Do you have a taste for hierarchy?

Everything about hunter-gatherer clans suggests that ad hoc hierarchies flourished. The desire to find security in a chain of status relationships seems to be a pronounced trait of primitive societies. For followers, the chances of safety and adequate food increased with attachment or deference to a leader.

If we are wired in some way to hierarchy, this helps to explain why every revolution trying to overturn hierarchy – whether the French or Russian Revolutions, or the modern flat, single-status organization – ends in creating new forms of hierarchy, often more effective or tyrannical. The twentieth century was the century of the common man, and also the century of the psychopathic leader – Stalin, Hitler and Mao alone murdered about 100,000,000 people. Even in our ostensibly liberal democracies, once official hierarchy is abolished or downgraded, new unofficial pecking orders flourish. Status is sought. More worryingly, status is acknowledged. The death of deference is routinely deferred.

In life as in all forms of organization, hierarchy without insight or genuine reform subtracts value. Yet most successful organizations – whether tiny teams or mega-states – combine near-dictatorship of ends with democracy of means. Consider Churchill. He defeated Hitler by autocratic leadership, yet stood for re-election in 1945 and graciously departed when outvoted.

History suggests dictatorship is easier to attain than genuine democracy, which requires centuries of gradual accommodation by factions that fight each other but ultimately compromise and tolerate. Our Stone Age genes can only be calmed by long periods of creeping democracy. Even then, there is always the danger of regression. For example, Russia has never had democracy and it shows. Germany had three centuries of increasing culture and liberalism; it was not enough to overcome German nationalism and desire for a supreme leader.

Do you still have a hankering for hierarchy? Could you combine dictator-ship of ends with democracy of means?

276 Don't be hostile to out-groups

The strength of the clan and its allegiance to the leader had the flipside of hostility to those outside the group. This, too, assisted survival. Charles Darwin noted:

> 'A tribe, including many members who, from possessing in high degree
> the spirit of patriotism, fidelity, obedience, courage and sympathy,
> were always ready to aid one another, and to sacrifice themselves
> for the common good, would be victorious over other tribes;
> and this would be natural selection.'

History suggests that only trade and the weakening of exclusive national identities can lead to peace. Our desire for group identity persists but has been sublimated in civilized societies into demonstrations, football team rivalry and, amongst the rich, business competition.

Neolithic habits die hard. Cohesion within a team is not too hard to build, but when do competing teams come together? The persistence of ancient rival-ries raises the question – can an organization, a local community or a nation composed of several cohesive groups be as effective, all other things being equal, as one comprising a single homogeneous group? *Why are many small nations richer and more united than comparable larger ones?*

Can you be friendly with out-groups? This is definitely the civilized option, but never an easy one.

CHAPTER 32

RISK, POSSESSIONS, EXPERIENCES AND RELATIONSHIPS

We'll see that 80/20 indicates we should take more risks, avoid panic, defend our 'territory', and value experiences above possessions, and relationships above experiences.

277   The self-defeating avoidance of risk

Evolutionary psychologists say that hunter-gatherers took risks only when their world was falling apart. Does this explain why today we are risk averse when we can afford risk, and yet risk takers when losses are endemic? Or why gamblers tend to back favourites, but when they are losing bet to extinction on outside chances?

It seems that a high degree of security – or insecurity – is necessary before we will take significant risks. Experiments in child psychology show that toddlers dare to explore only when their mothers are around. My Labrador will only leave the grounds of the house when we go for a walk; but will go far afield if I am in whistling distance. Maybe these are all hangovers from the Stone Age.

We do not seem to 'clock' that *uncertainty is not really risky*. In fact, uncertainty can be very reliable. Few places have such high and consistent returns as casinos. Placing a huge number of bets, which is what casino owners do, is not very risky.

Risk is everywhere, but not everywhere apparent. There is a risk in living, particularly if we have bad genes or bad habits. There is a big risk in the most important decision most of us make, which is to get married (or not) – yet the chances of being happier from a long-term commitment are very favourable. The risk is great unhappiness; but with the odds in your favour, and using decent commonsense, it is more hazardous not to take the plunge.

80/20 says it all. Be very careful in making the big bets, but make them. Then be blasé in spreading small bets at good odds without too much deliberation. As Nietzsche nearly said, what cannot kill you will make you stronger and happier.

How risk averse are you? Could you place a few big bets wisely and then take a lot of risks with the small stuff?

278   Don't panic

I confess that occasionally I panic. I don't do it often, but it takes a serious toll on me for a few minutes, and unless I dismiss it completely then and focus on all the good things in my life the panic casts a shadow over my day. To be honest, I am more concerned and slightly ashamed by my panic than by anything 'real'.

But now I am absolved; I have an excellent scapegoat. My genes. And you have the same get-out too. You see, primitive people did take risks and scramble furiously when their lives were at stake – which was a frequent occupational risk faced by hunters of large beasts. And, as always, natural selection worked: the more successful scramblers survived more often. Scrambling under threat – real or imagined – is part of our genetic makeup.

Yet today, such panic may not be so necessary or so functional. The modern world is not the savannah plains. A normally sane person under pressure when driving may exhibit road rage or panic, but if we stop to think for a moment, the panic is not in proportion to the situation – we are not about to be eaten by a wild animal on the motorway. And panic or road aggression are very unlikely to help at all: quite the reverse. Our genes may be flashing up EMERGENCY! EMERGENCY! The sensible thing is to ignore them and let the panic subside.

In gambling and trading on financial markets, if losses mount, gamblers or novices may hang on in an effort to avoid realizing the loss; they may even scramble to get funds to 'average down' by increasing the investment in their position. They are panicking. Professional investors are trained to take the opposite approach and coolly cut losses before they get out of hand.

Don't panic! It's a normal human reaction, probably a hangover from the Stone Age, but it will only make things worse. Keep calm and carry on.

Do you ever panic? Does it help?

Try to ignore the panic button presented by your genes.

279   Owners and intruders

Biology and game theory give a fascinating insight into contests between owners or incumbents of territory on the one hand, and challengers or intruders on the other. *Being the owner confers a psychological advantage that is independent of relative strength.*

If two similar butterflies contest a sunny spot, what usually happens is that they spiral around rather prettily for a short time, and then the intruder-butterfly departs. But if both butterflies are already resident in the spot or two equally near spots, the contest takes quite some time, with an equal chance of either winning. Experiments with baboons show the same pattern – the owner of the territory is likely to win, even if it is not quite as strong as the intruder. You can see the same phenomenon with dogs. The 'owner' of a garden will bark furiously and advance on an intruder, even if the latter is bigger or there are two or more; the intruders will be hesitant and rather easily dispersed. In a war, defenders of the homeland may fight harder and win against numerical strength.

Our genes appear to dispose us to hang onto what we already have and have a weaker disposition to take new ground.

How could this knowledge be useful? If an individual, team or company can convince themselves that 'territory' – a market, a disputed possession or inheritance, or anything valuable – is 'rightfully theirs', they are more likely to win.

If you are an 'intruder', do not be afraid of the 'barks' of incumbents. If you are stronger, don't hesitate to push in. Or demonstrate that ownership of the disputed territory is ambiguous, and that a compromise is better than a war.

Do you have some territory where you are clearly the owner? Find some such territory and defend it tenaciously. Believe that what you passionately want is rightfully yours.

280 The endowment effect: our possessions possess us

Psychologists have discovered a perverse glitch in our behaviour. Imagine that Alice has been given two tickets to a concert or top sporting event. A few days later she is offered the face value of the tickets, which is $500. In experiments, most participants refuse the trade.

Then the experiment is reversed. The subject – let's call her Carol – is given $500, and a little later the same tickets, worth $500, are offered to her at this price. What do you think happens? Logically, if Alice refused the money for the tickets, Carol should buy the tickets when offered the chance. But it doesn't work like that. Most often, Carol refuses the trade.

What explains this irrationality? Psychologists say that there is an 'endowment effect'. What people are given first, what they now own – whether the tickets or the money – they want to keep.

Car salespeople try to create the endowment effect by encouraging prospective buyers to take a test drive. The customer may form an attachment to the car and feel that it is 'theirs'. The endowment effect clearly parallels the 'owners' versus 'intruders' theory. We fight to defend the ownership status quo.

The ownership and endowment effects have implications well beyond the obvious game theory tactics and dodgy car sales. We like our possessions and they may well come to possess us. The key tenet of 80/20 is 'more from less'. Equally we may say that 'less is more'. All other things being equal, older people tend to own more than younger people. We accumulate more and better possessions as we age. If we really believe that 'less is more', we should divest ourselves of possessions as we get older, concentrating on things that matter more.

Possessions are less vital than experiences. Experiences are less vital than relationships. Relationships are most valuable if they are the few ones in which we can give and receive the most love.

Do you own too much? Are your priorities right?

281   Audit your possessions

Divide your significant possessions into the 20 per cent which are vital and the 80 per cent which are trivial or toxic.

The *vital possessions* are those that make you happy. Simple as that.

The *trivial possessions* are those contributing marginal happiness or marginal unhappiness.

Possessions create net unhappiness when the financial or psychic cost of maintaining them is greater than the happiness they give you.

Toxic possessions are those where their financial or psychic cost greatly exceeds the happiness they give you, or where they generate definite unhappiness.

When you have your lists of vital, trivial and toxic possessions the action steps are clear:

- Keep the 20 per cent of possessions that are vital and enhance your happiness.
- Immediately dispose of the toxic possessions.
- Less urgently, gradually dispose of the trivial possessions.

You probably wear 20 per cent of your clothes and other items in your wardrobe 80 per cent or more of the time. Keep the 20 per cent. Sell or give away the 80 per cent of trivial items.

You may have a large collection of music or books you will never listen to/read. Keep the ones you will use again and give or throw away the rest.

The 20 per cent of vital/happiness-inducing possessions should be easy to identify. Most of the other 80 per cent are probably trivial. Very few or none may be toxic, but if there are any – perhaps connected with self-destructive habits – destroy them now.

When will you clear out your non-vital possessions?

282   Audit your experiences

The experiences I recommend auditing are any significant ones that are recurring or constant in your life. These experiences include things such as holidays or trips; hobbies such as sports, collecting or maintaining anything; exercise undertaken at least once a week; going to concerts, films, festivals, museums, theatres or other events; gardening or walking the dog; volunteering; civic or political participation; and anything else that you do which has a marked positive or negative effect on your happiness.

Excluded are any which are directly related to personal relationships with family, friends or lovers, where the relationship angle is more important than the event/experience angle.

List all significant experiences, whether solitary or social, and divide them into vital experiences which significantly make you happier; trivial experiences which have little or no net impact on your happiness; and toxic experiences, which tend to make you less happy.

With experiences, the changes you can make are to do more/do less/end – that is, have more of these or similar experiences; or less of them; or stop having them altogether.

The 80/20 hypothesis is that there will be a few of these experiences which reliably and materially make you happier. The large majority of your experiences will probably not measurably and reliably increase your happiness. A few of your experiences may reliably make you less happy. *The remedies are obvious.*

Which type of experiences should you have more of?

283   Audit your relationships

Your relationships are far more important than your possessions and more important than even your experiences.

A relationship is a bond between you and another person which has high emotional value to you and affects your happiness. Relationships can be with family members, with lovers and with friends.

Note that the definition is quite restrictive – to qualify, a relationship has to have high emotional value. In an age where some people believe they have hundreds of friends, it is rare for more than 20 relationships to have high emotional value. Typically, you can count such relationships on your hands. The majority of happiness is likely to be generated by fewer than six relationships.

What are your most important relationships, ranked in order of their ability to make you very happy (or unhappy)?

How often do you see each of these people? Are there other people not on your list whom you see more often?

With your top five relationships, how could you deepen them and derive even more happiness and meaning in life for you and the other person?

Are any of the relationships a source of unhappiness for you or the other person? If so, can the relationship be made net-positive in terms of happiness? How? If so, you should move heaven and earth to make that happen. If it cannot happen, what should you do?

Sometimes intimate family relationships are fraught. It must be a high priority to do whatever you can to make them tolerable or positive. Be cautious in cutting off such relationships or allowing them to fester. If the other person died tomorrow, would you feel guilty for anything you had done or not done in respect of them?

Think long, hard and often about your relationships, and make them the centre of your life.

CHAPTER 33

NEUROPLASTICITY, TIT FOR TAT AND THE RIGHT PLACE TO LIVE

How to 'think yourself happier', collaborate effectively,
find your greatest relative advantage, find your best
'complementors' and the right place to live.

284   Your brain can be rewired to make you happier

Perhaps the most important scientific discovery – the most far-reaching in terms of its potential impact on human happiness – is *neuroplasticity*, the theory and practice of the brain rewiring itself.

We've looked at the impact of our genes and natural selection on our lives. Genes are definitely '80/20' – one of the few most important influences on our lives – but they are not our destiny. We can re-make our future by changing the shape of our brains.

Children have an innate ability to learn languages. But which language they learn determines how the brain stores sound. Neuroscientists have discovered why – the particular sounds made by any language forces a different rewiring of the part of the brain processing language.

Brain scans also show that obsessive-compulsive disorders can be moderated or cured if patients act deliberately to think about other things. Amazingly, we know that the brain circuits can be rewired by conscious effort. Neuroscientist Jeffrey Schwartz says, 'There is mind independent of the brain … if our mind can rewire the brain, then in an important sense the mind is master of the brain.'[1]

What you think determines how you feel and what you do. It is possible to 'think yourself happier' by what you believe and act on. There is no objective truth about you and your emotions. *Think whatever you can plausibly believe that will make you – and therefore those around you – happier.*

How will you 'think yourself happier'?

285   How to cooperate and win 'Tit for Tat'

Game theory, a branch of mathematics and statistics, explores what happens when two individuals are faced with a dilemma of whether to cooperate or pursue their own selfish interests. The typical game is a variant of the 'Prisoner's Dilemma', where if both parties collaborate, they each win a little, but if one is selfish and the other collaborates, the selfish person wins and the collaborator is screwed.

No useful conclusions emerged until the late 1970s when tournaments using computer programs were used. Each computer program deployed a different strategy, and the game was played 200 times or more between each strategy and each player. To general surprise the strategy that won was called Tit for Tat. It started by cooperating, and then mimicked the last move of the other player.

The tournament organizer explained that Tit for Tat won through a combination of being nice, forgiving and clear. Its retaliation discouraged selfish behaviour by the opponent. Its forgiveness restored mutual cooperation. And its clarity made it intelligible to the other player, thereby eliciting long-term cooperation.

Long-term advantage often requires cooperating players to take turns in collecting the payoff – I let you win the bigger prize this time, perhaps taking nothing myself, if you let me take the bigger prize next time. Cooperating focuses on making the pie bigger, and on understanding that when we have to divide it we will behave reasonably within the context of a long-term relationship.

All great relationships are founded on some variant of long-term reciprocity, together with humanity, humour, honesty and transparency. Game theory provides the skeleton of the relationship; personal chemistry puts the flesh on the bones.

How good a collaborator are you?

286   The unique advantage of being human

The science writer Matt Ridley says in his fascinating book *The Origins of Virtue* that humans are unique and 'virtuous' not because of parallels with the animal kingdom, 'but by the very lack of convincing parallels'.

The advantage of society rests, he says, in the division of labour and socialization, both of which humans have taken to a happy extreme.

According to Ridley, we humans have organized ourselves into large groups with complex inter-relationships between individuals, so that we cooperate in a qualitatively different way from other animals. Individuals and groups of individuals make trades with each other and exploit reciprocity, reaping the benefits of social living in a uniquely tangled way.

The difference can be seen objectively in the greatest miracle of life – the human brain. 'To thrive in a complex society,' Ridley writes, 'you need a big brain. To acquire a big brain, you need to live in a complex society.' Over time, human brains and the complexity of society have developed symbiotically. Virtue and reciprocity are the essential lubricants of human success, and they go with the grain of human nature, not against it.[2]

I think that one of the greatest mistakes of religion was the idea of the Fall and Original Sin, and the carry-over of this Jewish doctrine into later Christianity, against the ideas of grace and love developed by Jesus and Paul. Instead of wallowing in guilt – with all the advantages it gives to organized religion and rulers – we should take pride in our better natures and realize that we have infinite capacity for creation, forgiveness, love and reciprocity. All progress, personal and social, depends on human relationships, and the cornerstone of these is loving reciprocity.

What do you owe to your relationships and the love and reciprocity implicit in them? How could you take your relationships further and deeper?

287   Ricardo's law of comparative advantage

The links between cooperation, division of labour and trade were first made explicit in 1817 by David Ricardo, an economist, radical British politician and rich investor. His law of comparative advantage applied division of labour to groups and countries. Like 80/20, Ricardo's law is impressive because it is counterintuitive. Economist Paul Samuelson says that Ricardo's law is the only proposition in the whole of social science that is both true and not trivial!

Until Ricardo, it seemed obvious that countries could only trade profitably if one was better than the other at producing something. Ricardo demurred. He pointed out that there was a basis for trade whenever the relative ratios of productivity were different, whatever the absolute levels.

If country X is better than country Y at producing both products that they make, there could still be trade between them that would enrich both countries. If country X is twice as productive as country Y in clothing and four times as productive in leather goods, then country X should specialize in leather goods and country Y should specialize in clothing, where it has a comparative advantage, despite being inferior in absolute terms.

This idea can be applied to individuals as well as countries. You can view your whole life as a series of trades, around the discovery of where you are relatively the best at creating useful output. For example, if physics is your strongest suit, and you rank higher in physics than any other discipline, you don't need to be as brilliant as Einstein to make wonderful contributions to life.

Find out what your strongest suit is where you have the greatest relative advantage and enjoy working at that. Do not be discouraged if someone in the world is better than you.

288   Cultural advantage: knowing something extremely useful

We have looked at the way in which humanity has invented a new form of evolution – the human practice of passing on traditions, customs, know-ledge, insights and beliefs. The most effective 'memes' of this type and the ability to put them into effective practice constitutes, in a way, a new form of competition, not genetic but cultural. An individual or a group may prosper not because of genes, but because of knowing something extremely useful, and acting on it.[3]

You may well become much more effective and happier from selecting one or more guiding ideas of this type. It could be 80/20 or a particular subset of that – or any other powerful idea that can provide a focus to your life and your actions. Of course, it could be a particular religious conviction – or a philosophical one. The common theme is that advantage comes from a powerful idea and from devotion to purposeful, highly focused action arising from the idea.

One 80/20 message that bears repetition is that you don't need to know a lot of things. Modern life is confusing because we have a constantly expanding panoply of ideas, an over-production of concepts and advice.

The media and our hyperactive brains conspire to tell us something new each day, when what we need is something old – something that has stood the test of time and experience and been incredibly useful to millions of people. There comes a point in many people's lives, when, to a chorus of trumpets and then the sound of silence, an individual says, 'Enough! I will devote myself to this idea, which will bring me and my friends peace, a fulfilled life and serenity.' More ideas can provide less insight, less motivation, less value and less happiness.

What do you know that is hugely valuable and could be the theme-tune of your life?

289   Cultural advantage: being a superior cooperator

Cultural selection between groups happens, and the cooperators grow at the expense of the non-cooperators. The history of humanity is of ever-increasing and ever more complex inter-relationships. Society is not an artificial construct or a tyranny, but the highest form of evolution.

What drives personal and social progress?

We've already considered increased specialization and increased trade. It is pretty clear, though, that there is a third member of the trinity. The biggest influence on life since the invention of movable-type printing is technology, and the power and influence of technology has, ever since, grown at an exponential rate. Technology is probably the most potent and widespread purveyor of cultural advantage and the clearest advantage humans have over other animals. It is impossible to explain the explosion of population, wealth and the complexity of society in the last four centuries purely on the basis of increased specialization and trade. More and more, technology drives all before it.

Yet there is something else powering history. The greatest advances in technology and rises in wealth occurred between 1815 and 1914 and after 1945. It is no accident that these were also, for the most part, periods of peace between the most prosperous nations and large-scale cooperation between nations, groups and individuals. And who gained the most? Broadly, the best cooperators.

Are you a superior cooperator? How could you improve your ability to cooperate effectively, with the least new effort?

290   Find your complementors

A complementor is someone whose work causes your work to be more highly valued. A competitor is someone whose work causes your work to be less highly valued.

A complementor is not to be confused with a collaborator. You and your collaborator(s) constitute a team, working together to create and market one or more joint products. By contrast, a complementor does not participate in the creation of your work; he or she is an independent party, but one whose work increases the value of yours if they are displayed or marketed together.

Imagine that you are an artist who specializes in seascapes. If your style and that of another seascape artist are similar, and an art lover is browsing in a gallery with your work and that of the other artist, you are in direct competition. The customer is unlikely to want two pictures which are similar.

Yet imagine that the gallery has an exhibition of 'seascapes through the ages'. It features seascapes from J. M. W. Turner from the period 1790–1820, of later nineteenth-century Italian artists, of early twentieth-century Americans, of seascapes from the Second World War and your painting of a modern seascape. A collector of seascapes may want one of each period, and if yours is the only modern one, and good, the other works are complementors. Also, if the collector likes the idea of having one seascape, and yours is by far the least expensive and of comparable quality, the other seascapes are also complementors. The gallery owner is also obviously a complementor.

We tend to think about competitors, and possibly also about collaborators, but much less about complementors. Generally, we can do little about competitors, except to differentiate our work and avoid head-on competition. But we can find and benefit from complementors, if only we think about them.

Who are your complementors? How can you help each other?

291   The right place to live

The writer and professor Jared Diamond argues that in 1400, China had a huge technological lead over Europe, with the world's largest fleet of ships. Yet China was sunk by excessive centralization of power. In 1432, a new emperor sided with the anti-Navy faction and dismantled the shipyards.

By contrast, Europe at the time was divided into many different countries and principalities. When Columbus, who was Italian, wanted a fleet to sail across the Atlantic, he naturally tried to find Italian backers. Everyone in Italy thought it was a stupid idea. Then he tried in France, with the same result. He traipsed from court to court until finally, at the seventh attempt, the king and queen of Spain sponsored three small ships. This accidental event handed Spain and Europe a lead over China that lasted for five centuries.

Diamond says that fragmentation can be enormously valuable, but only up to a point. By rights, the German beer industry, with its long history of brewing and excellent products, should have dominated the world. Yet German beer production was shared by thousands of more-or-less equally sized companies, and the leading US beer producers, with huge scale and marketing budgets, were able to conquer the world with (to my taste) vastly inferior products.[4]

The ideal is Silicon Valley, with many fiercely competitive companies yet a free flow of information and ideas between them, as a result of job-hopping, and the influence of venture capitalists, journalists and bars where people from different companies congregate.

Where you live and work can be as vital as what you do and how good you are.

Do you live in an area with 'intermediate fragmentation' where individuals and groups compete but maintain free communication with each other?

CHAPTER 34

TIME OASES, THINKING AND CHAOS

How to identify your 'time oases' when you produce work of immense value, to think from first principles, to build flexibility into your plans and seize the 'first mover advantage'.

292   Time oases

If you are engaged in creative work of any kind, there is something you urgently need to know. Studies have shown that *only about 10 per cent of our time is used to great effect*. There is a 'value gulf' between the very best work we do on the one hand, and the great majority of our work on the other hand.[1]

Albert Einstein is an extreme example. How much time did he need to devise his incredibly powerful equation $E = mc^2$? What was the ratio of value to time spent? Not infinite, but a very large number!

This line of thinking leads to the concept of time oases. A time oasis is a lovely place – a small enclave, verdant, full of beautiful plants and flowers, relaxed, and immensely creative and productive.

It is quite impossible to convert all your days to time oases. By definition, an oasis is exceptional and defined by what it is not as much as by what it is. It is not common, it is not uninspired, it is not background material, it is not in any way *ordinary*. It is so precious, and of such high value that the idea or work you produce in the oasis is hugely, incomparably more valuable than what you produce outside the oasis.

But consider this – if you could double the time you spend in your time oases, you could create work that justifies the whole of the rest of your time to be spent not working, but doing what you would love to do otherwise. Maybe you will still decide to work on ordinary projects because you prefer doing that to doing anything else. But you have the option of being completely idle the rest of your time – and maybe that *idleness will generate the next oasis*.

What are your time oases? Do you need to truncate your 'time deserts' to allow the oases to arrive?

293   Thinking generates a new world

Who would you nominate as the most eccentric scientist of the twentieth century? Most people would nominate Einstein. Yet he had a friend who easily trumped him in his eccentricity.

Kurt Gödel is rightly celebrated as the author, in 1931, of the 'Incompleteness theorem', one of the twentieth century's most sublime and devastating pieces of logic. After working in Vienna as a professor from 1924, he fled to Princeton in 1938. The attempt to secure him US citizenship barely survived his long and pedantic exposition of the many grave flaws in the US constitution. Einstein eventually managed to get him to shut up in front of the judge hearing his application for citizenship. Gödel eventually starved himself to death, convinced his food was being poisoned.

Gödel showed that any consistent numerical system generates formulae – for example, 'a number is equal to itself', or 'zero is a number' – that cannot be proved, except by importing axioms from outside the system. Reality, he demonstrated is not a given – it is a construct. The most interesting application for 80/20 is that *the very process of thinking adds to what we think about ... and the process can never be completed.* We make our own reality. The future is not the past run backwards. The future is what we make it. There are many potential futures. There are multiple routes to success. The raw material of success is lying all around us, currently unused but available.

The most valuable thing we can do is *think*. Every time you think – really think, for example, about how you can create more value or happiness – you add to the world's stock of useful thinking.

Are you used to thinking, really thinking hard, about important improvements you can and will make to your life and that of people around you? There is nothing you can do in your life which will be so wonderful.

294   'The opposite of a great truth is also true'

The great Danish physicist Niels Bohr, working in the early twentieth century on quantum mechanics, once observed that 'the opposite of a trivial truth is plainly false. The opposite of a great truth, however, is also true.' Bohr demonstrated the very strange truth that electrons, tiny pieces of matter, can leap from one orbit to another, passing from one position to another without passing physically in between. He also proved that two contradictory beliefs about the microworld, for example, that light is like a wave and also like a particle, could both be true.

Whenever you see that something important is being demonstrated, realize that very probably the opposite is also true. This happens all the time in business. For example, Henry Ford simplified the car and produced it in great volumes, because he thought that extraordinarily low prices would attract millions of customers. He was absolutely right. But then General Motors went in the opposite direction, making cars that were more expensive but appealed to drivers because the cars said something important emotionally about their aspirations, whether for a Chevrolet or a Cadillac. Customers could buy on the basis of price ... and also on the basis of non-economic reasons.

This 'great truths can also demonstrate the opposite' phenomenon can be observed in politics – capitalism and socialism can both be popular – in fashion, in art, in architecture, in music and in every department of life. It can even be true about 80/20 – it is vital to work out what is most important in life – and yet also be true that trivial experiences of life should also be valued. Extreme positions can make huge differences; what has little or negative value is the mushy middle.

What great truths are being proclaimed around you, which you could stand on their heads? Plant your flag by taking an extreme position and making it important for other people.

295   Escaping the tyranny of 'either/or'

The discovery of 'both/and' as a sensible alternative to 'either/or' was partly due to the discovery by Niels Bohr and other quantum mechanics pioneers that light is both wave-like and particle-like, at the same time. Once this came from the scientific world, it found resonance quickly in the world of business. For example, if we are sufficiently creative or lucky, we can *both* keep the stock market happy *and* be socially responsible – claims that capitalism has irredeemably kept workers on low wages and working in shocking conditions have been disproved. Similarly, a firm such as Apple can make huge profits while also making customers happy with a stream of ingenious new products, and quality can be not just 'free', but also have negative costs. Previously 'inevitable' trade-offs can sometimes be transcended – simply by believing that they can, and by finding a way.

Many people believe that to be successful they have to work extremely hard and sacrifice a quality personal life. 80/20 proposes that you concentrate on the vital and relatively *easy* way to innovate. *It is possible to come up with brilliant new ideas and products where the value is so great that we can succeed without working hard* after the initial launch period.

The best way to have your cake and eat it is to believe that this is possible. It is not always true, but think creatively about how this might be possible, and you may very well find that it is.

When you think you are in an 'either/or' situation, ask your subconscious mind to devise a 'both/and' solution. Can you think of anything in your past life where 'both/and' worked for you?

296   How to recognize 'chaotic' patterns

'Chaos' is a very bad name for the study of complex systems in the universe – things like the weather, cities, economies, galaxies, insect colonies, packs of wolves, brains and the internet. The common characteristic of complex systems is that they are not linear, not easily predicted and not simply the sum of their parts. You yourself – and every other human – are a complex system.

Complex systems can't be analysed using our familiar tools – pretty much the only ones used in business and bureaucracies, for example – but that doesn't stop hard-working and often intelligent people from trying to do so. If you don't analyse, what the heck can you do instead? The answer is to *recognize patterns*.

Benoit Mandelbrot, one of the world's most brilliant mathematicians, coined the word 'fractal' to describe things that are very similar to each other, yet not identical – such as coastlines, clouds, earthquakes, trees and cotton prices (or any other collection of price data) over time.

Plotting price data reveals remarkably similar patterns regardless of the commodity being plotted. For example, the year-to-year graph of cotton prices looks eerily like the *shape* of month-to-month cotton price variations, even if the scales are different.

Whenever you face an important decision in your career or your life, try to find the nearest equivalent situation in your experience or that of your friends or co-workers. Draw up a 'top three' list of similar events and what happened next. As the near future unfolds, see which of the three previous patterns most resembles the new one.

You may not be right, so keep thinking about the other two patterns until you have a good match. Then use your intuition to make the final decision.

297   Chaos and complexity

In 1908, the French scientist Henri Poincaré said something quite profound: 'A very small cause, which escapes us, determines a considerable effect which we cannot ignore, and then we say that this effect is due to chance.' Chance and luck, in other words, may not be completely random. Random luck definitely exists, but what we call luck may sometimes just reflect our ignorance.

We should recognize the limitations of our knowledge and that our plans may hit brick walls. Expect the unexpected and when it happens, don't waste time trying to work out the cause. It may be undetectable. Therefore:

- Don't expect to be able to control everything.

- Build flexibility into your plans. Respect uncertainty. If *x* happens, do *y*. If *w* happens, do *z*.

- Don't try to establish blame. Annoyingly, there may be no wrongdoers. Or the 'wrongdoers' may have been following your instructions. Get on with working out what to do next.

- Most importantly, when something goes right, realize that it may not be much or at all to do with your skill. It may be 'sensitive dependence on initial conditions' – like the weather – that just happened to suit you perfectly. Exploit the trend for all it is worth, but don't claim personal credit or believe that you walk on water. The next apparently random event may scupper you.

What graphic examples of good and bad 'luck' have you experienced in your life? Do you see that such events are inherently unpredictable? Are you good at building flexibility into your plans?

298   Can you seize the 'first mover advantage'?

Complex systems are very sensitive to initial conditions. So, it makes sense to get in on the ground floor of any new development that appeals to you. The idea of the 'first mover advantage' is well known in business, but it can apply to individuals – like you – as well.

For example, Coca-Cola was not only the first cola, but also the first carbonated soft drink. This happened in the 1880s, when a batch of the soft drink – which originally was not carbonated – used fizzy water by mistake. Customers loved the new product; the rest is history. Ever since, Coca-Cola has been the world's leading soft drink, and the Coca-Cola Corporation has been the most profitable drinks company in the world.

First-mover advantage can be of similar importance to individuals – whether in pursuit of fame and fortune, or just doing something worthwhile that other people would like to imitate.

We all remember that Tenzing Norgay and Edmund Hillary were first to reach the top of Mount Everest, and that Roger Bannister was the first to run a mile in under four minutes.

Have you ever considered being the first person to do something that you think should be done, but hasn't yet been done?

What could that be? And if you were the first to do it, would you want to exploit the first-mover advantage and how could you do that?

CHAPTER 35

PARKINSON'S LAWS

Discover how Parkinson's laws align with 80/20, and how to avoid trivial tasks and unnecessary spending.

299   Parkinson's first law

In 1958, a book by C. Northcote Parkinson captured the world's attention. It was called simply *Parkinson's Law* and the law states that **Work expands to fill the time available.** Parkinson's book was both satirical and deeply serious.

His point was that in administrative work, including the professions, bosses strive to increase the size of their departments because they like having large departments, not because the work is inherently necessary or profitable. Officials make work for each other, and as there is always plenty of work to be found – whether worthwhile or not – that justifies (or appears to justify) enlarging the workforce, masking the real objective of empire building.

Parkinson did not link his law to 80/20, but he could have done. If work expands to fill the time available, it makes perfect sense that much of the work is of marginal importance, or even negative value – as 80/20 implies.

'Work expands to fill the time available' also applies, of course, to individuals. 80/20 implies that there simply isn't enough really important work to do, so we invent unimportant work to fill our working week. We don't realize it is unimportant, but if we are short of time – for example, if a hard deadline looms – we just do the important stuff. So, there is a kind of reverse Parkinsonian law that 80/20 proposes – *trivial work contracts when time available is short.*

It is only when we realize that 'work' is not 'work' that we can get to grips with what is important and what is not. There is a small proportion of vital work, and a large proportion of trivial work. Once we realize this, we are liberated. We can either do vastly more important work, or we can enjoy a great deal of leisure – or we can do a bit more important work and also enjoy ourselves more.

The best way to do more and better work and have a fulfilling life outside work is to decide what the vital parts of your work are, <u>and to do no more</u>.

What is the vital 20 per cent of your work? Can you resist the temptation to do more?

300   Parkinson's second law

C. Northcote Parkinson's second law is that *Expenditure rises to meet incomes*. We may make more money as we progress in our careers, but we may not necessarily feel better off or have any ability to save and invest money – which is the only likely way to escape from dependence on employers – because of the insidious way that if we have more, we spend more.

You might think this is a problem of middle-income people, but my experience in fancy consulting firms, and my observation of friends who are investment bankers or other very high earners, is that Parkinson's second law applies just as much, or more, when there is a surfeit of goodies. Do we really need all the trappings of upper-middle class life – a more-than-nice house in a 'good' area of town, two or more expensive cars, private education for the kids, expensive vacations and restaurants, golf club membership, personal assistants … you name it?

I have observed a phenomenon that operates relentlessly. The main earner in a couple feels under huge time pressure and therefore thinks that he or she 'deserves' mollycoddling; while the other partner in the couple may feel neglected by the inability of the partner to be present when he or she needs or wants it.

The 'solution' is the same in both cases – a willingness to spend, spend, spend as a lubricant of life. This is, of course, the Parkinsonian trap. There will never be a way out if there are no substantial savings and liquid investments.

80/20 is the salvation. Only spend money on vital possessions. Save and invest all incremental income as it grows, so that you become financially independent and can work at what you love.

CHAPTER 36

FIBONACCI'S RABBITS

This chapter is all about how you must 'grow or die', why you should back unexpected successes and stop your negative activities, why it's important to identify your scarcest resource, whether you should get involved in emerging technologies, how to be a life entrepreneur, the theory of increasing returns, why you have to do something first, the foolproof winning strategy that is almost never used, the importance of sleep, what you should and shouldn't worry about, doing what you love and 80/20 conflict.

301   Grow or die

I have an extremely intelligent and successful friend who argues that we are all machines – yes, he admits, extremely complex and sophisticated machines, but machines nonetheless. I cannot see this. Simpler organisms than humans are alive, and form into families and communities that are also alive – as for example in a tide pool. Humans are not just alive individually, but highly unpredictable, as are the families, communities and nations that we are also part of. Machines are controllable, and even artificial intelligence can be programmed.

Why does it matter? Well, for one thing, a living thing – even a pet or a slave – is harder to control than a machine. An organism is unpredictable and has a mind of its own. We cannot entirely control another person, and perhaps not even ourselves. Organisms have their own purpose.

Also, machines don't grow. Organisms can't do anything else – except decline and die.

Third, humans and a few other organisms can build networks and relationships. Machines can't.

Fourth, organisms learn. Individual humans and networks of humans can learn and create genuinely new artefacts and even whole civilizations.

Finally, as evolution teaches us, organisms and especially humans have their own character and uniqueness.

Being a slave is not much fun. Being a machine is no fun at all. But being a human organism can be wonderful, open-ended fun. 80/20 says – make the most of this phenomenon!

302   Back unexpected successes

Peter Drucker, perhaps the most brilliant management guru of two generations ago, drew attention to the phenomenon of unexpected successes. Drucker was shrewd as well as theoretical. He did not attempt to explain why unexpected successes happened. He just said – keep your eyes peeled for them, and then climb aboard.

Now the theory of emergence gives us some clues about how unexpected successes germinate. Chaos and complexity theories explain how, often quite unpredictably, complex systems can come together from the bottom up. They emerge. They evolve. They cohere. They come together, from many constituent parts. They seem to have no problem doing this. Structure emerges from no structure. The universe manages to bring forth ever more complex structures from simple causes – bacteria, plants, animals, stars, galaxies.

Planning and rational calculations may be inferior strategies compared to watching emergence. *When you see a new pattern, ask if it shows evidence of a new complex system evolving spontaneously from the bottom up.* If it does, and you like the pattern, you might want to become involved, whether as a worker, an entrepreneur, a promoter or an investor.

Personally, I believe in certain irrefutable and super-productive patterns such as 80/20 and the Star Principle. But I have also benefited, as an employee, as an entrepreneur and mainly as an investor, from backing unexpected successes. *If it is not too late, you can benefit enormously at relatively low risk from unexpected successes. And of course, backing unexpected successes is in itself a subset of 80/20 – more from less.*

303   Stop negative activities

The best way to become happier and more useful to other people is to stop your negative activities. It is also, with a bit of practice, the easiest way.

Every impact you have on your own life and the world can be divided into three activities. In mathematics there is something called the Trichotomy law. This states that every number is either zero, negative or positive. This may seem trivial but reflect on it in the context of your value creation – or destruction. We are back to 'less is more'.

Incidentally, where did 'less is more' come from? The phrase was made famous by Ludwig Mies van der Rohe, the twentieth-century minimalist German architect. In fact, the first use of 'less is more' comes from Robert Browning's 1855 poem 'Andrea del Sarto'.

The 'less' side of 'less is more' is significant. We do an awful lot of things in our lives that have negative value. Worry, for example, which may initially have some value in making you aware of danger. But if you can't (or won't) do anything to avert the cause of the worry, it just destroys your life, at least a little, for no gain at all. Being angry or rude usually serves no useful purpose and just subtracts happiness from life. Even displacement activities which seem neutral, such as mindlessly watching television or scrolling through social media, may take the place of potentially joyful activities or at least use up time and attention, which always has a cost.

Of course, you must always have positive activities to substitute for negative or neutral ones. But they are always to hand. Is there one single person in good health who cannot benefit from taking a walk or some other exercise, or from reading something they enjoy? Everyone can talk to a friend, do a good turn or dwell on the good things in life. *There is no sensible place in life for negative activities, and once you realize this, you are bound to make yourself happier.*

Start today – eliminate every activity which does not have positive value to you.

304 Your scarcest resource?

The legendary seventeenth-century French mathematician Pierre de Fermat discovered that *a ray of light travelling between two points will not go by the shortest route, but by the one taking the least time.* His proof of the Principle of Least Time led to the laws of reflection and refraction.

In going the quickest way, light minimizes its scarcest resource – time. You can apply the same principle in your life, by considering what is your scarcest resource. Is it Time? Money? Attention? Friends? Health? Excitement? Achievement? Love? Something Else?

For a teenager, the scarcest resource is unlikely to be time. But maybe for someone in their eighties time is indeed the thing which seems scarcest. Note that this is a deeply subjective call, but none the less real for that. A teenager may feel the answer is excitement or perhaps love. But so too may anyone of any age.

So, what is the scarcest resource in your life?

And what might you sensibly do about it?

I am not a huge fan of introspection, but this may be different. If you can decide what the scarcest resource in your life is, and if it is much scarcer than the next scarcest resource, the vital priority in your life is to find it, whether it is more time, more love, more excitement, better friends, better health, more achievement or even more money.

How you find it is up to you. But 80/20 says it is your top priority.

305   Work in emerging technologies?

Technological change is *the* main determinant of long-term growth.

Technology provides more for less – as well as driving up standards, it lowers costs to a degree that is magical. Indexed to 100, the cost of a transatlantic phone call fell from around 100 in 1940 to 2 in 2000 and is essentially free today via the internet.

The most vital technologies are those that are 'enabling', that generate changes in other technologies. Historically these included the alphabet and writing, bronze and iron, water wheels, windmills, the three-masted sailing ship, printing with movable type, the steam engine, electricity, refrigeration, the internal combustion engine, containers for shipping, genetics, the computer, the internet and artificial intelligence. The last three may be usefully subsumed under 'information technology'.

Information technology is the 20 per cent of technologies that have far more than 80 per cent of impact on our lives and wealth. Obviously not everyone wants and is able to be an information technologist, but if you fall into that category, you are fortunate. The universe is your oyster.

Do you fall into that category?

If so, work out which of the huge number of specializations within IT is your territory.

306   Fibonacci's rabbits

I have to include this fascinating puzzle about exponential growth.

In 1220, Leonardo of Pisa, later nicknamed Fibonacci, constructed this puzzle.

Start with a pair of rabbits. Each pair gives birth to another pair one year and a second pair the year after. Then they're too old to breed, but their progeny follows the same pattern.

How does the number of pairs of rabbits progress?

Work it out if you want, but here's the number of pairs in each successive year:

1, 2, 3, 5, 8, 13, 21, 34, 55, 89, 144 ...

Can you spot anything weird about this?

One amazing thing is that from the third year onward, each following number is the sum of the two preceding numbers.

Another incredible finding is that after year three, the following year's number is bigger than the year before by an almost constant ratio, which soon becomes very close to 1.618. In other words, there is a constant growth rate of just over 60 per cent.

Of course, this can't go on too long. After 114 years of such growth, the volume of rabbits would exceed that of the universe. All humans would have been long dead, smothered by bunny mass. Fur-fetched indeed!

Have you ever experienced growth rates of 60 per cent per annum?

I have, in three separate ventures, and it is intoxicating, because within a few years each business becomes extremely large and profitable.

If you want excitement and more, join or invest in the fastest-growing venture or movement you can find.

307   Become a 'life entrepreneur'

In 1803, French economist Jean-Baptiste Say wrote something profoundly modern, and, I think, applicable to life generally: 'The entrepreneur shifts resources out of an area of low productivity into areas of high productivity and yield.'

Now, forget about economics and business ventures; think about your life and ask yourself two questions:

- What are your areas of low productivity, judged by lack of happiness and good influence on other people?
- What are your areas of high productivity, judged by high happiness and positive influence?

Looking at life this way, whatever produces happiness is highly productive – and once you know this, you should spend more time on those activities.

And the converse also – whatever is low in happiness and good influence can be defined.

Then move from those areas towards the sunlit uplands!

Take a few minutes to define your areas of high and low 'productivity'.

How will you shift the balance towards the former?

308   W. Brian Arthur's theory of increasing returns

Around 1980, Brian Arthur, an economist from Northern Ireland working in the US, said that the 'new economy' exhibited increasing returns; that is, could become more and more profitable, and more and more like a monopoly.

Software, for example, has high up-front costs in research and development – the first sale of Windows cost Microsoft $50 million, the development cost. But the second cost just three dollars to produce. Network effects and the need for customers to learn how to use the product can lock customers into the leading product, even if other products are better.

It is clear that companies such as Microsoft, Google, Facebook, Apple and Airbnb can become incredibly more profitable and valuable in relatively short periods of time.

But let's forget about business. The theory of increasing returns is also applicable to our individual lives.

Attention has rightly focused on personal habits. It may be difficult, initially, to change from unhealthy to healthy habits – for example, to exercise more, improve your diet by eating healthier foods or to stop smoking or taking drugs. This is like the very high cost of inventing Windows or the iPhone. But also like these products, the payoff in terms of health from healthy habits exhibit increasing returns, become profitable very quickly and continue to deliver increasing returns over many, many years.

Similarly, avoiding things that destroy your happiness, such as worry, anger and behaving badly towards other people, may be hard to do initially – but the payoff in happiness (and also in health) comes fairly quickly and lasts a lifetime.

What changes in habits could you make that will give you increasing returns in health and happiness over many decades?

309   'Whatever you want to do, you have to do something else first'

There are many variants of Murphy's laws – the basic one is that 'If anything can go wrong, it will.' Others that I like are 'If several things can go wrong, the one that will cause the most damage will go wrong first' and 'If anything just cannot go wrong, it will anyway' – for example, the *Titanic*.

But the one I think is most salutary is the one headlined above.

Why? Because in contrast to the other Murphy's laws, which, although useful for taking precautions, are generally gloomy, *the idea that to do something you might have to do something else first is actually both insightful and highly positive.*

Viktor Frankl had this to say about how to be happy and successful:

'Happiness must happen, and the same holds for success: you have to let it happen by not caring about it' and 'Happiness cannot be pursued;

it must ensue. One must have a reason to be happy. Once the reason is found, one becomes happy automatically ... through realizing the potential meaning inherent and dormant.'[1]

Happiness, he implies, comes from developing your character and your potential. I agree with this but, as we have seen, there are also other things you can do to directly increase your happiness, such as spending more time with close friends and on activities you enjoy. This increase in happiness does not require prior self-improvement. Yet his valuable point is that to get permanent happiness you should do the necessary strategic 80/20 things first, such as love your work and your romantic partner – and then you will be happy.

In other words, happiness and success may be a *two-step manoeuvre*: to arrive at your desired destination, you need to go somewhere else first.

What is the 'something else' that you must do first?

310 Which strategy always works but is almost never used?

Whether in business or in any other group, organization or network, the strategy that always works is the 'A' team. Only hire or collaborate with the very best people in your field. When you bring in someone new, recruit to improve the – very high – average: the new person must rank in the top 20 per cent of the existing team.

You see, 'A' people love working with other 'A' people. It's rare to have that privilege, so it's highly valued. 'A' people have higher intelligence, commitment to excellence and standards, and are confident and fun to work alongside.

The 'A' team seems expensive yet is excellent value – remember 80/20! One often insuperable problem for nearly all groups is that you have to start from scratch with the 'A' team strategy. It's a strategy for start-ups. If you have some top people in a group who are really only B-plus, they can't start an 'A' team.

I've experienced the 'A' team magic in the Boston Consulting Group, Bain & Company, LEK and OC&C – all strategy consulting groups. I was the 'K' in LEK; we hired the very best people we could find. Nearly all of them have gone on to great careers subsequently. Working with people of this calibre was marvellous.

I believe that the same approach worked well in the early days for Microsoft, Apple, Amazon and Goldman Sachs and, no doubt, other groups. But as they grow, it gets almost infinitely harder.

And beware – 'B' people drive out 'A' people.

That is the rub. Capitalism is usually not as ruthless as imagined. Organizations are run by people, and people are generally not ruthless, even in a good cause. *Being ruthless means excluding anyone who is not genuine 'A' material. Can you be that ruthless?*

311　Sleep: another 80/20 secret

Only recently have we realized how vital sleep is for our wellbeing. As shown in Professor Matthew Walker's wonderful book *Why We Sleep*[2] it is as important as exercise and diet in improving our health, wellbeing and lifespan. Walker shows how sleep integrates everything we have learned during the day with our store of knowledge, and how REM sleep too detoxes us of painful experiences of the day just passed. *Dream sleep is incredibly valuable.*

Here are takeaways from Walker and others:

- Sleep at least eight hours a night.
- Before bed, avoid exercise, caffeine, nicotine, alcohol, substantial liquids, large meals, television and blue light from electronic devices.
- Wind down with music and/or relaxing reading (not thrillers or heart-thumping stuff) and think only pleasant thoughts before sleep.
- Have a hot bath before bed.
- Sleep in a completely dark, well ventilated, quiet and cool room, with no clock faces visible.

- Only go to bed when tired, but aim to *go to sleep and wake up at the same time every day*, including weekends.
- Do not use sleeping pills.
- If you find yourself awake for 20 minutes or more during the night, get up and do something relaxing, before returning to bed when tired.
- Go outside and get an hour of natural sunlight in the morning.

The progressive decline in the extent and healthiness of sleep may be the worst social change in the last 200 years. It contradicts the 80/20 view of time.

How healthy is your sleep and do you get enough of it?

312   *Don't Sweat the Small Stuff*

Richard Carlson wrote an excellent bestseller titled *Don't Sweat the Small Stuff ... And It's All Small Stuff.*[3]

In 80/20 terms, the small stuff is the 80 per cent which produces small or negative results. Carlson's book contains 100 nuggets of gold. Here are my favourites:

- Agree with criticism of yourself
- Don't interrupt others or finish their sentences
- Be happy where you are
- Allow yourself to be bored
- Imagine the people in your life as tiny infants and as 100-year-old adults

Doctor C gives an effective prescription for avoiding stress.

But avoiding stress is not the only important thing in life. Realizing your potential is vital, and there is almost nothing on this in his book. Ultimately, 'it's all small stuff' is wrong. It's <u>nearly all</u> small stuff. The difference between 'all' and 'nearly all' is immense. A few things are vital for happiness besides having a calm, tranquil mind.

What are the small things you sweat but shouldn't? And what are the big things you should sweat?

313   Do what you love but get paid for it!

My friend Perry Marshall has invented three categories of economic activity:

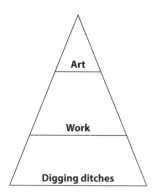

According to Perry, art is what you want to do but nobody will pay you for it (obviously, this does not apply to successful professional artists). Nobody would dig ditches except for the money. In between, intriguingly, there is something else, *'Your unique contribution to the world that you would still only do if somebody paid you money.'*

Perry quotes the example of Charles Dickens, who wrote his books as instalments in magazines that paid by the word. His great works *A Tale of Two Cities* and *Great Expectations* would not have been written unless someone had paid. Similarly, a lot of great classical music was written for kings and nobles putting on a special event: 'Johann Sebastian Bach drags himself out of bed, writes a symphony for dinner, and we're still playing it 300 years later.'

What Perry calls 'work' can be incredibly useful to other people – and to yourself – but you wouldn't have done it but for the financial incentive. I find it interesting: when I started writing books, I wouldn't have done it for free, but now the money is almost completely irrelevant – I do it to express myself and in the hope that you will find it helpful.

Have you ever done anything for money that also became a key part of your self-actualization? Can you think of a new activity that may do both?

314   80/20 Conflict

Is conflict good or bad? One view is that conflict is a terrible hangover from our Stone Age genes, particularly because we are geared for conflict with outsiders. Most of us, according to this view, engage in far too much conflict. We get irritated when life doesn't run smoothly. Irritation may turn to anger, and then conflict. Better to take unpleasantness in our stride.

There is an opposite view. George Bernard Shaw said that all progress depends on unreasonable people who don't accept the status quo and strive to improve it. Was it right for the majority of Germans between 1933 and 1945 to accept Hitler's terror and the enslavement of Jews and his political opponents? Was it right for nearly all politicians in France and Britain to appease Hitler, or Stalin immediately after the end of the Second World War?

It is easier to approve of conflict when it is not about petty personal matters, but about important matters of principle. But, either way, temperament has much to do with it. A conflict-avoiding personality such as Neville Chamberlain, British prime minister during the period of maximum appeasement, would naturally take a different line from Winston Churchill, who revelled in conflict. The natural tendency of people, even in democracies, is to obey authority, leading, for example, to appalling acceptance of invasions of freedom, whether under dictators or our national leaders under Covid.

80/20 provides guidance. For all trivial and semi-trivial difficulties, especially when they inconvenience you and few other people, avoid conflict. But for the few serious cases, where those in authority are doing things that are wrong and oppressive, take up your metaphorical sword and fight the good fight, particularly if your natural tendency is to avoid conflict.

Do you engage in too little or too much conflict?

CHAPTER 37

LUCK AND GOOD FORTUNE

Here we explore luck through the lens of 80/20. We see that you can't change your luck but you can change your future, that volatility breeds opportunity, and we learn how to 'sit loose in the saddle of life'.

315   80/20, luck and good fortune

What is luck? Is it a force or a factor we can control or influence?

Are there lucky and unlucky people?

In an uncertain world, how can you best increase your good fortune?

How can you prepare for the bad luck which will definitely come your way, and cope with it when it arrives?

The essence of 80/20 is selectivity – anticipating and dealing with the most important things in your life and pulling the levers which are most likely to lead to happiness for yourself and the people you care about. Nowhere is this more vital – and often most misunderstood – than in the context of luck and fortune.

To start the ball rolling, ask yourself:

- What good and bad luck have you experienced in your life?

- What are the most fortunate events – say, the top three – that have happened in your life?

- How did they come about and to what extent were you responsible for them?

- What are the three most unfortunate events in your life? Were you responsible for them at all, and if so, how far?

316   Endowment, fortune and luck

We must distinguish between three different things – endowment, fortune and luck. *Your endowment comprises the natural, innate advantages and disadvantages with which you were born and grew up* – where and when you were born, your genes, the talents, skills and temperament which are naturally yours, the pros and cons of having the parents you did during childhood, and the schooling and social conditioning you experienced.[1] Endowment is what you were given at the start and early stages of your life, not what you made of what you were given. For example, if you worked hard at school and consciously developed your skills in new directions, this is not endowment. It is not what you were given, but *what you made of yourself* – which is another way of saying your *fortune*.

Fortune comprises the good and bad things that have happened in your life, for which you were wholly or largely responsible. *Fortune, both good and bad, is the result of your own efforts and decisions in life.*

Luck, both good and bad, is the effect of random chance events on your life. Luck is pure chance. Luck happens to you. You cannot control or influence luck.

Unless you differentiate clearly between endowment, fortune and luck, you will confuse yourself and go round in circles. Clearly endowment and fortune sometimes work together to produce good (or bad) results in your life, and sometimes an initial piece of luck can be consciously built on by you to increase your fortune, but they are conceptually separate. You have never been responsible for your endowment or luck. You have always been responsible for your fortune, good or bad. People often use 'luck' in a loose sense to mean good or bad results, when they really mean fortune. But if you caused something to happen, that was fortunate (or unfortunate), and if you didn't, it was luck.

What are the three most vital bits of good fortune you have brought about in your life, and the three best pieces of pure luck you have received?

317   Was this luck or fortune?

Luck is the opposite of what you might reasonably expect. The essence of luck, good or bad, is its lack of predictability, combined with its significant impact on your life and with the absence of anything you may have done to deserve it. Luck is genuinely and surprisingly random, and fortuitous.

Some examples should help. Imagine – it may be hard – that you want to go to Newcastle in England. It is urgent because a dear auntie may be near death. You dash to Heathrow airport but, in your panic, you have no idea what the flight schedule is. You arrive just in time to catch the last plane of the day and see your auntie before she loses consciousness. This is lucky. But if you knew the schedule and planned the trip in advance, it would be fortunate, not lucky.

Was Columbus lucky in reaching America? This is not easy to answer. On the one hand, he expected to reach India, so he was lucky that there was land in between. He and his crew would have been dead otherwise, as they were almost out of food and water, so he was *extremely* lucky. But on the other hand, Columbus took the initiative in sailing across the Atlantic to discover a new route, so perhaps he was more fortunate than lucky. A reasonable judgment might be that he was fortunate because of his activism, and lucky because of his miscalculation of the distance. Being right for the wrong reason is often a characteristic of bold people, and fortune (not luck) favours the bold.

Abraham Lincoln, James Garfield, William McKinsley and John F. Kennedy were unlucky to be assassinated. Theodore Roosevelt, Harry Truman and Ronald Reagan were lucky to survive assassination attempts. In no case was their personal merit or the precautions they took an issue. It was plain luck. Similarly, the people who travelled on the *Titanic* when it sank were unlucky, as that eventuality was thought impossible, and a passenger who just missed the boat despite having a ticket was similarly lucky – it was not due to foresight.

Do you derive greater satisfaction from being fortunate, or lucky?

318   Are there lucky and unlucky people?

There are several books about lucky and unlucky people, analyzing their personalities and attributes. The books claim that you can learn to become luckier.[2]

The idea that there are lucky and unlucky people is remarkably common; yet it rests on a simple fallacy. There are many people who have had more than their 'fair share' of good and bad luck, but this fact, though unpalatable, has nothing to do with the attributes of the people involved. Luck is random chance and this, by definition, cannot be influenced. If 'luck' is not random, it is not luck. Luck, properly defined, is the good and bad things that sheer chance, pure accident, brings to your door. Luck is not avoidable. It is deeply rooted in the phenomena of life itself – the phenomena of earthquakes, weather, 'acts of God' and all 'chaotic' systems; all the unpredictable elements of business, social life and of human personality; all the miscalculations of life and, especially, of human beings.

If all elements of nature (including humans) were entirely predictable and 'ran like clockwork' there would be no such thing as luck, no unintended consequences and no surprises, good or bad. History would be smooth and malleable – in other words, unrecognizable as history.

Luck exists when human knowledge and calculations are imperfect, which is much or most of the time. It was sheer good luck of unimaginable proportions that our universe began and it had nothing to do with any human agency; when it ends, it will probably be through unimagined bad luck of similar magnitude.

Do you respect the role of luck in your life? Are you prepared for both good and bad luck of major proportions?

319   You can't change your luck, but you can change your fortune

Good fortune can result from human thought, calculation, intuition and, above all, action. Yet you will not eliminate the chance of bad luck. If you think you can, you are in for a terrible shock.

Consider your health. You may be in excellent health now, and eat healthy food, exercise every day and avoid excessive stress. Yet at any moment you could be struck down by bad luck, such as a virus, heart attack, cancer or road collision.

Does this mean that protecting your health is futile? Of course not! Your actions are your fortune; you can increase or decrease your chances of good health and longevity to a high degree. But you can never eliminate luck, and indeed, the more actions you take, both good and bad, the better or worse your pure luck in the event that something surprising happens. If you smoke two packs of cigarettes a day, or drink half a bottle of spirits or take harmful drugs, and live in good health to be 90, you will have had extraordinarily good luck. If you do everything that may enhance your health, and yet die prematurely in a bizarre accident, you will be extremely unlucky.

Actions which lead to fortunate outcomes – and especially the few fortunate outcomes which will most probably lead to great happiness – should be grasped with both hands. They shut the door to much bad luck, but they cannot rule it out. Good and bad luck are not fair; they are part of the human condition.

If you experience bad luck, take it stoically. If you (understandably) get angry at bad luck, you will just make it worse. If you are constantly aware of the possibility of bad luck, while acting to minimize its likelihood, you will, over the long run, come out ahead. This is the message of the book of Job in the Bible, arguably the most profound piece of philosophy ever written.

What are the best three steps you can take to improve your fortune/happiness?

320   Luck is not a force

We all tend to talk about luck as if it is a single discrete entity, like the wind, the waves or part of your genetic makeup, a characteristic of your personality – 'your luck'. But luck is none of these things. Luck is not a force, a person ('Fortuna' or 'Lady Luck'), something we can possess, or even a 'thing' like history, experience or the universe.

Each separate piece of luck you experience is '*sui generis*', its own little or big result of an untraceable process. If luck in aggregate is correlated with anything, it is the fruit of human ignorance. If we were omniscient – accurately forecasting future events – luck would not exist.

The German philosopher Hegel said that the aim of science is to reduce the scope of chance. If we chart the rise and rise of science since the seventeenth century, the flip side of this is a decrease in human ignorance and therefore the partial retreat of luck. With every discovery that wipes out a disease there is one less form of bad luck that can befall us.

Yet, as Einstein said, the difference between genius and stupidity (ignorance) is that genius has its limits. As science advances, it also becomes, for nearly all of us, increasingly incomprehensible. There is something about the complexity of the modern world, partly fuelled by our vast expansion in numbers and the virtually infinite web of human relationships, which makes forecasting increasingly hard, and therefore raises our ignorance and the prevalence of luck. Improbable events become ever more frequent.

What can you and I do? *Two things vital for happiness.* One, respect the role of different chance events in your life and not be fazed or upset by them. Two, influence the very small number of outcomes necessary for an active and fulfilling life.

What are those few outcomes that are most precious to you and you can influence?

321 Volatility and opportunity

There are times of peace and tranquillity, and times of extraordinary events, when one feels the whole world may be upended. Increasingly, perhaps, we live in times which are more turbulent. Volatility opens the door to chance, and chance beckons larger-than-usual losses and gains, financial and in all other respects. Increased volatility comes from the power of technology – the faster it runs, the more it veers towards 99/1, and the less predictable everything becomes.

Nassim Nicholas Taleb is the doyen of uncertainty and probability. He invented the concept of the 'black swan', highly improbable events which change the world. He has argued for some time that the growing trend towards 'winner takes all' in business, the professions and entertainment leads to highly unpredictable outcomes. In what he calls 'Mediocristan' – the normal, mediocre world where incomes are predictable and not extremely diverse – the traditional 'bell curve' of outcomes rules. But he has termed today's increasingly unequal world as 'Extremistan' and shows that in such a world not only are extreme outcomes more frequent, but it is also hard-to-impossible to compute their chance of success. Reading between the lines, he appears to suggest that, in the absence of any reasonable ways of computing the chances of unlikely outcomes, they may be seriously underestimated.

This is classic 80/20 or, to be more accurate, 99/1 territory, which is not appropriate for the novice investor or professional. The sensible advice is to follow a number of outside prospects, small organizations or movements which are growing fast, and gain more knowledge about them and their segment of the world than anybody else.

Volatility increases luck, both good and bad. But volatility also boosts the fortune of those who know more than anyone else about very specialized opportunities.

Is there any situation where you know more than anyone else about a high-growth opportunity?

322   'Sit loose in the saddle of life'

I have taken this very useful phrase from Nicholas Rescher.[3] You must come to terms with the existence of chance, of pure luck. There is no rhyme or reason behind chance. If you expect fairness in life, you will be disappointed. You should not expect luck to contain a 'message in a bottle'. If you expect bad luck to be immediately followed by good luck, you will be disappointed. If you think that there is no such thing as bad luck, that the unfolding of life may show you that it was planned by a benign Providence, you will be disappointed.

For sure, bad luck sometimes (but not often) turns out to be good luck, such as missing a train which then crashes with heavy casualties. Yet there is no goddess of luck keeping a tally of your good and bad luck and ensuring that eventually it all evens out. God may exist, but if so, he is plainly not that sort of God. If God exists and created the world, he put pure chance at the centre of the universe, perhaps in order to allow free will to exist. The essence of life is your ability to choose how you behave and what you do.

Some people have a life dogged by bad luck. Some people live a charmed life. Most people have a life in which there is oodles of good luck and oodles of bad luck. There is nothing that you or I can do to change our luck. If you think there is, you will be disappointed. Luck is luck, and it cannot be influenced by anything you do or think.

I repeat: the right response is *not* fatalism – let what will be, be what you accept. The right response is to influence what you can to make you and others happy.

Though luck cannot be influenced by your attitude to luck, your attitude to luck can strongly influence its effect on your life. It is wrong to let bad luck ruin your life, or even your next five minutes. The correct response is to sit loose in the saddle of life. If bad luck happens, shrug your shoulders. Get on with life and what you can influence in it.

Do you sit loose in the saddle of life?

323 The only certain thing about luck: it will change

Luck is random chance. Incidents of pure luck – some trivial, some life-changing – hit us all the time, though, as 80/20 dictates, few incidents will be life-changing. What is trivial, is commonplace. What is vital, is rare. Yet because we are hit with so many separate and independent incidents of luck, one thing is certain: while your life lasts, your luck will change.

Get one thing straight – *there is absolutely no inevitability about good or bad luck*. A run of 20 consecutive 'reds' or 'blacks' on a roulette wheel has a tiny probability. Similarly, a linear continuation of good or bad luck is incredibly unlikely to continue.

So what? Well, if you are enjoying good luck – not good fortune, which is what you can influence – do not assume that good luck will continue. Some time soon it will be followed by bad luck.

And the converse: if you are suffering bad luck, don't let it plunge you into despair. The universe and other people are not out to get you. It's not personal. It's just life, part of being a living human being.

You can't hurry love, and you can't hurry luck, good or bad. In either case, focus all your efforts, imagination and skill, on increasing your good fortune – the few things in life that really matter where you can shift the odds in your favour.

We will return to the questions of luck, fortune and opportunity soon. Whatever your luck, there are tricks you can use to place yourself in fortunate places, with fortune-friendly attitudes.

In the meantime, can you summarize your view on what you have learned about luck in the past few days?

CHAPTER 38

LIVE IN A SMALL WORLD

Is the theory of 'six degrees of separation' valid? What is 'the strength of weak links'? Is your world structured, random or small? What is a 'superconnector', and how do you become one? The answers to these questions greatly affect the excitement and success of your life.

324   Do you live in a small world?

Have you heard of 'six degrees of separation'? In 1990, the idea burst on to the public stage, quite literally, with John Guare's play, which later became a Hollywood movie.[1] The idea originated in 1929 with a short story by Hungarian novelist Frigyes Karinthy. The basic idea is that anyone can reach anyone else in the world through a short chain of acquaintances, five or six hops from the start of the chain: A to B, whom A knows, to C, whom B knows, and so on to the target F or G.

Do you think that six degrees of separation is realistic? Or just wishful thinking?

It matters. Do you live in a small or a big world? A small world means you can connect to anyone you want. A big world means a world of separate groups, surrounded by large social or geographical barriers.

Maverick social scientist Stanley Milgram first tested the idea with an experiment in 1967, saying that 'small world' suggests that networks are full of unexpected strands linking individuals who move in different places or social worlds. A large world would imply mainly unbridgeable gaps between people. Milgram said that his experiment in Nebraska had 160 chains started and 44 completed, and that the number of intermediaries required to complete the chain varied between 2 and 10.

Deeply impressive? Well, that was a matter of opinion. His results were disputed by another psychologist, Judith Kleinfeld, in 2002, who suggested that his findings had slipped away from their scientific moorings, and that 'six degrees of separation' might be an urban myth. Between 2002 and 2008 other psychologists conducted studies with larger sample sizes, coming to a definite conclusion.

Would you guess that 'six degrees of separation' is largely true or myth?

325   Is 'six degrees of separation' a valid theory?

Several studies between 1967 and 2008 investigated whether a small chain of acquaintances could reach a distant target – and therefore whether the world was 'small' or 'large'. The surprising conclusion was that if the people in the chain were truly motivated to make it work, it would. The average number of degrees of separation was 6.6. Taken at face value, this validates the 'small world' hypothesis. It means that anyone in the world – or at least those 180 million people connected to Microsoft's instant-message communications in June 2008 – could *on average* connect to anyone else in the world via seven 'hops' from person to person.

But not everyone was that well connected. While nearly 80 per cent of pairs of people in the database could be connected in seven or fewer hops, at the other extreme there were some pairs requiring 29 hops to connect. Some people, therefore, were connected to internet messaging, and yet largely isolated from other people in cyberspace as a result of geographical remoteness, poverty or lack of social connections.

The world is small, but only if you think it is and are motivated to connect with many other people. It's easier than you think to reach almost anyone; the main barrier is in your head.[2]

But why might you want to connect? Is it important for you to have a large network of contacts, or not?

It turns out that <u>more</u> *connections* are less important than the <u>right</u> *connections*.

And there is an even more striking and useful discovery than the small world …

326   The strength of weak links

Sociologist Mark Granovetter wrote one of the most important PhD theses of recent years. He wanted to know how executives got new jobs, particularly interesting and well-paid ones. He thought that it would be (1) largely through personal contacts rather than advertisements, and (2) mainly through family and close friends.

His investigation amazed him. He was right about point (1), but plain wrong about (2).

Only one in six of the good jobs came from the executives' family and friends.

The rest came from mere acquaintances, often very marginal ones that they had not spoken to for ages, such as an old college contact, or a former workmate or employer.

How could this be? Surely friends and family had a stronger wish to help the person get a good new job?

Granovetter concluded that the problem with family and friends – strong links – was that they wanted to help, but by and large couldn't. Family and friends largely move in the same circles as we do, and so have little more information than we ourselves do. If we want to get access to different information – in this case about job vacancies – we need to scour the distant fringes of our networks. The more tenuous the link between two contacts, the more value there is in getting back in touch.

I call these friendly but remote contacts 'weak links' or 'friendly contacts'. They can be gold.

Next time you want new information or help, make a list of your 'weak links'.

327   Identify your friendly contacts

The value that can come from 'weak links' – friendly contacts from the past – is Huge.

If you want information that you don't have about anything important to you, such as a job or investment opportunity, a way of contacting a dear friend who has fallen off your radar or any other kind of valuable knowledge, make a list of all the people from your past lives – school, college, former workmates, former friends and people you met doing sports or a hobby – with whom you are on friendly terms.

Arrange a catch-up call with them for half an hour. Explain that you have something in particular that you want to ask them, but that you are going through a series of catch-up calls which have proved interesting or useful to your former friends.

Start by telling them what has happened to you since you last met, and anything exciting or notable that you are doing now.

Then say, 'Your turn now – what have you been up to?'

Range far and wide, in a nice, casual, friendly way, as though you were having a drink with them. **Then ask your specific question.** If they can't help on that, ask them if they know anyone who might possibly know something about the subject.

Keep something of interest back with which to end the conversation, so it doesn't end on a flat note.

The calls will mainly just bring back happy memories. But quite often, you will learn something valuable.

Make your initial list of friendly contacts this weekend.

Schedule your first call soon after.

328   Build a new network of friendly contacts

The more friendly contacts that you have in your network, the greater the intelligence you can derive from 'distant parts of your social system'. So, you need to refresh your network with new contacts. A realistic target may be to add one new contact per week.

■ What kind of contacts should you aim to add to your network? The easiest is if they are friends of friends and you meet them in a social setting. But not all friends of friends are suitable. Which ones are? The most important attribute is that you like them. You may not know someone very well, or indeed at all, but the strange thing is that you know whether you like someone within a few seconds of seeing them. And if you like them, the chances are they will like you, partly because you will send off friendly signals to them without being aware of it!

■ If you want to cultivate a new contact, find an excuse to ask them for a cup of coffee or some other little event, either alone or with other friends. When you meet them, smile! Talk naturally about something. Don't be artificial. Don't talk too much. Just be pleasant. And – this is the most important thing – ask for their contact details.

Only do this when you feel in a good mood and confident. We all have our days when we feel comfortable being social, and days when we want to hide in our cave. Choose your moment.

Now start thinking about people you would like to add as new contacts in your own network.

329   Is your world structured, random or small?

Professor Duncan Watts and colleagues at Cornell University conducted pioneering research from 1996 using computer modelling to explore different types of personal networks. They identified three main network types:

1. A <u>*structured*</u> *network* (which Watts called a *regular* network) is one which is connected to 10 close other individuals and to only a few (or zero) distant contacts. This is a theoretical model which emphasizes the strong links between family, friends and co-workers. When we were growing up, we would have started with a structured network like this, where there is a small number of family and close friends with whom we had most of our interactions.

2. The researchers then constructed a theoretical opposite to the structured network, which they called a <u>*random*</u> *network*. Imagine setting up a thousand nodes (contacts) in a circle with 5,000 connections picked at random. The local clustering would be poor – there would be no strong links, but in compensation there would be few degrees of separation because you could be connected to all the individuals in the circle through a small number of intermediaries.

3. Finally, Watts and colleagues started with a structured network, and then added random links between the nodes. It turned out that by just increasing the total number of connections by a mere 1 per cent of random new links, the number of hops necessary to make connections between any of the nodes – that is to make a <u>*small world*</u> *network* – plummeted to seven. In fact, adding just *five* new links at random to a structured network cut the degrees of separation in half.

The small world network is by far the best in terms of ease of communication and access to ideas, and yet it is remarkably easy to construct. All you need is to add to your structured network of strong links a relatively small number of distant friendly contacts with whom you can get in touch when necessary.

Do you live in a small world already? If not, it is easy to construct one by adding distant friendly contacts to your network.

330   What is a super-connector?

A super-connector is my name for someone who connects a large number of people, either in a specific field or across a variety of contexts.

Perhaps the best example of the former is the semi-vagrant mathematician Paul Erdös who dominated his field until his death in 1966. He still holds the record for the number of mathematical learned articles with 1,475 in total. Of more interest is that the majority of these articles were authored with another mathematician, a stunning total of 511 such collaborators. Amongst the top thousand mathematicians of his time, everyone was connected to everyone else through Erdös.

Other examples are the German Andreas Meyer in photography, and my favourite example, Peter Harding, an Englishman who connects the rarified international field of vintage Lancia cars. Anyone who is a Lancia enthusiast anywhere in the world is likely to have come across Peter Harding. His customers come from all walks of life and often tour with him in France or Italy. He introduces them to each other and also connects many related matters – buyers with sellers, auctioneers and dealers with both, owners with suppliers of parts.

Then there are people such as Chicago's Lois Weinberg, the subject of a *New Yorker* article by Malcolm Gladwell titled 'Six Degrees of Lois Weinberg', and many others who connect people across the globe in particular areas, people who you will probably not have heard of unless you are in that segment.

Most super-connectors are not famous, and many are shy or introverted, but they make the world go round in their own spheres and their own ways. They link everyone within an existing world or bridge diverse worlds. Why is it good to be one of them? Because you will do a great deal of good, be at the centre of your own little web and get useful information before the crowd. Super-connectors have more fun, and there can be no better justification.

Are you a super-connector? Could you become one?

331   Would you like to become a super-connector?

'Everything is linked together,' wrote the eighteenth-century French philosopher Denis Diderot, 'beings are connected with each other by a chain.' The art of the philosopher, he said, was to add new links between people 'in order to reduce the distance between them as much as possible.'[3]

Experiments by Stanley Milgram, Duncan Watts, Mark Granovetter and many others have substantially proved the 'small world' hypothesis. It is possible for most people to connect with almost anyone else in the world by knowing someone, who knows someone … through a total of five or six such connections.

Intriguingly, experiments have proved there is a small number of individuals who are 'super-connectors', commanding hugely greater social sway through being in touch with people from different 'clumps' of society. By being in touch with at least one person in totally different groups, locations and occupations, they link together people who would otherwise not be connected with each other. They practise Diderot's 'art of the philosopher' by adding new links between people.

The advantage of being a super-connector, apart from the sheer fun of discovering spontaneous connections, is that they get new information faster. By taking information from one clump of friends who share information and passing it to another person or group not connected to the first clump, the super-connector is a crucial bridge between the two groups – and can realize the value of new information before anybody else.

Network society functions because of super-connectors. Without them, network society would not work so well, and might not work at all. So, super-connectors deserve all the benefits they can get from linking individuals and groups.

Do you see how you might become a super-connector in your own world?

CHAPTER 39

CHOOSING AND CREATING YOUR HUBS

You live in 'hubs' – the groups and networks to which you belong.
How can you avoid 'the gravity of hubs', create your own and benefit
from 'the network structure of ideas'?

332   Choose and design your hubs

'Hubs' are the groups to which we belong which comprise mainly strong links between individuals important in our lives. The number and variety of human hubs have steadily increased throughout history, especially in the last 300 years. In the Stone Age, people experienced just two or three hubs – the family, the tribe and – for men – the hunting group. Even when hunter-gathering was superseded by agriculture, the hubs for most people were still only the family, the tribe, the farm and, possibly, a market. For millennia, human existence was incredibly predictable and local.

Then came the growth of cities and the Industrial Revolution. Ordinary people started to move into the modern world – the cosmopolitan orbit of cities, schools, universities, multiple jobs in a career, voluntary groups and friendship circles freely adopted.

List all the hubs you have experienced – the family into which you were born, the family you may have entered through marriage; different groups of friends that you have belonged to; schools and colleges you attended; your organization or, if it is large, the department you are in or other work groups and projects you have been part of; sports clubs, gyms, societies or hobby groups; social or volunteer hubs; churches and other affinity groups or other groups you have met socially or while travelling. *How many hubs in total do you estimate you have belonged to? How many left a mark on your life?*

Do you think you generally made the right choice of hubs? How could you have made better choices – or could you still make them now?

Finally, the best thing about hubs is that you can create your own – a cadre of close friends, a study group which could be important throughout your life, even a new club, society or organization. It is an immense privilege and advantage in life to be able to create your own hub or hubs, which can add to your happiness and meaning in life. There is no barrier to anyone doing this, but not everyone does.

What one new hub would you most like to create?

333   Avoid the gravity of hubs

I have interviewed hundreds of people, asking about the hubs they have belonged to and still do, and whether they made good choices and are still doing so. What do you think is the most common drawback identified by these people regarding their hubs?

Yes, you probably got it! The most common drawback identified was that people stayed in past hubs too long, or even felt that they were staying too long in a current hub.

There are many advantages of hubs, but they have a strong tendency to want to keep people in them. This may be advantageous for the hub, but not for the individual.

Hubs often exhibit psychological forces such as groupthink and authority, which contributes to what I call the 'gravity of hubs', their tendency to maintain the status quo and hang on to their people. This is made worse because individuals in organizations often exhibit conformity, fear of change, wish to succeed and natural empathy with colleagues – which make them stay in the organizations longer than is good for them. Moreover, as researcher Mark Granovetter said, 'long tenure cuts off the accumulation of personal contacts and thus reduces the chances for mobility.'[1]

A friend I interviewed who had been successful in LEK Consulting then joined a smaller firm where he still works, 20 years later. 'In the last recession,' he told me, 'it was a tough time for the firm and I felt obliged to stay and put the business back on track. To be brutally frank, moving here was a mistake, and staying here was a worse one.'

What hubs are you currently in? Are you happy in them?

334   The network structure of ideas 1: The target market

There is a network structure for the way excellent ideas can be discovered and become powerful.[2] Christianity and Marxism provide great examples. Jesus of Nazareth had a revolutionary new message and, so too, 19 centuries later, did Karl Marx. Both Jesus and Marx failed utterly to make much of a dent in their worlds during their lifetime. This was, firstly, because their target markets were wrong.

The target market of Jesus was Jews. In his day, the gurus of Judaism were the Pharisees, who advocated strict adherence to Jewish law, together with good works; and the Sadducees, the priests and high priests, whose principal preoccupations were maintaining the glory of the Temple in Jerusalem and remaining on good terms with the Roman authorities. The two groups disliked each other, but Jesus' social-revolutionary message had no appeal for either side.

Paul of Tarsus modified Jesus' message to appeal to Greeks and Romans rather than to Jews. The emphasis shifted to using God's power to improve oneself, which was a modified form of Stoicism, a successful philosophy, plus the ideas of love and eternal life in Jesus.

Marx's great idea was that capitalism was replacing feudalism, and socialism would inevitably replace capitalism, which, he claimed, impoverished workers. Socialism would be driven by factory workers gathered in cities, who would make revolution in the streets. Marx failed because capitalism made factory workers richer, not poorer. His target market was wrong. Lenin took over Marx's idea that socialism would triumph, but changed the target market to peasants in Russia, not workers in developed countries. After three years of terrible war, he promised Russian peasants land, peace and bread.

If you wanted revolutionary change, what would be your target market?

335   The network structure of ideas 2: Hubs

Besides changing the target market of Christianity from Jews to Greeks and Romans, Paul also formed *hubs* – local bands of Jesus' followers, organized into a powerful, missionary group of 'churches' – people, not buildings. Paul used the Roman network of roads and shipping to organize churches in every major city in the Roman empire.

Lenin, like Paul, was a charismatic, organizing genius. Lenin formed his own hub, a political party, the Bolsheviks, and revolutionary cells in Russian cities, both under his personal control. The Bolsheviks were only a couple of hundred strong, but they were all dedicated revolutionaries, prepared to shoot and kill any opponents. In the exceptional circumstances of October 1917 in Leningrad, the major Russian city, that was all it took – besides huge luck and the political support of peasants – to establish a socialist tyranny.

Ideas such as Christianity and Marxism – or any other powerful and original idea – do not live and die on their own merits. They need a suitable target market, a terrifically competent organizer with great force of personality, and the creation of one or more new hubs. Without Paul – and later Constantine, the Roman emperor – Christianity would not have reshaped the world. Without Lenin, statues of Marx would surely never have been erected across Russia, Eastern Europe, China and parts of South America.

Paul and Lenin breathed new life into the failed ideas of Jesus and Marx respectively, totally changed the target market, and founded new hubs. Any idea, however great, needs an organization of disciplined and dedicated supporters to change the world.

Would you like to change the world, in any important way? Now you know how!

CHAPTER 40

HUNCHES

Hunches based on intuition and previous experiences are central to happiness and success. Hunches are not irrational; we all know far more than we realize or can articulate. Hunching skill, as we will see, is closely related to 80/20, and can be greatly improved.

336   Develop your hunching skill

Progress and happiness in life can be significantly enhanced if you can develop the ability to make very important (80/20) decisions better. This applies to your few most important interpersonal relationships – who to love, who to have as dear friends, who to learn from and conversely who to teach and help along the path of their personal development, and how to find and get on with the people who can advance your career.

Think back over your life and career. Identify the five most far-reaching good decisions that you made, and the five most far-reaching bad decisions.

When you have done this, take the life-changing decisions and recall *how you made them.*

For sure, you may have asked friends to help you decide, but ultimately you made the decision. How did you make it?

Broadly there are only two ways – using rational analysis, working out the pros and cons of alternative decisions, on the one hand; and on the other hand, using your intuition. In the end, also, most people make most decisions intuitively. Rational analysis, for example, can't be the main factor in deciding whom to marry. Thinking can take you only so far; nearly all critical decisions in life, including business, are intuitive.

How good do you think your intuition is? And in which areas of life is it excellent, and in which rather poor?

If you can improve your intuition – your hunching skill in making decisions – you can improve your life.

337   What exactly is a hunch?

Max Gunther sums it up nicely, 'A hunch is a piece of mind stuff that feels something like knowledge but doesn't feel completely trustworthy.'[1]

He gives the example of Conrad Hilton, founder of the eponymous chain of hotels, when he was bidding for a hotel in Chicago by sealed bid. Days before the deadline, Hilton submitted a bid of $165,000 (this was a long time ago!). That night he slept badly, waking up feeling that his bid was too low to win. Acting on this intuition, he changed his bid to $180,000.

He won the auction. The next highest bid was $179,800.

Can you remember the last time you made a vital decision based on a hunch? How did it go?

We all know far more than we think we know. Throughout life we collect millions, perhaps trillions, of pieces of information. These data may be facts, but very often the things we know, including the most important things, cannot be dignified with being called data – they are not precise and certain enough. They are something between feelings and facts. Nonetheless these scraps of useful information are stored in your subconscious mind, and accessible to you when you have to make vital decisions. Generally, you have to use your intuition.

When you hear someone's voice on the street, you know instantly who it is even if you can't see them. You have an emotional reaction and instantly recall a great deal about them. Your reaction comes from your subconscious mind, not your reasoning mind.

Do you realize how much you rely on hunches in making decisions, great and small? Can your hunching skill be improved?

338   80/20 applies to hunching skill

80/20 proposes these hypotheses about hunching skill:

- Everyone's success and happiness is related to their skill in making decisions based on intuitive hunches. Rational intelligence is much less useful in making key decisions in life than hunching skill.

- Rational intelligence is subject to the bell curve. Most people fall within a narrow range of intelligence. There are simply no people with intelligence many times that of other people.

- *Hunching skill is different.* Hunching skill is subject to 80/20. There are people who are many times more intuitive than others. This helps to explain why some people have the knack of making decisions leading to breakthroughs denied to people with less hunching skill. It is clear, for example, that Albert Einstein's power ally was intuition, leading to insights that had eluded much better educated and experienced physicists. Billionaires such as Warren Buffett and Bill Gates have hunching skills hundreds of times greater than the general run of their peers.

- Vastly superior hunching skill is usually confined to quite narrow areas or 'spots' of expertize. Buffett's expertize is making investments in relatively low-tech public companies such as Coca-Cola. Gates' brilliant hunching skills are confined to leading-edge areas of information technology.

- Identify where your hunching skill is strongest and develop that skill to a much greater degree.

In which area is your hunching skill most reliable and productive?

339 'A hunch is only as good as the sum of past experience that produces it'

'A hunch is only as good as the sum of past experience that produces it', says Dr Natalie Shainess. She says she makes intuitive decisions in treating patients and trusts her hunches because they are based on long experience in a narrow field.[2] If hunches are not random, but based on all the part-facts, near-facts, impressions and recognitions of previous patterns, and categorizations of new experiences on the basis of their resemblance to the closest previous patterns, then it makes perfect sense that good hunches require a great deal of experience in particular arenas.

It follows that your hunches can be improved by precisely defined specialization, and the accumulation of ever-greater experience in your sweet spots. It also follows that you should not trust your intuitions about areas in which you have little experience. Novices should beware of believing that there is such a thing as general intuition and should not make big bets – financial or personal – on the basis of limited experience. Many people believe that they can pick numbers likely to come up on the roulette wheel or in a lottery, but they are wrong. Random events such as these are not susceptible to hunches. They are matters of pure luck, and luck is impervious to hunches. Most gamblers eventually run out of money because they come to believe in their hunches. The few successful long-term gamblers have special knowledge not available to other gamblers.

Nevertheless, it may not be true that skilful hunches rely exclusively on experience and knowledge submerged in your subconscious. Some people appear to have the knack of superior judgment and shrewdness in particular areas even if they are not long on experience in them. There is one good way of seeing if this applies to you. If you think you have such a knack, *keep a record of your hunches, and see how often they work in high-experience and low-experience spots.*

Where do you have high experience? Are your hunches more successful there?

340   How to detect false hunches

The great enemy of successful hunching is wishful thinking. When you very much want something to happen, it's easy to imagine that you have a hunch it will do so. Here are five ways to distinguish between true and false hunches:

- Hunches where you have no vested interest can probably be trusted.
- Hunches which you hope will not happen are definitely to be trusted.
- If you have a hunch which is also a hope, ask a friend who is experienced in the area to give an opinion. Unless your friend is highly positive, distrust the hunch.
- Imagine how the hunch could go wrong and how serious these downsides could be.
- If, after due consideration, you develop the habit of confusing hopes and hunches, stop trusting all your hunches.

Do you trust yourself not to confuse a hunch with a hope?

341　How to improve your hunches

You can improve your hunches by deepening your experience in areas where your hunches are already good.

There is a second way – to expand and improve the use of your subconscious mind. The second way leads on to the third, which is to shun excessive analysis.

There is a kind of tug-of-war between analysis and intuition, both claiming 'market share' of your decision-making. Analysis goes back a long way but was particularly beloved of the late eighteenth-century Enlightenment schools in France, Britain and the US, which believed that science and reason would lead to endless progress, including perhaps making humans perfect! Benjamin Franklin, you will recall, advised his readers to make decisions only after listing the pros and cons of any move.

Despite the overwhelming evidence that we make decisions haphazardly and intuitively – and the perception that this is both inevitable and, on the whole, helpful – life and business in particular are besotted with quantitative analysis and increasingly ruled by algorithms rather than human judgment, from whether bank loans should be made to print runs for books. Algorithms are cheaper than humans but not necessarily better.

Detailed analysis, especially of the financial kind, can be dangerous. It often rests on slippery but hidden assumptions; for example, that the future will be like the past, and that the factors identified by analysis as important will continue to apply. When I make important decisions of any kind, I sit by my fish pond and ask the fish what to do. Perhaps because my quantitative skills are deficient, I rely on intuition for key decisions, and so far, intuition has served me well. *The more intuition based on relevant experience is used, the better it gets.*

Do you rely more on analysis or intuition? Could you improve your intuition through greater exercise of it?

342   Stay in your hunching sweet spots

We all observe people who are intuitive geniuses in their particular territory and have great success, yet fall flat on their faces when they try to apply their 'genius' to new areas, even ones which seem to be adjacent to their territory. From the trade union leader who becomes a government minister to the billionaire entrepreneur who opines about a pandemic, the assumption is that success in one area is readily applicable to another.

If you follow the hypothesis that intuition is related to feelings, impressions, and fragmentary facts gathered into the subconscious mind by decades of experience in a narrow field, you will understand why a track record in one area may not transfer to another.

This highlights the need to stay in your hunching sweet spots, or at least to gain considerable relevant experience in a new area before making large commitments in different territory.

Caution and modesty should be exercised until you know your way around any unfamiliar zone.

When I was in my mid-forties, I voyaged to a new assignment advising the executive chairman of a large South African organization. This was doubly new to me – I had never before been a coach/full-time adviser, nor had I been to South Africa. I had a lot of experience I thought was relevant – but needed to supplement it with understanding the new terrain. I was tempted to make premature recommendations, but just about managed to contain myself. It was just as well because I eventually reversed most of my early pet hypotheses.

Have you had a similar experience of moving to an unfamiliar role or environment? How did it go?

343   Be cautious in your hunches about people

A few people are extraordinarily good with intuitive hunches about people. But, as 80/20 would predict, most people are not. 'Most people' probably includes you, and it certainly includes me!

The problem is this. We are all geared to make snap decisions about people. It is a simple matter of chemistry. When you walk into a room and meet someone new (for the first time), you are likely to have an intuitive reaction. It could be favourable or unfavourable, but after 30 seconds you will have formed a view on whether you like them. You may also have formed an impression about how intelligent they are, and all manner of other ideas about them. It may have a lot to do with whether you think they are 'people like us' – or like you. We instinctively trust people who are like us and distrust people who are not. It's even possible that this reaction dates back to the Stone Age, when our genes told us to distrust people outside our own tribe.

Do not trust your reaction.

How often have you disliked or distrusted someone the first time you met them, but later, after getting to know them, come to like and rate them?

This has happened to me many times. We all tend to like people more once we get to know them. Familiarity usually breeds not contempt, but respect.

There is another reason to distrust your instant assessment. The main reason why your subconscious mind can give you an accurate hunch is that it contains trillions of bits of impressions, vibes and facts or semi-facts that you accumulate throughout life. It bears repeating, *a hunch is only as good as the experience you have leading to the hunch.* How can you possibly have a lot of information about someone you have just met? You are led astray by superficial or irrelevant data about them, such as how good-looking or confident they appear. If you have known someone well for years, your hunch about them is usually right. If not, it isn't.

Do you go by first impressions? How can you guard against this tendency?

CHAPTER 41

FORTUNE FAVOURS
THE BOLD

Boldness works. It fuses self-assertion, will and pursuing risky goals.
Boldness requires experiments and a wish to dominate life.

344 'Fortune favours the bold'

The ancient Romans originated this idea – *Audentes Fortuna Juvat.*[1] Julius Caesar, for example, boldly went where no man had gone before. He conquered the barbarians of Gaul (France), Germany and Britain (well, almost), and laid down a network of roads that still exists today. As he said, 'I came, I saw, I conquered.' Simple if you were bold, and aggressive, enough.

Boldness still works today, for three simple reasons.

First, bold people are much more likely to take risks and to create their own path in life, whether by joining a fast-growing firm or social movement, becoming self-employed or starting their own venture, large or small.

There is a false market in risk. The potential rewards exceed the risks, because too few people take risks. Taking risks is the fastest way to learn more and create more value. You may make a wrong decision, but even then, if you act accordingly, you may come across a way to be right for the wrong reason. Always remember Christopher Columbus. He aimed for India but found America, just in time. Where there is life, where there is action, there is hope.

Second, bold people are much more likely to become aware of the huge galaxy of opportunities that exist. They are more likely to search out and meet people who can give them a leg-up in life, and more likely to go to events and parties where they come across serendipitous opportunities.

Third, bold people are more likely to seek unreasonable, outrageous success – see my book *Unreasonable Success & How to Achieve It.*

On a scale of 1 to 10, how bold are you? Could you become bolder?

345 Boldness means experimentation

Life, it has been observed, is not a rehearsal. It is the real thing.

Every day matters. Every day can change and develop you, if you experiment.

Experimentation helps you find your destiny. It relieves boredom. It forces you to adopt new roles, new masks, new identities.

How many different organizations have you worked in? In each new one, did you learn something different? Even if you didn't like it, you learned what to avoid, and perhaps much more.

How many different fields or disciplines have you experienced? Marketing is a discipline. Anything academic is a discipline. Selling is a discipline. So too is administration, engineering, acting, any form of art, anything that has its own rules and methods.

How many different teams – of any sort: sporting, hobbyist, work – have you belonged to? What did you learn? Which did you like most?

How many cities, towns and countries have you lived in? Each is different. Each teaches you something.

How many different groups or individuals have you lived with? What did you learn about yourself?

It is great to find your niche in life – the place, and the people, with whom you identify and feel fulfilled.

Have you found your niche?

Experiment until you do.

346   Boldness means dominating life

Everyone dominates life; or, more usually, is dominated by it.

Domination need not be in any way macho. It can be a very quiet, introspective and gentle thing. The small, still voice of calm can be more effective than the voice of a chatterbox or the shout of a lout.

Domination means leaving your imprint on life. It is impossible to be bold and not to do this.

Boldness means being wilful. It means being self-possessed.

Being bold always involves being somewhat unreasonable. Being bold means being demanding and assertive, but also imaginative. Being bold means doing new and sometimes apparently impossible things. It means reaching for the stars.

Julius Caesar was bold. So – in an opposite way – was Jesus Christ. Leonardo da Vinci was bold. So too was, or is, every pioneering artist, musician, explorer and thinker.

Boldness is not necessarily good. Lenin, Stalin, Hitler and Mao were all bold. They changed the world – markedly, perhaps irrevocably, for the worse.

The answer to bad boldness is not meekness or self-abnegation. It is good boldness.

On a 1–10 scale, how bold are you?

How could you notch up your boldness towards 10?

347   Boldness and luck

Boldness and luck are totally different. Boldness is action by an individual, an attempt – futile or fulfilled – to control the uncontrollable, to dominate destiny, to improve your life.

Luck, on the other hand, is pure chance. You do not change luck or influence it. It changes or influences you, and it does so purely at random. You do not attract or repel luck. Luck is arbitrary. It rewards good and bad people, good and bad actions, intelligence and stupidity.

You might argue that boldness and luck inhabit different universes. Boldness is boldness and luck is luck, and never the twain shall meet.

Boldness is a virtue, because it produces good results for individuals, at least if they are well-intentioned. Luck is totally amoral. To be lucky is not to be virtuous, because the essence of luck is passivity; it happens to you, not because of you or your actions.

And yet, this is not quite right. Boldness requires experimentation. Boldness means attempting to dominate life. And this means putting yourself in the path of luck, both good and bad. Good and bad luck may come in equal volumes – this is the nature of luck, in aggregate, for everyone. Yet good and bad luck need not be symmetrical in their results. If you have the right attitude, it is possible to slough off bad luck. And if you have the right attitude, it is possible to ride good luck for all it is worth. Imagine two people of equal intelligence and abilities. One stays in her cave and neighbourhood, never venturing beyond them. The other experiences life to the full. Which one is likely to do more and to be more? Exposure to luck is net positive.

Fortune favours the bold, not just because thought and action expand the possibilities for you and the universe, but also because your exposure and reaction to luck is pivotal.

How do you react to bad luck and to good luck?

348   Rejoice that life isn't fair

You might expect random chance to be neutral for society and humanity. By definition, random chance is equally likely to be good or bad. There is no evidence that God or anything else loads the dice of luck, and if anything did, it would not be random.

But I will stick my neck out and assert that the existence of luck is a good thing.

Imagine the opposite – a world without luck, without random chance. In this world, we would all get our just deserts. What could be wrong with that?

Everything.

As Michael Young showed in his brilliant 1958 satire, *The Rise of the Meritocracy*, a society based on merit – which could only be judged by qualifications – would be insufferable. Those at the top would be smug and overbearing. Those at the bottom would be oppressed and hopeless, and rapidly fall into a passive or rebellious underclass.

Moreover, a free-market economy works better than a socialist or fascist planned one, because of the role of trial and error. We find better ways of doing anything by experimenting. Experiments which prove to make life better are encouraged and rewarded. The reasons for this may include better ideas or skills, but nearly always include a larger slice of luck. It is good for society for its less academic but more active movers and shakers to sometimes come out ahead of those who are better qualified but make fewer experiments. Luck is a great leveller. And luck encourages enterprise.

Individually, we may experience more or less good luck, more or less bad luck. But collectively, luck is a luscious lubricant of life. Therefore, if you have bad luck, shrug your shoulders, stand tall and recognize the equity in inequity.

Rejoice that life isn't fair!

Do you think the existence of luck is good, bad or neutral?

349   Life is a trapeze

Jim Lawrence, one of my two partners in starting LEK, has a nice saying: 'It's not a corporate ladder; it's a corporate trapeze. You jump from one swinging trapeze to another. If you're lucky you catch the new trapeze as it's about to go up, swinging to an even higher level.'[2]

Another way of saying this is that life – not just a career – is a matter of snakes and ladders. It is unrealistic to expect an upbroken upward path. It is not even good for you. Nothing fails like success, and nothing succeeds so well after a failure.

Failure is feedback. You are either doing the wrong thing, or doing it the wrong way. Which is it?

Doing the wrong thing means doing something that you have little interest in or talent at.

Doing it the wrong way means violating 80/20 – putting in a lot of effort for poor results. How could you do the reverse?

You are great at something. It might be building a happy family. It might be art of some kind. It might be persuasion. It might be science. It might be running things. Do anything that you like, so long as it is not law, dentistry or investment banking, where most professionals are miserable.

Life is a trapeze. Swing down. Swing up. Reach the summit that is attainable. It is higher than you think.

Is it time to swap your trapeze for another swinging upwards?

CHAPTER 42

PASCAL'S WAGER AND ASYMMETRIC BETS

Philosopher and theologian Blaise Pascal told us to
consider the upside and downside of bets. To get rich, or
just enjoy life, go for high upside, low downside bets.

350   Pascal's wager

Blaise Pascal was a distinguished seventeenth-century mathematician, scientist, philosopher and theologian. A devout Catholic, he formulated a justification for believing in God under conditions of uncertainty. His 'wager' argued that if someone bet that God existed, and behaved accordingly, and God did indeed exist, they would enjoy eternal life in heaven – a big win. If God did not exist, they would lose relatively little – a little less pleasure in life.

On the other hand, if the person bet that God did not exist, and was wrong, the downside was enormous – not just missing out on heaven, but being condemned to eternal life in hell. As many people have observed, this was dodgy theology.[1] What sort of God would be impressed by belief based on this kind of bet? What sort of God would send people to eternity in hell because they had made the wrong intellectual decision?

Yet Pascal hit upon a method which can be applied to vital decisions in life, and has, substantially, been responsible for making many people, including me, a great deal of money: think of the upside and the downside from any uncertain decision. Even more important, apply the method to things in life that are more important than money – things related to your happiness and fulfilment.

You might not know whether it will be 'right', but you may be able to gauge roughly the result of making the decision if you are right and if you are wrong. *Go for high upside and low downside bets.*

Do you think this way? Should you?

351   When the going gets tough, quit

Investors are often taught about a little bit of equipment called a ratchet. It allows a wheel to turn forward but stops it from slipping back.[2] When investing on the stock market, it is often a good idea to set a rachet in the form of a 'stop loss' – for example, if you buy shares and they decline by 15 per cent, sell them. That way you can't lose more than a small part of your investment. On the other hand, it is often a good idea to 'run your gains', so you set no limit to your upside.

The same principle applies in more important areas of life. If you make a significant decision – to befriend someone, to change your job, to join a club or a network, or anything else that really matters – and it turns sour, what should you do?

Conventional wisdom is to stick at it: 'When the going gets tough, the tough get going' (that is, keep at it with greater energy). 'Winners never quit' – and other such nonsense. 80/20 wisdom is to quit. Set a ratchet in your mind. If something is making you unhappy, end it and do something different and better.

Why is this wise? Because when things start to go wrong, they usually get worse. If you set out in a small boat and the sea begins to get rougher and rougher, is it sensible to continue out into the ocean, or to retreat to the harbour? If you are a manager, how many times have you had an under-performing person, and out of human decency given them a chance, and then another? How often does that turn out well? How many marriages start to go wrong, and then suddenly turn around and miraculously go right? If you make a mistake that causes you stress and unhappiness, how often is it sensible to keep at it?

In your experience, how many times have bad situations become worse? And how often have they become better?

352   Three reasons we perpetuate our mistakes

Why do we perpetuate our mistakes? First, we all find it hard to say, 'I made a mistake, I was wrong', especially if you have to do so publicly.

Second, when we make an investment of any kind – but especially an emotional investment – it is hard to give up on it.

We are all averse to making losses. We hate it. We deny it. We refuse to recognize it. Psychologists have proved, at least to their own satisfaction, that we hate losses more than we like gains.

This miserable philosophy seems deeply set in our bones – again, quite possibly, because in the Stone Age mistakes were often fatal. In the modern world, mistakes can usually be rectified with no loss of face or angst – if you are prepared to change your mind and do what is more likely to make you happy and secure.

The third reason is that none of us really 'grok' (fully understand, deeply value, constantly keep in mind) 80/20. There are a few arenas of life – love and work being the obvious ones – where a small number of things affect and colour our whole life.

It is in these vital areas that mistakes simply must be corrected – otherwise, you will be much less happy and useful than you should be.

It is not that you should correct all your mistakes. Heaven forbid! You would always be changing your mind and what you do. Small mistakes that don't affect your peace and position in life can be allowed. Let loss aversion and pride persist in these areas, else you will think you are completely hopeless. In many ways we all are, but it doesn't matter. Keep your fallacious self-esteem!

But in the big areas you *must* correct what is going wrong.

When things are badly deteriorating in very important areas of your life, do you cut your losses?

353   Before you turn 30, 40, 50...

Max Gunther makes an arresting observation: 'In the common pattern, the main structural timbers of one's life are bolted in place by age 30 or earlier.'[3] He argues that after this point, it is hard for you to change career or redesign your life.

This may or may not be true – it is hard to measure it empirically since the definitions of changing career or re-engineering life are so fuzzy. But it is certainly not inevitable that, as he says, 'Only minor tinkering takes place from then on.'

Was there a marked discontinuity in your life at a particular age? By 'discontinuity' I'm talking about career change, a new love life, a move to a significantly different country or region, a shift in attitude and disposition, or any other major punctuation point or breaking away from your previous path.

When I turned 30, I was in crisis. I had failed in the only really important job I had and was just picking up the pieces of my career. At 30 I landed a new job in the same field of 'strategy consulting' and at 33 I was a partner in that firm.

If your career has stalled or self-destructed, try again in a significantly different environment. In my mid-forties I moved to South Africa for two years and took on a totally different challenge. Since then, I have had two new concurrent careers, as a writer and as a venture capitalist.

Turning 30, 40, 50 … or 80 may be a good time to take stock and change direction, but you can do it at any time. *If your life is not working well for you, break with the past and do something else.*

Do you want to do that? Then do it!

354   How much should we try to know?

I came across this intriguing quote today from Werner Heisenberg, who was one of the world's top physicists in the 1920s and 1930s: 'Only a few know how much one must know to know how little we know.'

Of course, Heisenberg was one of the great explorers of the microworld, the tiny parts of matter which behave so unpredictably. For him, and many since, it seems the more we know about science the less we understand it.

It made me wonder what the 80/20 view of knowledge is. Try these hypotheses:

- In the eighteenth century, it was possible for an educated person to know the rudiments of all branches of knowledge. Such individuals comprised a tiny proportion of society, but knowledge was general, not specialized.

- Today knowledge is fragmented into a million different disciplines and sub-disciplines. Only a tiny proportion of the highly educated can cross subject boundaries with confidence.

- Yet there are 'life skills' which are accessible to everyone – a kind of general wisdom which enables the motivated learner to become much more successful and happier than most people. These skills include the tiny parts of psychology, medicine, exercise, diet, probability theory, science, history and a few other disciplines that are crucial in life. *I include understanding 80/20 as a key component of these skills.*

Obtain two kinds of knowledge. One, a mastery of the few key life skills. Two, mastery of a very useful specialism which helps other people enjoy life more. Very few people have both kinds of knowledge, but they transform lives, starting with their own.

What knowledge do you have? What new knowledge do you want to acquire?

CHAPTER 43

THE BLACK SWAN AND HISTORY

With strong parallels to 80/20, Nassim Taleb argued in his great book, *The Black Swan*, that history jumps occasionally through unpredicted random events. Few things matter, as 80/20 insists, but they matter enormously.

355   Taleb's big idea: the black swan

In 2007, Nassim Nicholas Taleb unleashed a powerful new idea related to 80/20 in his masterwork *The Black Swan: The Impact of the Highly Improbable*. His big idea is that changes in society and history come from rare, unpredictable and unpredicted events, not from the slow accumulation of known, repeated and predictable events. He called them 'black swans' after the Latin poet Juvenal, 'a bird as rare as the black swan'.

This is a book about probability. Taleb takes aim at the famous 'bell curve' of Carl Friedrich Gauss, which describes how most events fall within a narrow distribution of values, with extreme values at either end of the curve. Human height, weight, and that dubious measure of intelligence, IQ, all fall neatly within the bell curve.

But wealth of individuals does not fit the bell curve. If it did, there would be (in 2007) 1 in 16,000,000,000,000,000,000,000,000,000,000 people with incomes greater than €8 million – that is, none. In fact, there was 1 in 500.[1] The distribution of wealth, like 80/20, follows a power law, like 80/20. With the bell curve exceptional results can't budge the average more than a tiny bit. With power laws, the top players or events can dominate the total and make the average irrelevant.

80/20 presents a static picture. What Taleb did so well was to paint a dynamic picture of extreme variations in impact. In many ways, his book is *The 80/20 Principle Part Two*. He also potentially changed our understanding of history. He made a plea to use exceptional results as the starting point for understanding the modern world, instead of shoving them under the carpet as inconvenient, atypical, and incomprehensible. His theme is that because we can't predict black swans (whether positive or negative), we just can't predict, period.

Can you think of any black swans in your experience, or in history?

356   The black swan and history

History, according to the black swan theory, alternates between crawling and jumping. It crawls most of the time – changes are gradual, cumulative and predictable. It makes huge and unpredicted jumps at rare intervals. But these lurches change history. They are also beyond explanation. The causes are not obvious and may always remain opaque. Yes, Taleb says, historians can explain what happened. But they are in danger of reading history backwards, implying a degree of predictability and inevitability that is simply untrue.

Take the rise of Christianity, says Taleb. Who predicted its rise to become the dominant religion in the Roman empire? Roman chroniclers of the time took almost no notice of Jesus. As far as I can tell (this is my view, not Taleb's), just before the emperor Constantine converted to Christianity around 310–13 AD, only 1–2 per cent of people in the empire, at most, were Christians. If the emperor (and his successors) had not converted, Christianity would probably have disappeared – and in any case Constantine's religion would have been abhorrent to Jesus and Paul of Tarsus. The rise of Roman Imperial Christianity was a true black swan – unpredicted, unpredictable and highly consequential.

Where I part company with Taleb on history is this – it is the job of historians to identify causes, and this is not a hopeless task. Black swans do happen as he says – for example, the Industrial Revolution, the French Revolution, the two World Wars, the rise of Lenin and communism, and of Hitler, the reconstruction of Europe after 1945, the fall of communism, and the internet as we know it today. These events were unpredicted and incredibly important, but this does not mean we cannot identify their causes. In doing so, we should remember that they were freak events, incredibly unlikely and certainly not inevitable.

Do you agree with me that understanding history and how it unfolds is vital to understanding the modern world? Do you think you have a good understanding of history, the context of our lives today?

357   History and the theory of black ducks

It is not enough to divide history into two types – the crawling, predictable type on the one hand, and, on the other hand, the world of black swans, huge and massively consequential lurches in unexpected directions.

There are also 'black ducks'.[2] Black ducks are the building blocks of black swans. They are important events which together largely or wholly explain black swans. They are more predictable than black swans and were sometimes noted by contemporaries; if the latter had connected the dots between several black ducks they might well have predicted the black swans – and therefore accelerated them if they were benign, or prevented them if malign.

For example, these were some of the black ducks which were the most vital causes of the Industrial Revolution – crop rotation and other elements of the Agricultural Revolution of the seventeenth century, the rise of canals, the invention by James Watt of a usable steam engine, the water-powered mill and other inventions such as the flying shuttle, the spinning jenny and iron machine tools that made mechanized cotton production possible, the existence of tinkerer-entrepreneurs such as Richard Arkwright, the availability of early 'venture capital' finance, and the invention of steam-powered boats and railway locomotives. All of these were necessary for the Industrial Revolution to take off. Each one of these events or inventions was unlikely, so the cumulative probability of an industrial revolution would initially have been close to zero, but after each black duck materialized the odds shortened markedly. Some contemporaries in the mid-nineteenth century, including Karl Marx and Friedrich Engels, noticed these events and predicted astounding consequences. Without the Industrial Revolution life as we know it today would have been impossible.

What do you think were the black ducks leading to the internet? Can you spot some black ducks today which may lead to black swans in your lifetime?

358 Counterfactual history and lucky escapes in history and life

What about black swans that did not happen? For example, the Cuban missile confrontation of October 16–28, 1962, is widely considered the nearest that the world came to nuclear disaster. It is said that President Kennedy thought the chances of war were between 33 per cent and 50 per cent. If he really believed that, it is incredibly scary.

Should historians investigate these and other near-disasters – or indeed positive breakthroughs for humanity which did not happen but came close? If historians are sometimes criticized for implying that terrible events such as the First or Second World Wars were inevitable, can they also be criticized for not telling us enough about wonderful events that nearly happened, such as, perhaps, the opposition to Mao Zedong or the assassination of Hitler that averted the Holocaust?

Here we are in the enchanted garden of counterfactual history – versions of history that could have changed its whole course. Counterfactual history started in earnest in the 1920s and 1930s and recent books by reputable historians such as Niall Ferguson and Robert Cowley have explored many intriguing *What If?* scenarios, of varying degrees of historical rigour. The genre easily slips into whimsical mode or the parading of hobby horses, but *The Black Swan* should make us think very seriously about how to make counterfactual history respectable and scholarly. Can we quantify probabilities of events that happened a year or so before they did, or of events that nearly happened?

Have there been any serious 'What If' events in your life? Any lucky escapes from disaster, or freak events that should not have happened but did? Are they worth reflecting on, and are there any lessons for the future?

I have dodged a few bullets in my time. It is worth feeling grateful for extreme good luck which you did not deserve.

359   The prehistoric origins of 80/20

The Black Swan has some fun imagining where scalable events – in other words, the 80/20 Principle – originated. It could be with DNA, which enables humans (and other beings) to replicate themselves through the generations without being alive to do so. Evolution, he says, is scalable; that is, the DNA that wins will multiply itself, while other DNA will disappear.[3] Reflect on how humans have increasingly colonized the earth, or how more 'advanced' civilizations have extirpated others, and you will see his point.

Humans took a big, unfair step forward when the alphabet enabled us to store and multiply information. Then came written books, and with even more momentous consequences, the movable printing press. Once a book is written and printed, its message can spread without the author needing to do anything else. There is almost nothing 'more 80/20' than book publishing, where a favoured few sell millions of copies – and earn huge royalties – while the vast majority of authors fail to earn minimum wage. The gramophone, radio, television and the internet exacerbate scalability – which spreads its tentacles remorselessly and inequitably into society and its future. And don't even get me started on venture capital, and the huge rewards to a tiny number of lucky or fortunate entrepreneurs.

Goodness knows what future manifestations of scalability will do to us. As science fiction writer William Gibson wrote, 'The future is already here – it is just not equally distributed.' Like champagne socialists enjoying both success and moral status, it pays to be on the right side of 80/20, while deploring its unfair tendencies. Perhaps the purpose of civilization and religion or philosophy should be to soften the downsides spread by 80/20.

Do you worry about the unfairness inherent in 80/20? What can be done to mitigate it?

360   Mediocristan versus Extremistan

Nicholas Nassim Taleb has invented two mythical worlds.[4]

Mediocristan is the realm of the mediocre, the vast majority of events and observations that are obvious, routine, collective, gradual and predicted. This is the domain of the bell curve, where everything is close to the average, and the very high and low observations are rare and can never overwhelm the bulk of average results.

Extremistan is the world of the very few improbable but highly consequential events – singular, accidental, unpredicted, staccato, sudden, disruptive and often driven by an individual or small group.

Weight loss (or gain) belongs in M'stan (as the Arabs call it). Whatever you do, you will never lose much weight in a single day, nor will you make a fortune, except very slowly, over many years, with many years of effort as, say, a good dentist. M'stan is where most people live, perhaps where nearly everyone lives most of the time.

Ex'stan is the unfair world where time and effort are often irrelevant. If you are a financial speculator you live in Ex'stan and can make or lose a fortune very quickly, perhaps in 60 seconds. Taleb does not say this explicitly, but Ex'stan is the world of 80/20 (really 99/1).

M'stan is the world of the past; Ex'stan the world of the future.

M'stan is subject to gravity and the tyranny of the material world; Ex'stan has no physical constraints – they are all mental and subject to wacky imagination.

M'stan is impervious to a single event or person; Ex'stan is not.

M'stan reveals itself easily; in Ex'stan it is hard to figure out what is going on.

Which world would you prefer to live in?

361   Mediocristan in history

Here are a few of the most important events in history which were largely gradual.

Fortunate Mediocristan Events

- The founding and expansion of cities – a gradual but important trend over millennia increasing human connections and prosperity
- The development of civil and religious rules regulating social life and preventing anarchy

- The gradual expansion of liberty and decline of feudalism from 1000 AD
- The rise of science and technology – mainly a very long cumulative process
- The spread of trade and common languages between countries and regions
- The agricultural and industrial revolutions throughout the world from the seventeenth century, exponentially increasing human numbers and wealth
- Population migrations after 1800 to richer and more liberal countries

Unfortunate Mediocristan Events

- The gradual rise of the slave trade up to around 1840
- The rise and rise of deadly war technology throughout history

Do you think there is significant evidence of human progress over time?

362   Extremistan in history: some positive black swans

Here are some notable 'black swan' events in history – unexpected, disruptive, highly consequential and, on balance, good for humanity:

- The Big Bang, the origins of life in cellular organisms and vertebrates, the most notable developments in evolution and consequential inventions such as fire, the wheel, the alphabet, movable-type printing, eyeglasses, windows, crop rotation, the inflection points of the Industrial Revolution (including the steam engine, steam- and water-driven cotton mills, steamships and railways), electricity, the telegram, the bicycle, automobiles, planes, radio, modern agriculture, the microchip, the internet, the smartphone, and all medical-related advances saving lives and making them more pleasant (such as proper sanitation, germ theory, the water closet, modern dentistry, aspirin, antibiotics, antidepressants and keyhole surgery)
- The Renaissance
- The American Revolution and the consequential growth of liberalism and democracy; the failure of European revolutions in 1830, 1848 and 1870–1

- The abolition of slavery
- The defeat of Hitler in 1945 and the peaceful reconstruction of Western Europe
- The fall of the Berlin Wall in 1989 and rise of democracy in Eastern Europe

Most of these events would not have happened without the role of intelligent consciousness, individuals and small cliques. Do you agree?

What would you add to or subtract from my provisional list?

363   Extremistan in history: some terrible black swans

- The Black Death; other major epidemics including the 'Spanish flu' after the First World War
- All major wars in which there were large casualties as a proportion of the population, and especially Civil Wars which left enduring divisions in society
- The virtual holocaust of native Americans following Columbus' voyages; and similar massacres after the discovery of Australasia; all ancient and modern genocides
- The Russian Revolution in October 1917 and the rise of Lenin, Stalin and communist tyranny in Eastern Europe
- The Wall Street Crash of 1929 and the consequent Great Depression of the 1930s; the Crash was also a significant cause or catalyst for:
  - The rise of Hitler to power in January 1933 and the resultant Holocaust
  - The Nazi–Soviet pact of 1939, which precipitated the Second World War
  - The rise of Mao Zedong and communism in China in 1949; the subsequent 'Cultural Revolution' of 1966 in which millions were persecuted or murdered

With the exceptions of epidemics and in some cases wars, and the Wall Street Crash, nearly all the negative black swans, like the positive ones, were the work of charismatic individuals and cliques associated with them.

The negative black swans were nearly all unpredicted. If they had been convincingly predicted, many of them might have been prevented.

What negative black swans would you add to the list?

364   With information, less is more!

The story I like best in Taleb's *The Black Swan* is about bookmakers. In a psychology experiment, Paul Slovic asked bookmakers to select 10 out of 88 variables in horses' performance that they found most useful in compiling their odds, and then predict the outcome of races. Then he gave them 10 more variables in addition to the first 10. The extra 10 variables did not increase the bookmakers' accuracy, but it did markedly increase their confidence in the predictions.[5]

I am a great believer in the virtues of not knowing. I constantly try to pare down the information needed to assess whether or not to make a venture capital investment. The objective information I need is no more than the following – the historic growth rate of the business, the historic growth of the market segment it is in, and how large the company is compared to its largest rival company in the segment. I don't want to know anything more. The only subjective information I need is a face-to-face chat with the chief executive. Then I decide. I never use – in fact I *cannot* use – computer spreadsheets. I never look at 'decks' of information presented in business plans. They always contain a huge amount of irrelevant or misleading information, forecasts which nobody can credit and tendentious logic. Over 37 years I have compounded my after-tax wealth at 22 per cent annually.

In any analysis, financial or otherwise, fewer variables of the highest quality should be preferred to more variables of inferior quality. Knowing what to look for, and especially what not to look for, is crucial.[6]

When you are deciding anything vital to your happiness, how many factors do you take into consideration? Which factors are most valuable? Could you just stick to using those?

365   Deep laziness and the order of nature

Just as I am finishing this book, I have come across a fascinating piece on the internet about 'Deep Laziness' by Sarah Perry.[7] Following the work of Christopher Alexander, Sarah comments that 'There is intense laziness apparent in the natural world (which one might come to understand simply by watching household pets).' In science, there is the 'principle of least action' – a soap bubble minimizing its use of surface area, for example, or a river meandering slowly and lazily towards the sea.

In nature, we can observe a structure which has a 'strong centre' – a shape, such as a diamond or a cloud or a tree that is fractal (eternally appearing in a similar pattern, but with the potential for endless variations on the theme). Trees in a forest may then form an avenue quite naturally. By preserving the same shape, but elaborating it, nature exhibits beauty, flexibility and economy (laziness). Nature is never a mess. Styles of architecture, such as Gothic, Renaissance or Georgian, can mimic nature's deep laziness. Modern architecture does not do the same thing – there is often no central template; there is often a mess.

Apart from appreciating that 'intelligent and lazy' is a brilliant and beautiful way of paying tribute to nature, how can we use this idea? Sarah suggests that we all have a small number of 'behavioural centres' – her main two are running and knitting. When we have spare time or money, it may make sense to build new activities in the shape of one of our behavioural centres, or a combination. In my case, my main two behavioural centres may be sitting and thinking by the fish pond, and reading. I usually read late in the day, often before sleep, whereas it might make sense for me to be lazy and stop work in mid-afternoon, so that I can *read by the fish pond*, which is better for my mind, my eyes, and my sleep than reading by strong electric light at night. I may also have more good ideas that way.

How can you use the idea of deep laziness?

THANK YOU AND FARE WELL

366   Keep on the road to happy and good results

Thank you for reaching the end – and the beginning.

This remarkable journey need never end in your life.

80/20 is an invitation to share in delights without downsides – success as you define it, with as little or as much effort as you want to put in; the quest for personal fulfilment of your potential, a target moving from one height to another, maximizing the meaning that your life can have, which is far more than any of us realize at the outset, or even now; the abolition of stress and anxiety, because you believe in yourself and choose the path which leads to the results you want, bypassing the slough of despair and anything which depletes your energy; a journey shared with other people you love and admire, achieving great outcomes together; a life full of delightful days and years, enriching the lives, in small or great ways, of anyone you meet along the way. You are happy because you like and love your fellow-travellers, and because you have good reasons to be happy with them, and important to them.

With 80/20 implanted in your thoughts and actions, all things are possible. Your weapons are optimism, the search for outrageous opportunity, and doing only what you can do cheerfully and with distinctive aplomb, without angst or exertion that is beyond you. Every day you do things that make you and other people happier – things that can be little in time, toil and trouble, such as smiles, small encouragements and empathy, yet are disproportionately great in results.

There is of course another universe around you – that of evil, and sometimes even worse than evil, because it is more widespread and dispiriting: the world of mediocrity, low horizons, anxiety, depression and hard but pointless work. This universe can only be countered by doing the opposite in a way that is so attractive that more and more people join the 80/20 way.

<u>Your mission in life is to travel to happy and good results. Go now!</u>

ENDNOTES

Chapter 2 Intelligent and lazy

1. See Richard Koch (2013) *The 80/20 Manager*, New York: Little, Brown, pp 209–11.

2. My co-author Greg Lockwood invented the concept of a 'virtuous trade-off' in Richard Koch and Greg Lockwood (2016, 2018) *Simplify: How the Best Businesses in the World Succeed*, London: Piatkus, pp 83–5.

3. This essay keeps moving around on the web. To find it easily and without payment type into Google 'Bertrand Russell + In Praise of Idleness'.

4. John Ruskin (1851, 1903) *The Works of John Ruskin*, edited by E. T. Cook and Alexander Wedderburn (eds), vol 12, London: George Allen.

Chapter 4 Happiness

1. Charles Murray (2012, 2013) *Coming Apart: The State of White America, 1960–2010*, New York: Crown Forum, pp 268–9.

Chapter 5 Ambition, self-belief and your career

1. Walter Isaacson (2011) *Steve Jobs*, New York: Simon & Schuster, p 4.

2. G. H. Hardy (1941) *A Mathematician's Apology*, Cambridge (England): Cambridge University Press, pp 8–19.

Chapter 7 Optimism and opportunity

1. Martin E. P. Seligman (1990, 1998) *Learned Optimism: How to Change Your Mind and Your Life*, New York: Pocket Books, p 15.

2. Richard E. Nisbett (2003) *The Geography of Thought*, London: Nicholas Brealey, p 100.

3. Richard Koch and Chris Smith (2006) *Suicide of the West*, London: Continuum, pp 48–67.

4. Jordan B. Peterson (2018) *12 Rules for Life: An Antidote to Chaos*, London: Allen Lane, p 96.

Chapter 8 Difficulties, stress and moods

1. M. Scott Peck (1978, 1990) *The Road Less Travelled: The New Psychology of Love, Traditional Values and Spiritual Growth*, London: Arrow Books, p 13.

2. Ian Robertson (2016) *The Stress Test: How Pressure Can Make You Stronger and Sharper*, London: Bloomsbury.

3. Robert E. Thayer (1996, 1997) *The Origin of Everyday Moods: Managing Energy, Tension, and Stress*, Oxford: Oxford University Press.

Chapter 9 The subconscious mind

1. See, for example, Lionel Mlodinow (2012, 2014) *Subliminal: The New Unconscious and What It Teaches Us*, London: Penguin, pp 3–51, and David Eagleman (2011, 2016) *Incognito: The Secret Lives of the Brain*, Edinburgh: Canongate Books, pp 1–19.

2. Nancy C. Andreasen (2005, 2006) *The Creative Brain: The Science of Genius*, London: Penguin.

Chapter 11 Success and 80/20

1. Eric Barker (2017) *Barking Up the Wrong Tree: The Surprising Science Behind Why Everything You Know About Success Is (Mostly) Wrong*, New York: HarperCollins, pp 9–11.

2. Ibid., pp 10–14.

3. Author's calculation based on ibid., p 24.

4. See, for example, ibid., pp 107–8.

Chapter 14 Fantasy mentors, failures, winners and sex

1. Bob Dylan (2004) *Chronicles*, New York: Simon & Schuster, pp 17–18.

2. See Richard Koch (2020) *Unreasonable Success and How to Achieve It: Unlocking the Nine Secrets of People Who Changed the World*, pp 34–7.

Chapter 15 More on happiness … and romance

1. Many thanks to Hans Jonas for part of this analogy: Hans Jonas (1958, 1963) *The Gnostic Religion: The Message of the Alien God and the Beginnings of Christianity*, Boston: Beacon Press, p 267.

2. Martin E. P. Seligman (2002, 2017) *Authentic Happiness*, London: Nicholas Brealey, p 187.

3. Meyer Friedman and Ray H. Rosenman (1974) *Type A Behavior and Your Heart*, New York: Alfred A. Knopf/Random House.

Chapter 17 Money and happiness

1. Ed Diener (24 April 2005) 'Income and Happiness', http:///www.psychologicalscience.org/observer/income-and-happiness, pp 1–2.

2. Betsey Stevenson and Justin Wolfers (2013) 'Subjective Well-Being and Income: Is There Any Evidence of Satiation?', www.nber.org/papers/w18992, April 2013, abstract, p 16.

Chapter 19 More on optimism and opportunity

1. The Gospel of Thomas: saying 113.

2. See Ivan Alexander (1997) *The Civilized Market: Corporations, Conviction and the Real Business of Capitalism*, Oxford: Capstone, pp 28–33.

3. Peter Thiel (2014) *Zero to One: Notes on Startups, or How to Build the Future*, London: Virgin Books, p 68.

4. William Gibson (1984) *Neuromancer*, New York: Ace Books, p 51.

Chapter 22 Growth and how to compound yourself

1. Richard Koch (2020) *Unreasonable Success and How to Achieve It: Unlocking the Nine Secrets of People Who Changed the World*, London: Piatkus, pp 158–9, 211–19.

Chapter 23 How to increase your effectiveness with less effort

1. Richard Koch and Greg Lockwood (2016, 2018) *Simplify: How the Best Businesses in the World Succeed*, London: Piatkus, pp 3–11.

2. Ibid., pp 22–32.

3. Ibid., pp 12–21.

4. Richard Koch (2008, 2010) *The Star Principle: How It Can Make You Rich*, pp 59–64.

5. Ibid.

Chapter 24 The art of 80/20 Thinking

1. Marshall McLuhan (1962) *The Gutenberg Galaxy: The Making of Typographic Man*, Toronto: University of Toronto Press, especially p 124.

Chapter 25 Decisions

1. Barry Schwartz (2009) *The Paradox of Choice: Why Less Is More*, New York: HarperCollins.

2. See Chip Heath and Dan Heath (2013) *Decisive: How to Make Better Choices in Life and Work*, New York: Crown Business, especially pp 168–73.

3. Ibid., especially pp 92–114.

4. Ibid., pp 35–6.

Chapter 26 Networks

1. *McKinsey Quarterly* interview with Eric Schmidt, September 2008, quoted in Richard Koch (2022) *The 80/20 Principle*, London: Nicholas Brealey, pp 335–6.

2. Quoted in Richard Koch, *The 80/20 Principle*, op. cit., p 329.

3. Parag Khanna (2016) *Connectography: Mapping the Global Network Revolution*, London: Weidenfeld & Nicolson, p 49.

4. Richard Koch and Greg Lockwood (2010) *Superconnect: How the Best Connections in Business and Life Are the Ones You Least Expect*, London: Little, Brown, especially pp 246–61.

Chapter 27 Territory, hierarchy and how to thrive in the brave new world

1. Steven Pressfield (2002, 2012) *The War of Art: Break Through the Blocks and Win Your Inner Creative Battles*, New York: Black Irish Entertainment, pp 147–59.

Chapter 28 What is the source of meaning in your life?

1. Viktor E. Frankl (1946, 1959) *Man's Search for Meaning*, New York: Washington Square Press, pp 87–9.

2. Viktor E. Frankl (1946, 2019, 2020) *Say Yes to Life in Spite of Everything*, London: Penguin, pp 68–71.

3. Ibid., p 123.

4. Viktor E. Frankl, *Man's Search for Meaning*, op. cit., p 154.

5. Ibid., p 101.

6. Ibid., p 134.

7. Viktor E. Frankl, *Say Yes to Life in Spite of Everything*, op. cit., pp 76–7.

8. Viktor E. Frankl, *Man's Search for Meaning*, op. cit., pp 170–2.

9. Ibid., pp 120–7.

10. Ibid., p 175.

11. William Boyd (2018, 2019) *Love Is Blind*, London: Penguin.

12. Will Durant (1932, 2005) *On the Meaning of Life*, Dallas: Promethean Press. Charles Beard's answer is on pp 45–6.

13. Ibid., pp 97–109.

Chapter 29 Evolution's lessons for you

1. Richard Koch (2014) *The 80/20 Principle and 92 Other Powerful Laws of Nature*, London: Nicholas Brealey.

2. Ibid., p 20.

3. Ibid., p 21.

4. Ibid., pp 22–3.

5. Ibid., p 23.

6. Ibid., pp 27–9.

7. Richard S. Tedlow (1990) *New and Improved: The Story of Mass Marketing in America*, New York: Basic Books, p 69.

8. Richard Koch, *The 80/20 Principle and 92 Other Powerful Laws of Nature*, op. cit., p 32.

Chapter 30 A genetic perspective on how to make more money and have more fun

1. If you are interested, read Richard Koch (2008, 2010) *The Star Principle: How It Can Make You Rich*, London: Piatkus.

2. Richard Dawkins (1976, 1989) *The Selfish Gene*, Oxford: Oxford University Press, pp 189–201.

3. Richard Koch, *The 80/20 Principle and 92 Other Powerful Laws of Nature*, op. cit., pp 50–7. In that book, I called them 'business genes'.

4. Ibid., pp 50–9.

5. Ibid., pp 18–19.

Chapter 31 Niches and breast-beating

1. Richard Koch, *The 80/20 Principle and 92 Other Powerful Laws of Nature*, op. cit., pp 64–5.

2. Ibid., pp 66–7.

Chapter 33 Neuroplasticity, tit for tat and the right place to live

1. Jeffrey Schwartz and Sharon Begley (2002, 2009) *The Mind and the Brain: Neuroplasticity and the Power of Mental Force*, New York: HarperCollins. See also Jeffrey Schwartz and Rebecca Gladding (2011) *You Are Not Your Brain: The 4-Step Solution for Changing Bad Habits, Ending Unhealthy Thinking, and Taking Control of Your Life*, New York: Avery Books.

2. Matt Ridley (1996, 1997) *The Origins of Virtue*, London: Penguin, p 144.

3. This insight derives from Richard Dawkins and Matt Ridley. See Richard Koch, *The 80/20 Principle and 92 Other Powerful Laws of Nature*, op. cit., p 110.

4. Jared Diamond (1999) 'How to Get Rich', *Edge* 56, June 7. www.edge.org/documents/archive/edge56.html.

Chapter 34 Time oases, thinking and chaos

1. Richard Koch, *The 80/20 Principle and 92 Other Powerful Laws of Nature*, op. cit., pp 153–5.

Chapter 36 Fibonacci's rabbits

1. Viktor E. Frankl, *Man's Search for Meaning*, op. cit., pp 17, 162.

2. Matthew Walker (2017, 2018) *Why We Sleep: The New Science of Sleep and Dreams*, London: Penguin.

3. Richard Carlson (1997, 1998) *Don't Sweat the Small Stuff … And It's All Small Stuff: Simple Ways to Keep the Little Things from Taking Over Your Life*, Hodder Paperback. I have shortened some of the 'nuggets'.

Chapter 37 Luck and good fortune

1. See Nicholas Rescher (1995) *Luck: The Brilliant Randomness of Everyday Life*, New York: Farrar, Straus & Giroux, especially pp 69–77.

2. The best of these books is probably Max Gunther (1977, 2009) *The Luck Factor: Why Some People Are Luckier Than Others and How You Can Become One of Them*, Petersfield: Harriman House. The second-best is Richard Wiseman (2003, 2004) *The Luck Factor: Four Simple Principles That Will Change Your Luck – And Your Life*, London: Arrow Books.

3. Nicholas Rescher (1995) *Luck*, op. cit., p 22.

Chapter 38 Live in a small world

1. Richard Koch and Greg Lockwood (2010, 2011) *Superconnect: Why the Best Connections in Business and Life Are the Ones You Least Expect*, pp 13–24.

2. Ibid., pp 20–4.

3. Ibid., p 13.

Chapter 39 Choosing and creating your hubs

1. Richard Koch and Greg Lockwood, *Superconnect*, op. cit., pp 132–54.

2. Ibid., pp 155–77.

Chapter 40 Hunches

1. Max Gunther, *The Luck Factor*, op. cit., pp 133–55. I highly recommend this book for pages 117–201. I believe Gunther is wrong in thinking that hunching skills and the other skills he discusses in these pages are matters of luck. I think it is clear that they are skills which can be developed, and therefore not luck. His advice in these pages, however, is generally excellent.

2. Ibid., p 146.

Chapter 41 Fortune favours the bold

1. Max Gunther, *The Luck Factor*, op. cit., pp 157–73.

2. Richard Koch and Greg Lockwood, *Superconnect*, op. cit., p 132.

Chapter 42 Pascal's wager and asymmetric bets

1. For example, Nassim Nicholas Taleb (2007, 2010) *The Black Swan: The Impact of the Highly Improbable*, London: Allen Lane, p 210.

2. Max Gunther, *The Luck Factor*, op. cit., pp 175–86

3. Ibid., p 181.

Chapter 43 The black swan and history

1. Nassim Nicholas Taleb, *The Black Swan*, op. cit., p 233.

2. I owe this term and the idea behind it to my friend and fellow student of history Jamie Reeve.

3. Nassim Nicholas Taleb, *The Black Swan*, op. cit., p 30.

4. Ibid., pp 33–7. I have amplified and simplified Taleb's account.

5. Ibid., p 145. Taleb quotes a huge number of psychology papers which boil down to the same point – more information is bad for us!

6. My approach is described in Richard Koch, *The Star Principle*, op. cit.

7. https://www.ribbonfarm.com/2018/04/06/deep-laziness/ retrieved 17 October 2023.